GERARD MANLEY HOPKINS

TO MY PARENTS AND SJEF
IN MEMORIAM

GERARD MANLEY HOPKINS

A Critical Essay
towards the Understanding of
his Poetry

by

W. A. M. PETERS
S.J.

Basil Blackwell
Broad Street, Oxford, England

johnson Reprint Corporation
111 Fifth Avenue, New York, N.Y. 10003

© Copyright by the Society of Jesus

ISBN 0 631 12790 9

First published March 1948,
by Oxford University Press

Second Edition 1970 by Basil Blackwell and Johnson Reprint
Corporation with the authorization of Oxford University Press

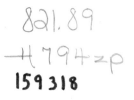
Printed by offset in Great Britain by
Alden & Mowbray Ltd, Oxford
and bound at Kemp Hall Bindery

CONTENTS

 Importance of *inscape*—definition—the meaning of 'scape'—inscape and beauty—inscape and pattern or design—instances of the use and meaning of inscape—the appreciation of inscape by Hopkins—inscape 'word of God'—inscape and *impersonation*—difference between impersonation and personification.—Impersonation proved by the absence of the article—by the frequent use of the form of address—by the perception of objects as ever active and alive—the result of impersonation *instress*.

 The meaning of instress, derived from the use of the noun stress—two different senses of instress—its meaning in philosophical writings—instress as synonymous with impression—description of external reality in terms of inscape and instress—instress as a source of imagery—marked difference between Hopkins and other poets in their attitude towards external reality and its interpretation.

 Philosophical justification of instress and inscape in Scotism—further influence of Scotus on Hopkins—the 'self'—the effects of his self-analysis on his poetry—Conclusion.

 Hopkins's attitude towards criticism—his reaction to the criticisms of Bridges and Dixon—and Patmore—his fundamental canon—inscape is the aim of poetry—'the individualising touch'—earnestness, sincerity and humanity in poetry—praise of the poetry of Bridges and Dixon—wavering attitude towards that of Patmore—his views on the poetry of his age.

 His own poetry examined by the standard of his own theories—his own misgivings—first group of poems—second group—the background to the third group—the struggle *poet-priest*.

 His zeal for objective truth—truth and imagery—the medium of poetry—schools and echoes in literature—no artificial or archaic language—but 'current language heightened'.

 Conclusion—Hopkins the experimentalist—his oddity and obscurity.

 Current language—Hopkins's objections to the poetic language of his day—his language examined by his own standard 'we do not speak that way'.

 Current language *heightened*—various forms of language—the difficulties inherent in the employment of affective language as the medium of poetry—use of rhythmical and syntactical marks—the

poet's anxiety to be read aloud—the rhythm of Hopkins's poems
—current language heightened and modern poetry—division of
this subject into three sections.

Logical language heightened by the use of the interjection—
of the exclamatory phrase—of the question—of the form of
address—subordination and co-ordination—the colon—the dash
—the meaning and function of *and*—co-ordination as a source of
obscurity.

Affective language as the medium of poetry—order of words in
the sentence—order of words within the word-group—inversions
—various omissions—sequence of thought in some of his poems.

Mixing two sentences—mixing two grammatical structures—
mixing two expressions—'confusing' object and image—run-on
imagery—Conclusion.

Hopkins's difficulty in expressing the individual by means of a
universal term—his solution—the compound word—the restrictive adjectival expression—attribution in his poetry—predication.

The adjective-noun compound—the noun-noun compound—
other noun compounds—use of the hyphen—the adjectival
compound—the compound ending in -ed.

Inscape expressed by means of a converted adjective—and by
means of an abstract noun—the hypallage—the omission of the
relative pronoun.

The expression of the inscape of an object in action—the transitive verb—the gerund—the predicate preferred to the adverb—
Conclusion.

Hopkins's essay on the nature of words—the inscape of a word
—its results.

Analogy in Hopkins's poetry—his conversions—the use of
prefixes and suffixes—new expressions formed after analogy of
existing ones.

His notes on Homer—a word used with different grammatical
functions—with different syntactical functions—with different
meanings—the employment of the syllepsis—convergence of
meanings and the use of homophones.

More notes on Homer—the workings of assonance in
Hopkins's poetry—Conclusion.

PREFACE

THE purpose of this essay is indicated by its subtitle. By analysing Hopkins's mind, his attitude towards reality, the avowed aim of his poetry, I hope to have succeeded in making this poet more accessible and more intelligible. He should not be a poets' poet only: his poetry is too rich for that.

It will be clear that only through the kindness of many could this book have been written. Father Martin D'Arcy gave me every facility to study the autograph papers of Hopkins at Campion Hall, Oxford. The librarians of the Amsterdam University Library, the British Museum Library, the Bodleian Library and the Glasgow University Library never failed in courtesy and were ever ready to help me. Mr. A. G. van Kranendonk, Professor of English Literature at the University of Amsterdam, zealously watched the growth of my book and carefully read the manuscript. To all of them I am very grateful.

Though many of their names are only mentioned in the bibliography and some of them occur in the text only to be attacked as adversaries, yet I wish to acknowledge my indebtedness to the authors of books and articles on Hopkins. It is impossible to trace how much I owe them exactly, but there can be no doubt that their studies have been very stimulating and must have contributed both to my choice of the subject and the way in which I have treated it.

Special thanks are due to Mr. G. W. S. Hopkins. He took an interest in this study from its very first stages when he gave me free access to all the autograph papers of Hopkins in his possession, down to the actual printing of it, which also means that he saved it from being destroyed by bombs. I only hope that the final result is, in some slight way at least, worthy of his great and lovable uncle.

January 1948

PREFACE to the SECOND EDITION

A quarter of a century ago one might have wondered whether interest in Gerard Manley Hopkins and his poetry would really last. Numerous scholarly writings on the poet and his *oeuvre*, thickly scattered over this period, a visit to Gonzaga University, Spokane (Washington), where a formidable Hopkins library has found its home, the recent foundation of the Hopkins Society prove that Hopkins's stature has grown. This explains the publication of a new edition of *Gerard Manley Hopkins. An essay towards the understanding of his poetry*, which has been out of print for more than fifteen years.

This new edition does not differ from the first except for some corrections of minor importance. It has not been brought up to date. This does not mean that the author is unappreciative of the fine scholarly work that has been given to Hopkins over the last twenty years or that he is deaf to criticism. On the contrary. But in his modest opinion the main thesis of this study is in no need of modification after all those years. Moreover, publication in its original form has certain advantages of weight and interest. As it stands, the book gives in passing an idea of what had happened to Hopkinsean studies during the twenty five years that passed since the poems were published by the then Poet Laureate Robert Bridges (1918). At the same time it informs one of the literary standards and the literary tastes during and immediately after the second World war. And those who are well acquainted with the interpretation and appreciation of Hopkins today will be interested to observe how far prophecies concerning the poet's future have come true, how far remarks and observations made at that time have proved to be valid and right, now a quarter of a century of careful scholarship has been devoted to the man and his work.

Even the original bibliography has been maintained. There was no point in bringing it up to date as this heavy task has been recently completed by Edward H. Cohen (*Works and criticism of Gerard Manley Hopkins: a comprehensive bibliography*. Washington, D.C., The Catholic University of America Press, 1969). To drop the bibliography altogether appears to be a loss, as the original bibliography will be of sufficient interest as giving an idea of the state of Hopkins studies at that time. The poems are still numbered according to the

second edition of the *Poems of G. M. Hopkins,* but the table of numbering at the back of the book has been revised and the numbers correlated
with those of the fourth edition (1967).

Naturally, if the book were written today, or at least re-written,
it would be different in matters like tone, diction, and style.   For one
thing, the author being now a good deal older, would have done his
best to be more modest and less apodictic in propounding his views;
for another, he would certainly be much milder in his judgment of
others and more appreciative.   And so the second edition goes forth,
with quite a number of imperfections on its head.   Among these
imperfections I would especially like to mention that I seemingly pass
by the most valuable work done by others mainly on matters treated
in my final chapter.   That all who have considerably added to a right
understanding and true appreciation of Hopkins during these past
twenty five years and yet find no trace of this in the second edition
rest assured that this in no way reflects the author's gratitude for what
they have done on behalf of the great man and poet Hopkins was, and
for the many hours of stimulating reading and thinking they have
given to the author of this book.

November 1969

INTRODUCTION

DURING the last two decades numerous articles and papers have appeared dealing with the life and poetry of Gerard Manley Hopkins. It is no longer possible to pass him by or dismiss him with a brief reference to his eccentricities, even though his poetic *œuvre* contains no more than fifty poems, mostly sonnets, and some fragments. It was not until 1918 that Bridges published this small collection of poems, which he had treasured and kept to himself since the poet's death almost thirty years before. Since then Hopkins has attracted the attention of both critics and poets. Opinions differ as to his merits, but his innovations in the technique and the medium of poetry have so influenced the poetry of this day that, at least for the present, there is no danger of his falling back into the ranks of the unknown.

Hopkins's poetry apparently allows for a very wide margin of appreciation. Articles have been published hailing him as a major poet. Some papers have appeared that are as extravagant in denying him praise as a poet as others had been in lavishly bestowing it upon him. Thus, for instance, F. R. Leavis bluntly states that Hopkins was 'one of the most remarkable technical innovators who ever wrote ... and he was a major poet'.[1] Another critic, slightly more guarded in his pronouncements, writes that Hopkins was 'intrinsically a great poet'.[2] This is one extreme. The other extreme is the point of view adopted, for example, by D. S. MacColl, who gives his essay entitled 'Patmore and Hopkins' the sub-title 'Sense and Nonsense in English Prosody', where the nonsense stands for Hopkins.[3] Most critics, however, have taken a sometimes rather shaky middle position; recognizing many good qualities in Hopkins's poetry, but utterly baffled by his oddity, they are really at a loss what to think of him. Thus Hopkins is highly praised because he had 'an exquisite literary sense' but condemned because in spite of it he lapsed 'into nearly every literary fault'.[4] Middleton Murry is driven to the conclusion that, in spite of some outstanding poetic qualities, the achievement as a whole is a complete failure, and the failure is due to the 'starvation of experience which his vocation imposed upon him'.[5] Of the same opinion is the anonymous reviewer in *The Times Literary Supplement*, maintaining that Hopkins's poetry, 'with all its power and suggestiveness

is in fact just such a failure as Bridges said it was' (9 February 1933).
Hardly more flattering, but for one redeeming quality, is this criticism:

Hopkins at a glance is maddening. The glance shows the most
individual of all English poets: that alone makes something in his favour.
And against him the equally obvious torture of words, torture of meaning
and rhythm, wilfulness, sometimes childishness, all packed into no more
than fifty complete poems, make no less strong an objection. . . . No
matter what words are used, what perfection or imperfection of image, what
style, what age, what integrity, the true speed, the subtlest nicety of nice
minds, is what turns a poet to greatness. . . . And this alone, however
ridiculous he sometimes makes himself, gives him, with all other good poets,
his excellence.[6]

These are only a handful of extracts, but they are so typical of the
criticisms of Hopkins's poetry, that there is no need to multiply them.

Turning from the critics to the poets, we notice at once how they
have claimed Hopkins as one of themselves and are eager to be taught
by him; they have bestowed the highest praise on Hopkins's originality
and on his innovations. We have come to acquiesce in the curious
fact that in anthologies of modern poetry Hopkins is found in company
with Cecil Day Lewis, Stephen Spender and W. H. Auden. It is not
so easy to trace the influence that Hopkins has exercised over the poets
of to-day, and on this point as on so many other points connected with
Hopkins's poetry opinions again differ widely. Herbert Read is convinced that Hopkins's influence has been very powerful on the poets of
this generation and he holds that 'when the history of the last decade
comes to be written by a dispassionate critic, no influence will rank in
importance with that of G. M. Hopkins'; [7] and elsewhere he has
written that 'Hopkins is amongst the living poets of our time, and no
influence whatsoever is so potent for the future of English poetry'.[8]
Dr. Leavis is of the same opinion: 'Hopkins is likely to prove, for our
time and the future, the one influential poet of the Victorian age, and
he seems to me the greatest.' [9]

Granted that the influence has been powerful of recent years, we
may well ask whether it has been to the benefit of English poetry, and
on this point not everybody agrees with Dr. Leavis and Herbert Read.
Thus Edith Sitwell writes with reference to the younger poets that
proudly confess to following the lead of Hopkins: 'They produce
exterior and therefore unliving rhythms, instead of rhythms which
live in, under, and over, the lines. Imitations of them have resulted,
too, in a complete loss of melody, arising from falsified, clumsy, or too
thick vowel-schemes, clumsy and huddled-up assonance-patterns,

useless alliterations, and a meaningless accumulation of knotted consonants.' [10]   Hardly less devastating is the criticism of Max Plowman: 'The paltry caricaturists of greatness, the disenchanted, detached intellectualists have called passing attention to themselves, and their petulant trifling, because as a monkey may learn a trick, they have succeeded in mangling their verse structures into some sort of technical imitation of Hopkins's sprung rhythm.' [11]   Louis MacNeice is more moderate and to my mind he comes near the truth where he maintains that 'Hopkins's influence on younger poets to-day has often been unfortunate.   A close imitation of his manner is dangerous because both his rhythms and his syntax were peculiarly appropriate to his own unusual circumstances and his own tortured but vital personality.' [12]

It is this lack of agreement of poets and critics among themselves where the merits and the influence of Hopkins are concerned, and even more where the value of his technical innovations is in question, that has done great harm to his reputation.   For the intelligent and interested reader of Hopkins's poetry, who, puzzled by his obscurity and oddity, looks for guidance from these poets and critics that claim to understand him, is in the end sadly disappointed.   He suspects the greatness of this poet, but his queer diction and very odd technique are a barrier preventing him from completely enjoying Hopkins's poetry.   Critics have not helped him to any extent in surmounting this barrier.   And this not so much because they do not agree among themselves, but what is worse, because they have not tried to prove their point of view by arguments based on facts which anyone can verify for himself.   Critics of Hopkins have stated, but have attempted no proof; and another critic has denied these statements and propounded his own views of Hopkins, similarly without satisfactorily accounting for them.   The result is that many readers of Hopkins's poetry have given up the struggle to arrive at some definite opinion about Hopkins's poetic gifts, because no help was forthcoming and, to all appearances, no help could ever be expected.   G. W. Stonier has attacked the critics of Hopkins's poetry and warned us with a 'Beware of critics'; indeed, I too have fault to find with those who have interpreted Hopkins in an off-hand way and have given no arguments to show how their interpretation is borne out by facts.   It is not very helpful to say that Hopkins's intensity of language was 'the expression of an important moral conflict, related to an outer social and intellectual conflict',[13] unless it is shown how and why this conflict demanded this most peculiar form of language.   And Hopkins's poetry is not interpreted—and interpretation should be the critic's duty—by vague references to a *fractured personality* or a *tortured personality*,[14] if the critic safely refrains from telling us how such a personality could not but employ this mode of expression. Bridges himself inaugurated this very unsatisfactory form of criticism; he registers in Hopkins's poetry lack of taste, perversion of human feeling, exaggerated Marianism, a naked encounter of sensualism and asceticism, absence of literary decorum, wilful oddity and obscurity, all of them the outcome of artistic wantonness (*Poems*, p. 96); is it not possible that Bridges missed some essential aspect of Hopkins's technique, failed to detect the why and wherefore of these *defects*, which would give them their meaning and perhaps even their beauty? Such a catalogue of faults and defects is hardly more helpful to an understanding of Hopkins's poetry than the above references to his personality and psychological make-up. What is said by these critics is not necessarily untrue; but the point is that their statements are useless, unless an attempt is made to prove that they are true and are really relevant to Hopkins's practice. In his book *New Literary Values* David Daiches does try to give a reasoned explanation of the innovations of Hopkins and of his influence on the poets of to-day. He writes as follows:

If in the poetry of to-day there is one single highest common factor that can be isolated, that factor consists less of loyalty to a predecessor than of an *attitude*, an attitude to the poetic medium and also an attitude to society. The connexion between the technical and social aspects of this attitude may seem remote, and indeed it is remote enough to justify their separate consideration, but an ultimate connexion does exist (p. 23).

This introduction sounds promising enough, the more so because it is to lead to the conclusion that the modern poets have so much in common with Hopkins for this reason, that they 'came to adopt an attitude towards the poetic medium which Hopkins for reasons of his own had adopted and exploited' (p. 24). There may even be a suggestion in the argument that, since Hopkins and the moderns had adopted a similar attitude towards the poetic medium, their attitude towards society was the same; and if this point were proved, we should certainly have gained in our understanding of both Hopkins and the moderns alike. But the argument adduced by Daiches is fallacious, though couched in terms that at first sight seem convincing enough. He has to show how a certain attitude towards society involves a definite attitude towards the poetic medium, and this is how he does it: 'An attitude to society on the part of a poet involves a definite view of the function of poetry, and a view of the function of poetry is bound to have a reaction on poetic technique' (p. 23). The argument sounds plausible: indeed, a view of the function of poetry *is* bound to have a reaction on poetic technique; I shall try to prove in the second chapter that this holds good in the case of Hopkins. And it is also true that an attitude to society involves a definite view of the function of poetry. But unknowingly the critic here confuses two senses of the word 'function'. When he says that an attitude to society involves a definite view of the function of poetry, 'function' means the effect that poetry is intended to achieve in society; it is not unlikely that the critic had in mind the left-wing propaganda of certain modern poets. But where he says that a view of the function of poetry must react on poetic technique he takes 'function' in the sense of its proper end in and by itself, as normally laid down in a definition of poetry. Now that function in this latter sense has its reaction on technique will be readily granted. That this holds good of function in the other sense is not true. I fail to understand how the technique of poetry is changed by poetry being intended to serve some social cause or other instead of being meant to give aesthetic enjoyment only, as long as it remains poetry.

Even if I cannot agree with the arguments of Daiches, I at least appreciate the effort he has made in trying to establish a connexion between Hopkins's technique and his outlook on this world. He may not have succeeded, but at any rate he was well aware that Hopkins's poetry cannot be properly understood unless it is made plain why the poet turned to this very strange form of language, and how this language was the result of his attitude towards external reality. On a far more ambitious scale and much more thoroughly this subject was treated by Dr. J. Pick in his *Gerard Manley Hopkins: Priest and Poet*, and by Dr. W. H. Gardner in the first volume of his *Gerard Manley Hopkins, 1884–1889*. In my opinion neither book is in this respect a success. Dr. Pick treats the relation between the poet and the priest. He hardly touches, however, upon the relation between the poet's religious experience and his peculiar poetic technique. Dr. Gardner registers various devices, deviations from normal grammar and syntax; but the ultimate *why* and *wherefore* is not explained. And to explain this is precisely what I have made the object of this study. My aim has been to place within the reader's reach the clue to Hopkins's most peculiar medium of expression; I intend to show that obscurity and oddity are not the result of artistic wantonness or bad literary taste, but the logical outcome of his poetical theories, which, in their turn, can be logically deduced from Hopkins's view of life.

Consequently I have not contented myself with giving lists of various grammatical and syntactical irregularities occurring in Hopkins's poetry; these too are useless unless it is pointed out why Hopkins had recourse to these deviations from common usage. It is for the same reason that I have not set myself the task of giving an exhaustive treatment of the grammar and syntax of Hopkins. I have in the very first place been careful to give the principles that underlie the poet's practice and have adduced so much material to support it as is necessary and useful. An exhaustive treatment of his syntactical or grammatical idiosyncrasies is only given where partial treatment of the material would tend to give a false impression.

The first two chapters of this study are almost exclusively devoted to an investigation of Hopkins's mind. Yet these chapters are indispensable, and I attach to them the greatest value, because they put before the reader those data without which a correct interpretation of his poetry is, to my mind, impossible. Thus in the first chapter little else is attempted save an explanation of *inscape* and *instress*—terms that very clearly bring out Hopkins's attitude towards external reality and his philosophy of life. In the second chapter Hopkins's poetic theories are examined, again in relation to inscape and instress. Finally in the last three chapters I hope to show how Hopkins employed this most personal form of language as the only means by which he could realize the aim of his poetry.

I have been very fortunate in having had at my disposal the three published volumes of letters and the published *Note-Books and Papers*. They contain a wealth of material without which it would have been altogether impossible to discover the secret of Hopkins's poetic language. I have been careful to make the poet speak for himself; in putting forward my opinions I have always tried to prove their soundness from his own writings so as to minimize the possibility of reading into Hopkins what is not there. I hope thus to have taken all precautions against false or faulty interpretation.

It is nowadays the fashion to detect literary echoes and on their strength to relate a poet to other poets most like him in a certain respect. This appears to have been a favourite method with critics of Hopkins. Thus Hopkins is most like Shelley, according to Middleton Murry,[15] and akin to Milton according to Charles Williams;[16] Miss

E. E. Phare is of the opinion that he has some affinity among others to Wordsworth and she agrees with Babette Deutsch that he was also very close to Keats.[17]   But T. S. Eliot's view is that he 'should be compared with . . . the minor poet nearest contemporary to him, and most like him: George Meredith'.[18]   According to Walter de la Mare and Osbert Burdett, Hopkins reminds us of John Donne.[19]   He has much in common with the Metaphysicals, especially Crashaw and Vaughan.[20]   He has been mentioned in one breath with Walt Whitman,[21] and a curious likeness has been discovered between him and Patmore.[22]   Among 'his literary ancestry' are also mentioned Charles Doughty and William Barnes ;[23] 'he is obviously inspired by Welsh poetry',[24] and his supposed great likeness to Aeschylus in many respects is the subject of again another article.[25]

I am sure that this list is not complete; but in any case it must be obvious to all who like to compare him to others, that it is a hopeless task to assign Hopkins to his right place.   But suppose it were possible to compare him to another poet, would such a comparison be very useful?   Every good poet can be like another only in accidentals; each poet is essentially his own species, as Hopkins once said, and any likeness with others cannot but be superficial.   It is for this reason that I think it regrettable that so much fine scholarly work should have been spent on a cause not worthy of it: for Dr. Gardner's book on Hopkins's poetry bears as subtitle: 'A Study of Poetic Idiosyncrasy in Relation to Poetic Tradition.'   It is for the same reason that I have abstained from drawing any parallel between Hopkins and other poets, and from interpreting his poetry by referring the reader to that of others.   Throughout the book I confine myself to Hopkins himself, to his mind, his character, his personality, his outlook on life, his perception of external reality, his philosophy, and similar subjects, and to the effect these factors had on his poetry.   But there is one danger against which the reader must be forewarned.   Various practices or poetical devices of Hopkins will be explained as the result of his very personal way of looking at things or of his definite attitude towards the aim of poetry; now the same practice and the same device may occur in another poet without my making any reference to it. From this no conclusion whatever should be drawn; reticence does not mean that this practice, occurring in another poet, must be due to the same cause, neither does it mean that it cannot be due to the same cause.   I readily grant that at times an investigation into the methods of another poet might be interesting; thus it would undoubtedly be of interest to hear that Hopkins very often omits the

B

article for reasons that made another poet very careful to put it in; but such digressions lie outside the scope of this book.

After these paragraphs the title of the book will need no explanation and no apology. I can only hope that the reader of Hopkins's poetry will find in these pages what he expects to find in them and that this book will be a valuable help in both rightly understanding and appreciating the poet.

Throughout I have appended notes which are printed at the end of the book. They are usually references to words or passages quoted in the text; in no case do the notes contain remarks that are directly relevant to the contents of the paragraph in question. As I am not dealing with Hopkins's rhythmical innovations, I have thought it better to leave out the rhythmical marks in quoting from his poetry. The Roman figures I, II, III refer to the three volumes of letters edited by Claude Abbott; the *Note-Books and Papers* edited by Humphry House are referred to as *N*. (see p. 188). All quotations taken from early drafts of poems belong to either the 'A' MS. or the 'H' MS. All other references are to the *Poems* edited by Robert Bridges, second edition with Appendix, &c., by Charles Williams, 1930, not to the third edition edited by Dr. W. H. Gardner, 1948. A comparative table of the numbering of the poems in these two editions is given at the end of this book.

THE MEANING OF 'INSCAPE' AND 'INSTRESS'

IN a letter to Bridges dated 15 February 1879 Hopkins wrote: '. . . But as air, melody, is what strikes me most of all in music and design in painting, so design, pattern or what I am in the habit of calling "inscape" is what I above all aim at in poetry' (I. 66). And in a letter to Patmore, written some seven years later, he criticizes the poetic talent of Sir Samuel Ferguson as follows: '. . . he was a poet as the Irish are—to judge by the little of his I have seen—full of feeling, high thoughts, flow of verse, point, often fine imagery and other virtues, but the essential and only lasting thing left out—what I call *inscape* . . .' (III. 225).

From these two quotations it is already abundantly clear, how important it must be for the understanding of Hopkins's poetry to know what he meant by inscape and what inscape meant to him as a poet. Curiously enough, critics have almost all of them refrained from examining this notion. There is no excuse for such negligence, as Hopkins confessed inscape to be the very aim of his poetry. Those critics who have paid attention to inscape, which in another place Hopkins calls 'the very soul of art' (II. 135), have, in my opinion, not grasped its meaning, nor have they realized its far-reaching implications: their treatment of inscape has been too cursory and superficial and even incorrect.[1] Nearly all of them have taken 'inscape' for little more than one of the many words which Hopkins coined because the English language did not contain any one word representing this objective fact or thing, or because he was dissatisfied with the existing word for reasons of euphony.[2] They have failed to see that this word represented something that was not observed by other men, therefore caused a very personal experience, and so was to stand for something not experienced by others, for which consequently there existed no word, because the need for it was never felt. For 'inscape' is the unified complex of those sensible qualities of the object of perception that strike us as inseparably belonging to and most typical of it, so that through the knowledge of this unified complex of sense-data we may gain an insight into the individual essence of the object. We are ever inclined to compare and contrast objects and to put before us what is

universal in them.   Our minds turn unconsciously as it were and
instinctively to what this object has in common with others: it needs
special concentration of our faculties to bring before the mind an
object's distinctiveness.   Now Hopkins habitually looked at objects
with the fixed determination to catch what was individually distinctive
in them in order thus to arrive at some insight into their essence as
individuals.   To express this set of individuating characteristics in a
suitable term he coined the word 'inscape'.

   Hopkins has nowhere defined 'inscape'.   I could only draw up the
definition given above after a detailed study of the many places in
which the word occurs.   I shall now attempt to show that the above
definition is right.   The best starting point to arrive at a correct
definition is the analogy on which the word 'inscape' has been formed.
The suffix 'scape' in 'landscape' and 'seascape' posits the presence of a
unifying principle which enables us to consider part of the countryside or sea as a unit and as an individual, but so that this part is perceived to carry the typical properties of the actually undivided whole.
By placing special emphasis on this second aspect of 'scape': 'the part
is perceived to carry the typical properties of the actually undivided
whole', 'scape' comes to stand for that being which is an exact copy or
reflection of the individual whole on which it is dependent for its
existence.   In this meaning 'scape' is frequently used by Hopkins in
his notes on the *Spiritual Exercises* of St. Ignatius Loyola as the
translation of the *species* of the scholastic theory of knowledge: the
species being the reflection made by a sensible object in our senses and
on our mind, which actualizes our power to know the object with a
sensitive or intellectual knowledge respectively, and in which the
object is known.[3]   Bearing in mind this aspect of the meaning of
scape I infer that '*in*-scape' is the outward reflection of the *inner* nature
of a thing, or a sensible copy or representation of its individual essence;
and thus I define it as the unified complex of those sensible qualities
of an object that strike us as inseparably belonging to and most typical
of that object, so that through the knowledge of this unified complex
of sense-data we may gain an insight into the individual essence of the
object.   The correctness of this definition is confirmed by the relation
between inscape and beauty as expressed by Hopkins in the following
quotation: 'But if it (*sc.* verse) has a meaning and is meant to be heard
for its own sake it will be poetry if you take poetry to be a kind of
composition and not the virtue or excellence of that kind, as eloquence
is the virtue of oratory and not oratory only and *beauty the virtue of
inscape and not inscape only*' (*N.* 250) (italics mine).   For beauty, as

Hopkins sees it, lies in the 'relation between the parts to each other and of the parts to the whole' (*N.* 68), or, as he expresses himself more carefully, in the 'apprehension of the presence in one of more than one thing' ('On the signs of health and decay in the arts' (unpublished)). Hence for Hopkins beauty presupposes unity in the object, just as it presupposes inscape, which is clear from the above quotation. The reason why he related beauty to inscape must consequently be that in inscape there is inherent unity, a unity, that is, proceeding from the nature of the object itself.

It is now not hard to understand why Hopkins compared inscape to design and pattern, yet could not be satisfied with either of them. These terms do, indeed, denote a principle which creates unity and order; but the unity and order brought about by them are imposed from without and they are in no way the necessary outward manifestation of an intrinsic principle of unity, while it is precisely the outward manifestation of this intrinsic principle of unity which is signified by inscape. Thus there may be pattern and design while no inscape can be discovered; this is made clear by the following quotation in which 'scaping' is synonymous with pattern: [4]

I saw also a good engraving of his *Vintage Festival*, which impressed the thought one would gather also from Rembrandt . . . . of a master of scaping rather than of inscape. For vigorous rhetorical but realistic and unaffected scaping holds everything but no arch-inscape is thought of (N. 194).

But from this quotation it is equally clear that inscape *can* be present in a picture. Provided that in the poet's artistic vision the object of art shows forth an intrinsic unity that extends further than a mere harmonious ordering of parts as designated by pattern, the poet will grasp its inscape. Hence not only an organic being, as a flower, tree or animal, each a *unum per se*, will present itself to Hopkins's vision as an individual, but also objects of art, and even nature-scenes, can in his perception display a marked individuality. It is well to bear this point in mind. For if individuality—and similarly inscape—is taken in its strict philosophical sense only, one will be frequently faced by inconsistencies in Hopkins's use of this word.

The following quotations, all taken from his diary, well illustrate the use of 'inscape'; they have been chosen so as to bring out clearly the difference between inscape and mere shape.

Spanish chestnuts: their inscape here bold, jutty, somewhat oak-like, attractive, the branching visible and the leaved peaks spotted so as to make crests of eyes (*N.* 108).

This is the time to study inscape in the spraying of trees, for the swelling buds carry them to a pitch which the eye could not else gather . . . in these sprays at all events there is a new world of inscape (*N.* 141).

The bluebells in your hand baffle you with their inscape, made to every sense: if you draw your fingers through them they are lodged and struggle/ with a shock of wet heads; the long stalks rub and click and flatten to a fan on one another like your fingers themselves would when you passed the palms hard across one another, making a brittle rub and jostle like the noise of a hurdle strained by leaning against; then there is the faint honey smell and in the mouth the sweet gum when you bite them. But this is easy, it is the eye they baffle. They give one a fancy of pan-pipes and of some wind instruments with stops—a trombone perhaps. The overhung necks. . . . Then the knot or 'knoop' of buds some shut, some just gaping, which makes the pencil of the whole spike, should be noticed: the inscape of the flower most finely carried out in the siding of the axes, each striking a greater and greater slant, is finished in these clustered buds, which for the most part are not straightened but rise to the end like a tongue and this and their tapering and a little flattening they have make them look like the heads of snakes (*N.* 145–6).

The Horned Violet is a pretty thing, gracefully lashed. Even in withering the flower ran through beautiful inscapes by the screwing up of the petals into straight little barrels or tubes. It is not that inscape does not govern the behaviour of things in slack and decay as one can see even in the pining of the skin in the old and even in a skeleton but that horror prepossesses the mind, but in this case there was nothing in itself to shew even whether the flower were shutting or opening (*N.* 149).

There is one notable dead tree . . ., the inscape markedly holding its most simple and beautiful oneness up from the ground through a graceful swerve below (I think) the spring of branches up to the tops of the timber (*N.* 154). Of these [*sc.* mountains] the first four names are round-headed; the Little Matterhorn couples the two inscapes, being a sharpened bolt rising from a flattened shoulder . . . the range on the other side of Zermatt and skirting the Zermatt valley are concave, cusped; they run like waves in the wind, ricked and sharply inscaped . . . (*N.* 109).[5]

The participle 'inscaped' here means carrying an inscape; it occurs in other places also:

Note that a slender race of fine flue cloud inscaped in continuous eyebrow curves hitched on the Weisshorn peak as it passed . . . (*N.* 110).

From a height in Richmond Park saw trees in the river flat below inscaped in distinctly projected, crisp, and almost hard, rows of loaves, their edges, especially at the top, being a little fixed and shaped with shadow (*N.* 120).

The verb 'to inscape' means to catch the inscape of an object, as in these lines:

Sham fight on the Common, 7000 men, chiefly volunteers. Went up in the morning to get an impression but it was too soon, however got this—caught that inscape in the horse that you see in the pediment especially and other bas reliefs of the Parthenon and even which Sophocles had felt and expresses in two choruses of the *Oedipus Coloneus*, running on the likeness of a horse to a breaker, a wave of the sea curling over. I looked at the groin or the flank and saw how the set of the hair symmetrically flowed outwards from it to all parts of the body, so that, following that one may inscape the whole beast very simply (*N.* 189).

But what I note it all for is this: before I had always taken the sunset and the sun as quite out of gauge with each other, as indeed physically they are, for the eye after looking at the sun is blunted to everything else and if you look at the rest of the sunset you must cover the sun, but today I inscaped them together and made the sun the true eye and ace of the whole, as it is. It was all active and tossing out light and started as strongly forward from the field as a long stone or a boss in the knop of the chalice-stem: it is indeed by stalling it so that it falls into scape with the sky (*N.* 129).

Because man is ever inclined to turn to what an object is like, he rarely contemplates things with that concentration of mind which is necessary to get a glimpse of their uniqueness and distinctiveness. Hopkins almost habitually looked at nature with this intense concentration; he looked hard at things and patiently waited till the inscape had strongly grown on him (*N.* 152, 140): 'Unless you refresh the mind from time to time,' he wrote in his diary, 'you cannot always remember or believe how deep the inscape in things is' (*N.* 140). And again: 'Stepped into a barn of ours, a great shadowy barn, where the hay had been stacked on either side, and looking at the great rudely arched timberframes . . . I thought how sadly beauty of inscape was unknown and buried away from simple people and yet how near at hand it was if they had eyes to see it and it could be called out everywhere again' (*N.* 161).   The world is full of inscape (*N.* 173) but one has to be alone to 'discover' it (*N.* 135).   He complains in his diary that 'even with one companion ecstasy is almost banished: you want to be alone and to feel that, and leisure—all pressure taken off' (*N.* 111); and again he writes: 'I saw the inscape though freshly, as if my eye were still growing, though with a companion the eye and the ear are for the most part shut and instress cannot come' (*N.* 171).

These last quotations well show how highly Hopkins valued the perception of inscape: he regrets that, though the world is full of things and events that deserve attention, they 'go without notice, go un-witnessed' (II. 7).   If by the contemplation of the individuality of things in nature he became rapt in ecstasy we can understand that

Hopkins was sincere when he wrote these pathetic lines: 'The ashtree growing in the corner of the garden was felled. It was lopped first: I heard the sound and looking out and seeing it maimed there came at that moment a great pang and I wished to die and not to see the inscapes of the world destroyed any more' (*N.* 174). In his short poem on Binsey Poplars he is grieved for the same reason: the poplars were felled and so the rural scene was 'unselved', its inscape was destroyed.

Such a profound admiration and love of the inscapes of the world is most striking and requires a closer study. Why did Hopkins consider the inscapes so precious that their destruction pained him so severely and acutely? When man contemplates an object, he usually does it to grasp the beauty of the thing and to rejoice in its perception; in the case of Hopkins this is not altogether true. Inscape is not primarily valuable because it is so closely related to beauty; for in the quotations given Hopkins entirely prescinds from beauty. Inscape is appreciated for its own sake, for a value entirely its own. It was his spiritual outlook on this world that made inscape so precious to Hopkins; the inscape of an object was, so to speak, more 'word of God', reminded him more of the Creator, than a superficial impression could have done.

How intense his awareness was of the actual presence of God in each individual thing and how he realized that each individual thing in its own peculiar way brought him news about the Creator appears from a careful reading of his writings. God's utterance of Himself outside Himself is this world, he writes, so that then this world is 'word, expression, news of God'.[6]

I do not think I have ever seen anything more beautiful than the bluebell I have been looking at. I know the beauty of our Lord by it (*N.* 133–4).
As we drove home the stars came out thick: I leant back to look at them and my heart opening more than usual praised our Lord to and in whom all that beauty comes home (*N.* 205).
This busy working of nature wholly independent of the earth and seeming to go on in a strain of time not reckoned by our reckoning of days and years but simpler and as if correcting the preoccupation of the world by being preoccupied with and appealing to and dated to the day of judgment was like a new witness to God and filled me with delightful fear (*N.* 135).

It is a theme which continually recurs in his poetry:

> I kiss my hand
> To the stars, lovely-asunder
> Starlight, wafting him out of it; ...   *Deutschland* st. 5

> I walk, I lift up, I lift up heart, eyes,
>> Down all that glory in the heavens to glean our Saviour;
>>> *Poems* 14

>> The world is charged with the grandeur of God.
>>> It will flame out, like shining from shook foil;   *Poems* 7

> Always and everywhere he is reminded of
>> him that present and past,
>> Heaven and earth are word of, worded by.
>>> *Deutschland* st. 29

To this poet all things 'are charged with love, are charged with God and if we know how to touch them give off sparks and take fire, yield drops and flow, ring and tell of him' (*N.* 342).   But nowhere has he more emphatically spoken of the actual presence of God in things than in the following quotation:

Neither do I deny that God is so deeply present to everything ('Tu autem, O bone omnipotens, eras superior summo meo et interior intimo meo') that it would be impossible for him but for his infinity not to be identified with them or, from the other side, impossible but for his infinity so to be present to them.   This is oddly expressed, I see; I mean/a being so intimately present as God is to other things would be identified with them were it not for God's infinity or were it not for God's infinity he could not be so intimately present to things (*N.* 316).[7]

Quotations such as these fully justify our conclusion that Hopkins appreciated inscape so highly because in perceiving inscape he knew the individual well; and the better he knew the individual, the more sparks it threw off, to use his own words, 'sparks that rang of God' (for this image I refer the reader to p. 19).   This consciousness of the presence of God in things markedly influenced his loving admiration of the inscapes of the world, for as his attention concentrated more and more intensely on the individual and on the individual as 'charged with love, charged with God', he came more and more to look upon the object as worthy of a *personal* love.   There is evidence in his writings that Hopkins was acutely aware of the fact that, in spite of profound generic and specific differences, man and beast and inanimate nature were all alike 'selves', 'supposits', so that *from this angle of vision* there was between man and the rest of creation a difference of degree, not one of kind.   In man the self was joined to a free nature, while in all other things the self was not so raised.   Thus he writes : 'A person is defined a rational (that is/intellectual) supposit, the supposit of a rational nature.   A supposit is a self . . .' (*N.* 322).

'Now if self begins to manifest its freedom with the rise from an irrational to a rational nature, it is . . .' (*N*. 323).   This most peculiar attitude towards the self—whether joined to a rational or to an irrational nature—immediately proceeding from his habitual search for the inscape of things, drove Hopkins instinctively to their *impersonation*, a personifying, that is, of the irrational selves on the level of sensitive perception, unconscious therefore, in so far as Hopkins neither reflected upon it nor intellectually accounted for it. I wish to stress the words 'on the level of sensitive perception'; this restriction implies that the impersonation did not take place by an explicit act of comparison by and in which the intellect presented the irrational object as a person.   For this reason I have chosen the term 'impersonation', and I preserve the term 'personification' for that figure of speech which cannot exist without a conscious act of intellectual reasoning.   As soon as the poet reflects on his perception and becomes thereby conscious of his impersonation, he at once opens the way to complete personification.   Personification is in Hopkins frequent enough:

> 'Some find me a sword; some
> The flange and the rail; flame,
> Fang, or flood' goes *Death* on drum. . . .
>
> *Deutschland* st. 11

> `Earth, sweet *Earth*, sweet *landscape* . . .   *Poems* 35

> . . . Natural heart's ivy, *Patience* masks,
> Our ruins of wrecked past purpose.   id. 46

> *Fury* had shrieked 'No ling-
> ering!   Let me be fell: force I must be brief'.   id. 41

> When will you ever, *Peace*, wild wooddove, shy wings shut,
> Your round me roaming end, and under be my boughs?   id. 22

> Not, I'll not, carrion comfort, *Despair*, not feast on thee. . . . id. 40

> I caught this morning morning's minion, king-
> dom of daylight's dauphin, dapple-dawn-drawn
>
> *Falcon*. . . . id. 12

> *Hope* had grown grey hairs,
> *Hope* had mourning on,
> Trenched with tears, carved with cares,
> *Hope* was twelve hours gone. . . .
>
> *Deutschland* st. 15

> This, by *Despair*, bred Hangdog dull; by *Rage*,
> Manwolf, worse; . . .   *Poems* 42

These are some instances of complete personification and in most of them the use of the capital is ample proof of it.   A proof so tangible as this cannot of course be given in the case of impersonation, because the use of capitals would argue that Hopkins had reflected on his impersonations and so we should be back again to personification. But there are in his poetry indications enough that place the fact of impersonation beyond any reasonable doubt.   Among these indications I mention in the first place the extremely frequent absence of the article.   This absence has the effect of making the common noun into a kind of proper name.   'The omission of *the* is I think an extension of the way in which we say "Father", "government", etc.', so Hopkins remarked himself (*N.* 148).   But the use of such proper names surely points to the fact that in inscaping an irrational being its outstanding individuality impressed him so much that he unreflectingly looked upon this being as a person.   Instances abound:

. . . For *earth* her being has unbound . . .	*Poems* 32
. . . while *moon* shall wear and wend . . .	id. 11
Bright *sun* lanced fire in the heavenly bay.	*Eurydice* st. 6
Delightfully the bright wind . . . beats *earth* bare . . .	
	Poems 48
Earth hears no hurtle then from fiercest fray.	id. 49
I have put my lips on pleas	
Would brandle adamantine *heaven*. . . .	id. 23, st. 12
. . . is the shipwreck then a harvest, does *tempest* carry the grain for thee?	
	Deutschland st. 31
Commonweal	
Little I reck ho! lacklevel in, if all had bread:	*Poems* 42
I wake and feel the fell of *dark*, not *day*.	id. 45
and *thrush*	
Through the echoing timber does so rinse and wring	
The ear . . .	id. 9
Star-eyed strawberry-breasted	
Throstle . . .	
Forms and warms the life within.	id. 18
No wonder of it: sheer plod makes *plough* down sillion	
Shine . . .	id. 12

Very striking is the very frequent absence of the article before parts of the body:

. . . *mind* has mountains . . .	id. 41

> Nor *mouth* had, no nor *mind*, expressed
> What *heart* heard of, *ghost* guessed.   *Poems* 31

> Father and fondler of *heart* thou hast wrung . . .
>   *Deutschland* st. 9

> . . . nor can *foot* feel, being shod.   *Poems* 7

> To what serves mortal beauty —dangerous; does set danc-
> ing *blood*—   id. 38

I have only given a selection of examples; a cursory reading of the poems will impress any reader with the frequency of the absence of the article.[8]   This scant use of the article cannot be explained or accounted for by the fact that the article 'took up room in the lines which [Hopkins] could not afford them'.   Bridges in his preface to the notes to Hopkins's poetry has thus tried to account, not for the omission of the article explicitly, but for the omission of what he calls 'purely constructional syllables' (*Poems*, p. 97). This explanation is most unconvincing; for while other poets had to fit their matter in closely defined 'room', the expanse of which was limited by the metre based on a certain fixed number of syllables to the line, Hopkins was free— though free within bounds, which he could not transgress with impunity—to increase or decrease the number of syllables; it was the elasticity of sprung rhythm.   In maintaining that Hopkins was free in fixing the length of the line I repudiate the false conclusion that he could therefore squeeze as many syllables into any one line as he liked, provided he took care not to exceed the fixed number of stressed syllables; even sprung rhythm has its rules and even strict rules, as he told Bridges more than once.   'Lack of room', however, yields no explanation of the many omissions in a poet like Hopkins, who even lengthened his lines by 'outrides', which are purely extrametrical syllables.   Lack of room should be the last resource in our attempts to account for the omission of articles, conjunctions, pronouns, &c.

The omission of the article is not the only indication pointing to Hopkins's practice of impersonation; strongly in favour of it is his habit of addressing the objects he contemplates.   For we do not ordinarily address inanimate objects unless we feel that there is present some ground for considering them as in sympathy with us and capable of responding to our sympathy towards them.   Though by itself this practice does not strictly prove impersonation to the exclusion of personification proper, the fact that Hopkins does not use the capital, in my opinion makes impersonation the more likely explanation.   It

serves no purpose to give a complete list of all the lines in which
Hopkins addresses the objects of his contemplation: some more striking instances may be given:

> My aspens dear, whose airy cages quelled. . . .   *Poems* 19
>
> . . . graceless growth, thou hast confounded
> Rural rural keeping . . .   id. 20
>
> The heart's eye grieves
> Discovering you, dark tramplers, tyrant years.   id. 54
>
> Brute beauty and valour and act, oh, air, pride, plume, here
> Buckle!   id. 12
>
> My heart, but you were dovewinged, I can tell,
> Carrier-witted, I am bold to boast . . . *Deutschland* st. 3
>
> Heart, you round me right
> With: Our evening is over us . . .   *Poems* 32

But in the examples given so far it is not only the omission of the
article or the form of address that points to impersonation; through his
keen awareness of the individuality of the objects of contemplation
Hopkins was naturally led to attribute to them qualities which by right
only belong to persons.   Thus to repeat some quotations: 'earth her
being has unbound', 'what heart heard', 'does set dancing blood',
'discovering you, dark tramplers, tyrant years'.   Elsewhere Hopkins
speaks of the 'behaviour' of clouds (*Poems* 14) and again impersonation of the air and breakers and snowflakes is implied in the following
lines:

> She to the black-about air, to the breaker, the thickly
> Falling flakes, to the throng that catches and quails
> Was calling 'O Christ, Christ, come quickly'
> *Deutschland* st. 24

If we study the quotations more closely we find that frequently the
object is seen in action: 'wind beats earth bare', 'bright sun lanced fire',
the aspens 'quelled or quenched . . . the leaping sun', 'thrush . . . does
so rinse and wring the ear', tempest 'carries the grain', &c.   If
Hopkins saw things as 'charged with love, charged with God', he saw
them thereby also as charged with activity.   His poetry teems with
examples: he speaks of 'wild air', 'live air', a bird's 'wild nest', 'wild
starlight', &c.   Nature was to him 'a Heraclitean Fire'.

> The glassy peartree leaves and blooms, they brush
> The descending blue; that blue is all in a rush
> With richness; . . .   *Poems* 9

'The heart rears wings bold and bolder' and, to Hopkins's keen perception as a beholder 'hurls earth for him off under his feet' (*Poems* 14).

In the *Deutschland* there occur these lines:

> [they] fell to the deck
> (Crushed them)   st. 17

It might sound strange that the deck 'crushed' the victims of the waves as if it were falling on top of them with its 'crushing' weight and not the other way about.   To Hopkins the deck displayed an activity and actively took part in the ruin of the crew and the passengers as much as the storm-winds and the waves and the falling snow.   Instances of this kind, not too obvious and easily overlooked in the reading, are by no means rare.   In his poem *God's Grandeur* Hopkins wrote: 'There lives the dearest freshness deep down things', where *lives* should receive its due emphasis; for once the inscape had been caught, the object began to be active and to live; each mortal thing 'Deals out that being indoors each one dwells' (*Poems* 34).   This constant attribution of activity and life as a rule found its origin in Hopkins's impersonation of the object; this is the explanation which he himself has given to it in an essay written in his undergraduate days, entitled: 'On the connexion between mythology and philosophy', which does not appear among the papers edited by Humphry House.   The following paragraph is relevant here:

Those things which like the common chattels of the house are in the control of man entirely and offer no resistance except weight, become generalized, that is cease to have individuality or personality, but all things which by their freedom from man's control, their irregular and unaccountable sequence, and their influence on man himself most of all, look like persons and seem to have will of their own, these receive only personal names.

Though this paragraph was written when Hopkins was still at Oxford, it already shows his peculiar attitude towards the things of nature, which he developed as time went on.   We need add nothing to it; only be it noticed how again Hopkins seems to identify individuality and personality.[9]

I have mentioned only some of the more obvious indications of impersonation in Hopkins's poetry.   Impersonation was the natural result of his having inscaped an object, of his perceiving the object as charged with God.   Because of this impersonation he was grieved to see the inscapes of the world destroyed and because of it he regretted that the inscapes 'went unnoticed'.

Once Hopkins had inscaped an object and unreflectingly personified it, there was created the possibility of communication between the poet and the object as between two persons. The object is no longer passive, but is perceived to act independently of the poet. Hence the poet, who now unreflectingly looks upon the object as a person, will ascribe to it properties only applicable to man: examples of this we have seen. But inversely this object, this quasi-person, will impress the stamp of its own individuality, of its own 'self', on the poet. The impression thus made by inscape upon the poet, not by means of any poetic activity on the part of the poet but in virtue of its own individual essence, is interpreted by him in terms of human *affects*. But before further entering into this important but not easy question I must first turn to another coinage of Hopkins's, intimately bound up with inscape and as fundamental to a right understanding of the poet; we have arrived at the notion of *instress*.

As in the case of inscape, Hopkins has nowhere defined 'instress', although it is of no rare occurrence. The starting point in trying to get at its precise meaning will be the use of the noun 'stress', which in Hopkins's philosophical writings stands for the perfection of being, proper to a thing.[10] He identifies it with the Greek ἐνέργεια, in scholastic terminology rendered by *actus*, which is the principle of actuality in a thing. The preference of 'stress' to 'act', the normal word in scholastic terminology, most likely finds its reason in the greater expressiveness of the Saxon word, 'stress' well marking the force which keeps a thing in existence and its strain after continued existence. The noun 'instress' adds little to this meaning of stress except in so far as the prefix emphasizes that this force is intrinsic to the thing. A good instance of its use is found in his notes on the *Spiritual Exercises* of St. Ignatius, which have been partly edited by House; the following quotation occurs among the unpublished notes: '. . . as in man all that energy or instress with which the soul animates and otherwise acts in the body is by death thrown back upon the soul itself; so . . .' The verb 'to instress' is oftener found; the following quotations all bear out the fundamental meaning of 'to come to stress', 'to actualize':

And as a mere possibility, passive power, is not power proper and has no activity it cannot of itself come to stress, cannot instress itself (*N.* 310).

. . . for the constant repetition, the continuity, of the bad thought is that actualising of it, that instressing of it . . . (*N.* 321).

This access is either of grace, which is 'supernature', to nature or of more grace to grace already given, and it takes the form of instressing the affective will, of affecting the will towards the good which he proposes (*N.* 325).

It is to be remarked that *choice* in the sense of taking of one and leaving of another real alternative is not what freedom of pitch really and strictly lies in. It is choice as when in English we say 'because I choose', which means no more than . . . I instress my will to so-and-so (*N.* 328).[11]

In this sense the verb occurs twice in his poetry:

> What the heart is! which . . .
> To its own fine function, wild and self-instressed,
> Falls light as ten years long taught how to and why.
>
> *Poems* 27

This example is clear enough, which, perhaps, cannot be said of the second, occurring in the *Deutschland* st. 5:

> Since, tho' he is under the world's splendour and wonder,
> His mystery must be instressed, stressed;

yet the same meaning should be attached to the verb here; 'actualized' as a translation would be clumsy, but 'realized', while preserving its original signification, hits the sense exactly.

It is most important that one should firmly grasp and continually bear in mind this fundamental meaning of 'instress' before turning to its use by Hopkins elsewhere, where it is not always employed with the same accuracy and well-defined meaning. The original meaning of instress then is that stress or energy of being by which 'all things are upheld' (*N.* 98), and strive after continued existence. Placing 'instress' by the side of 'inscape' we note that the instress will strike the poet as the force that holds the inscape together; it is for him the power that ever actualizes the inscape. Further, we observe that in the act of perception the inscape is known first and in this grasp of the inscape is felt the stress of being behind it, is felt its instress. I speak of 'feeling the instress' and I do so with good reason. Inscape, being a sensitive manifestation of a being's individuality, is perceived by the senses; but instress, though given in the perception of inscape, is not directly perceived by the senses, because it is not a primary sensible quality of the thing. Hence it follows that, while inscape can be described, however imperfectly, in terms of sense-impressions, instress cannot, but must be interpreted in terms of its impression on the soul, in terms, that is, of *affects* of the soul.   We can now understand why and how it is that 'instress' in Hopkins's writings stands for two distinct and separate things, related to each other as cause and effect; as a cause 'instress' refers for Hopkins to that core of being or inherent energy which is the actuality of the object; as effect 'instress' stands for the specifically individual impression the object makes on man.   The first meaning is illustrated by the following instances:

[Description of Ely Cathedral]   The all-powerfulness of instress in mode and the immediateness of its effect are very remarkable (*N.* 119).
. . . a pair of plain three-light lancets in each clearstory of the S. transept, which dwell on the eye with simple direct instress of trinity . . . (*N.* 154).
Take a *few* primroses in a glass and the instress of—brilliancy, sort of starriness: I have not the right word—so simple a flower gives is remarkable (*N.* 142–3).
To Westminster Abbey, where I went round the cloisters . . . took in the beautiful paired triforium-arcade with cinqfoiled wheels riding the arches (there is a simplicity of instress in the cinqfoil) etc. (*N.* 209).
Millais—*Scotch Firs: 'The silence that is in the lonely woods'*—No such thing, instress absent, firtrunks ungrouped, four or so pairing but not markedly . . . (*N.* 192).

In some of these quotations Hopkins tries to express the instress in some sensible form; but the lines about the primroses well show how difficult it was to give precisely the nature of that fugitive perfection of instress.   In the following quotations there is an interesting mingling of the two senses of instress:

Bluebells in Hodder wood, all hanging their heads one way.   I caught as well as I could . . . the lovely / what people call / 'gracious' bidding one to another or all one way, the level or stage or shire of colour they make hanging in the air a foot above the grass, and a notable glare the eye may abstract and sever from the blue colour / of light beating up from so many glassy heads, which like water is good to float their deeper instress in upon the mind (*N.* 174).
. . . the greatest stack of cloud, to call it one cloud, I ever can recall seeing . . . The instress of its size came from comparison not with what was visible but with the remembrance of other clouds (*N.* 150).
Tall larches on slope of a hill near the lake and mill, also a wychelm, also a beech, both of these with ivory-white bark pied with green moss: there was an instress about this spot (*N.* 204).

In the following examples 'instress' should be taken in its second sense and is nearly synonymous with impression:

I saw the inscape though freshly, as if my eye were still growing, though

C

with a companion the eye and the ear are for the most part shut and instress cannot come (*N.* 171).

The comet—I have seen it at bedtime in the west, with head to the ground, white, a soft well-shaped tail, not big: I felt a certain awe and instress, a feeling of strangeness, flight (. . .), and of threatening (*N.* 198).

We went up to the castle but not in: standing before the gateway I had an instress which only the true old work gives from the strong and noble inscape of the pointedarch (*N.* 216–17).

In the second example we again feel that Hopkins is doing his best to find words to express the peculiar sensation which instress gives. But as instress is of necessity as distinctive as inscape, general terms will never crystallize its peculiar quality; the poet can only approach its nature by stating what it is like and what it recalls:

The blue was charged with simple instress, the higher, zenith sky earnest and frowning, lower more light and sweet (*N.* 143).

Very instructive in this respect is the following quotation:

On this walk I came to a cross road I had been at in the morning carrying it in another 'running instress'. I was surprised to recognize it and the moment I did it lost its present instress, breaking off from what had immediately gone before, and fell into the morning's. . . . And what is this running instress, so independent of at least the immediate scape of the thing, which unmistakeably distinguishes and individualises things? Not imposed outwards from the mind as for instance by melancholy or strong feeling: I easily distinguish that instress. I think it is this same running instress by which we identify, or, better, test and refuse to identify with our various suggestions / a thought which has just slipped from the mind at an interruption (*N.* 153–4).

Hopkins is working out a problem here; on the one hand he is sure that the effect of instress has its origin in the object itself, is as distinctive of the object's individuality as inscape and consequently does not proceed from the onlooker's subjective mood, in terms of which something objective is interpreted; on the other hand he cannot describe this peculiar effect which the object causes in him except in terms of personal subjective impressions. These impressions, as he notices himself, being personal and subjective, never touch the real essence of the instress, which in its objectivity is individually distinctive. And relevant is the last phrase: in trying to recover the thought that has just slipped from our mind we can turn to the impression it has left there and having grasped the instress of the thought in its distinctiveness we may thus be able to recover the inscape of the thought. It is in this passage more than anywhere else that we see Hopkins at work to disentangle the essentially twofold aspect of instress. Indeed, it is not improbable that as yet Hopkins had not reflected upon its precise nature; he felt what instress meant and not writing for any public he took no trouble sharply to distinguish its double meaning. It is only when he is engaged upon writing on philosophical and theological subjects—and he had great hopes that this work would be published— that he took care to delineate what precisely he meant by 'instress'. But in this exposition I have not followed the chronological order; the instances of 'instress' taken from his diary are all of them dated earlier than 1875, the first year that was completely devoted to the study of theology; and the instances from which I derived the fundamental meaning of 'instress' are all dated later than this year. Consequently we find that in his later letters he no longer wavers which meaning to attach to 'instress' and which meaning to put in the first place: if 'instress' is used in non-philosophical writings, he identifies it with the sensation or *affect* aroused in him by inscape. If he feels the need to try and describe this individually distinctive impression he has recourse to like impressions made on him by other inscapes. The first traces of this exclusive use of 'instress' as synonymous with feeling are found in the closing pages of his diary, written in 1875:

Looking all around but most in looking far up the valley I felt an instress and charm of Wales (*N.* 210).
Then . . . I looked into a lovely comb that gave me the instress of *Weeping Winifred*, which all the west country seems to me to have . . . (*N.* 200).

In his correspondence he mentions among the many beauties of Dixon's poetry 'the instress of feeling' (II. 37 and 63), and to Patmore he writes that in his [Patmore's] poems the intelligence is in excess of the 'instress or feeling' (III. 173). And notice how Hopkins associates various instresses:

His [i.e. William Barnes's] poems used to charm me by their Westcountry 'instress', a most peculiar product of England, which I associate with airs like Weeping Winefred, Polly Oliver, or Poor Mary Ann, with Herrick and Herbert, with the Worcestershire, Herefordshire and Welsh landscape, and above all with the smell of oxeyes and applelofts: this instress is helped by particular rhythms and these Barnes employs . . . (I. 88).

At the risk of a slight digression I draw the reader's attention to the logical inference from the above section about 'instress'. If Hopkins is going to describe the individually distinctive aspect of an object, he can do so by giving a word-picture in terms of its inscape, or he can choose a second way and describe it in terms of instress, which, as we have shown, was to Hopkins as distinctive as inscape. Most of the passages quoted in this chapter establish Hopkins as a writer who takes great pains to describe things objectively in minutest detail. This is what we should expect; for most of the quotations I have so far given were taken from his prose writings, in which the emotional appeal is made subject to objective representation and so there is little room for instress. But the passages in which 'instress' occurs in its second sense already show that even in his diary the second way of representing things is not lacking; thus, for instance, he speaks of 'sad-coloured' sky (*N.* 171), 'pinings of snow' (*N.* 172), 'grave green' (*N.* 142), 'happy leaves' (*N.* 165). It is to be expected that in his poetry this way of giving the essence of things should come more to the fore than in his prose writings: thus he describes the heavy boots of the plough-man as 'bluffhide' (*Poems* 43), the ploughed unsown fields as 'surly mould' (id. 36), the iron tools and boot-nails of workmen as 'surly steel' (id. 42); hail he calls 'grimstones', which was afterwards rejected for 'hailropes' (*Eurydice* st. 7); he speaks of 'proud fire' (*Poems* 21), the 'shy wings' of the wooddove (id. 22), the blacksmith's 'grim forge' (id. 29) &c. I single out two instances for full quotation:

> Flesh falls within sight of us, we, though our flower the same,
>   Wave with the meadow, forget that there must
> The *sour scythe* cringe, and the *blear share* come.   *Deutschland* st. 11

A magnificent combination of these two forms of description is found in the opening lines of his poem *Spelt from Sibyl's leaves* (*Poems* 32):

Earnest, earthless, equal, attuneable, | vaulty, voluminous, . . . stupendous Evening. . . .

The pause marked by Hopkins himself indicates the transition from description by instress to that by inscape; in *stupendous* the two waves reach a common crest, for *stupendous* is expressive of both inscape and instress.[12]

I must point to another inference from Hopkins's consciousness of instress: it serves him as a source of imagery. For just as things may be described in terms of another thing which visually or auditorily is like or unlike it, so this writer describes an object in terms of another because the instress that each possesses for him affords a ground for comparison or contrast. I am well aware that this is not peculiar to Hopkins nor do I hold that a good deal of imagery in other poets may not be explained in the same way. I only wish to point out that as a source of imagery, association of impressions, such as found in

Hopkins, finds its logical explanation in the attention he was ever paying to the instress of things.   We are not then surprised that in Hopkins there occur instances of *synaesthesia,* which is always based on association of impressions.   Thus we read in his diary:

Above the Breithorn Antares sparkled like a bright crabapple tingling in the wind (*N.* 109).
But this sober grey darkness and pale light was happily broken through by the orange of the pealing of Mitton bells (*N.* 158).

And in his poetry Hopkins speaks of the 'moth-soft Milky Way' (*Deutschland* st. 26), of 'bugle blue eggs' (*Poems* 18),[13] 'thunder-purple' (id. 21), 'very-violet-sweet' (id. 14); the song of the thrush strikes the poet 'like lightnings' (id. 9).   Most interesting is the way in which Hopkins appears to have associated the sound of bells with flames of fire.   Thus in the *Deutschland* (st. 26) he writes of 'belled fire', and in a quotation from his diary, given on page 7, we read of '*sparks* that *ring* of God'.   Similarly, an object displaying great activity recalls to him the flames of fire: poetic inspiration is 'live and lancing like the blowpipe flame' (*Poems* 51).   We thus have the series: activity—flames of fire—the pealing of bells; the curious thing is that this series we find complete in his magnificent sonnet *The Wind-hover* (*Poems* 12).   Having described how the bird rides and strides the steady air, he exclaims: 'how he rung upon the rein of a wimpling wing', where 'rung' very possibly might cause obscurity.   In the sestet the poet bids the bird's 'beauty and valour and act', the 'air, pride, plume' join, and seeing the bird fly forth in its majesty he continues:

> . . . AND the fire that breaks from thee then, a billion
> Times tolled lovelier, more dangerous, O my chevalier!

The words 'fire' and 'tolled' show how the instresses of the bird in action, of fire and of tolling bells, are joined in one poetic experience. It will be objected that I have changed the text by making an alteration in the word 'told'; indeed I have.   But that this alternative spelling is legitimate I shall prove in my final chapter.[14]

'Inscape' and 'instress' are two terms which well bring out Hopkins's preoccupation with the 'self' of things.   These coinages clearly point to his intense awareness of what was individually distinctive in every object and to his consciousness of the object's independence in being and activity.   This should be remembered in the reading of Hopkins's poetry, for in it is situated a characteristic and essential difference

between Hopkins and other poets. It might, indeed, be objected
that what I have put forward as typical of Hopkins is found in most
poets. It does not, for instance, appear that Hopkins's reaction to
the impressions received from external objects is so very different from
that of other poets: they all interpret such impressions in terms of
various *affects*; at the most it would seem to follow that, because
Hopkins was more conscious of the individuality of these objects and
their effect upon man, his reaction following the contact with objects
was more reasoned and less spontaneous than the reaction of other
poets. But such a way of presenting things is superficial; the difference between Hopkins and other poets goes deeper. Hopkins contemplated objects separately, each with its own individuating characteristics, each independent in its existence and activity, even granted that
he used 'individual' in a somewhat extended sense. Through his
impersonation he was ever in communication with them as with
persons, each with 'life' entirely its own. The result of this attitude
was that the object appealed to the poet in virtue of its own emotional
atmosphere; if any object stirred Hopkins emotionally, the appeal
arose in and from the object as from a real person. The poet is
passive, receptive; he has opened wide his heart the better to respond
to this quasi-personal appeal of the object. There is no question of
inferring from impressions received that the object possesses certain
qualities; Hopkins cannot ascribe to an object qualities which to his
mind it does not really and literally possess. Here Hopkins differs
essentially from other poets. They may indeed be similarly affected by
external reality, but they interpret those impressions altogether otherwise. Approaching nature through the imagination they interpret
the emotions arising in themselves as due to a great poetic sensibility
and not as due principally to any independent activity on the part of
the object. Poetic fancy makes them attribute the emotion to a
fancied, imagined, but unreal emotional appeal directly forthcoming
from the object itself; they cast round it an emotional atmosphere
which the object possesses only in virtue of the poet's imagination and
of the poet's imaginative interpretation. In Hopkins there remains a
clearly marked separation between the activity of the poet and the
independent activity of the object; they do not become one in a poetic
experience in which the subjective element and the objective element
have been fused by the imagination. The emotional activity ascribed
to an object by Hopkins is real to him and not fancied, as real as its
inscape.

The importance of these remarks is not to be underestimated in the judging of Hopkins's poetry. It is this peculiar non-imaginative attitude towards the selves that gives his poems that severity, even rawness of tone which is the very opposite of, for example, Keats's luxuriousness. I do not discredit one method of approaching and interpreting external reality nor do I favour the other as more poetic, nor do I hold of course that Hopkins lacked poetic imagination. I only wish to stress the fact that Hopkins's living conviction that things were 'selves' prevented him from bestowing upon them imagined life and imagined activity; hence that breath of seriousness which blows through the whole of his small but exquisite poetic *œuvre*.

That Hopkins should look for a philosophical justification of this original attitude towards the individual as revealed in his conception of inscape and instress is what we naturally expect from such a scholar as he was. The study of philosophy appealed to him. If we read his philosophical essays written in his Oxford days, we are struck by the thoroughness, very remarkable for a young student, with which he entered into problems of morality, art, knowledge and so on. There remain four essays on four Greek philosophers, one of which, that on Parmenides, has found a place among the published papers (*N.* 98–102). The fact that only this essay has been published might perhaps lead one to think that it is the only one written and that therefore Hopkins as an undergraduate was a follower of Parmenides. This conclusion is wrong; Aristotle was his philosopher. In a letter to Alexander Baillie dated 12 February 1868 he writes:

This reminds me to say that I find myself in an even prostrate admiration of Aristotle and am of the way of thinking, so far as I know him or know about him, that he is the end-all and be-all of philosophy. But I shd. be sorry to bore you with philosophy, of which you no doubt have had enough what with reading for fellowships: with me on the contrary an interest in philosophy is almost the only one I can feel myself quite free to indulge in still (III. 84).

It is with this profound admiration of the philosophy of Aristotle that in 1870 he began the course of philosophical studies in the Society of Jesus, lasting for three complete years. We should expect that the philosophy taught in that Order, being that of St. Thomas Aquinas, would have attracted Hopkins, precisely because St. Thomas built his system on the philosophy of Aristotle. The fact, however, is that at the end of his second year he had transferred his loyalty to Duns Scotus. In his diary under 3 August 1872 we find this entry:

At this time I had first begun to get hold of the copy of Scotus on the

Sentences . . . and was flush with a new stroke of enthusiasm.   It may come to nothing or it may be a mercy of God.   But just then when I took in any inscape of the sky or the sea I thought of Scotus (*N.* 161).

For the rest of his life Hopkins was a Scotist, and an ardent one.   To Bridges he once wrote:

I do not afflict myself much about my ignorance here, for I could remove it as far as I should much care to do, whenever it became advisable, here-after, but it was with sorrow that I put back Aristotle's *Metaphysics* in the library some time ago feeling that I could not read them now and so probably should never.   After all I can, at all events a little, read Duns Scotus and I care for him even more than Aristotle and more *pace tua* than a dozen Hegels (I. 31).

It is with delight that he notes in his diary that in one week he had the privilege of meeting the only two Scotists in the country (*N.* 198).   In his philosophical writings he frequently refers to Scotus and when he is stationed as a preacher at Oxford he expresses his loving admiration of this 'of realty the rarest-veinèd unraveller' in a sonnet (*Poems* 20).

The reason why the philosophy of Scotus attracted him even more strongly than Aristotle's is given by Hopkins himself where he says that the inscape of things made him think of Scotus.   This argues that Scotus's philosophy gave the philosophical basis to his inscape. And it is not hard to see how the theory of inscape harmonizes beauti-fully with the system of Scotus.[15]   For Aristotle and St. Thomas the first and proper object of our knowledge is the essence of things, abstraction made of its individuality.   According to the theory of knowledge of Scotus the first object of all human knowledge is the individual as it here and now presents itself to our senses. As a man gains sensitive experience of the object, at the same time he arrives at an intuitive knowledge of the concrete individual and on this knowledge the mind works and reaches intellectual knowledge of the universal essence by the method of abstraction.   We see at once why it was that Hopkins gave serious attention to these claims put forward by Scotus in favour of the relatively high value of sensitive experience, not merely as the material for the mind to work upon, but as valuable in itself.   He had long since concentrated his attention on the perception of inscape, and had long since been conscious that in the inscape he really knew the individual essence, not completely, indeed, not even with a true intellectual knowledge; but in the intuitive glimpse following sensitive contact with the object he was aware of knowing it as a self.

But more than the theory of knowledge it was the theory of the individuating principle that made Hopkins turn eagerly to Scotus. This is evident from the passages in his published and unpublished notes in which his occupation with this principle in things made him refer to the authority of Scotus as an argument in favour of his views (*N.* 321 and 328). Hopkins was convinced that inscape was a direct sensible manifestation of the entity that makes a thing one and individual. But this theory clashed with that of Aristotle and St. Thomas, who maintain that the individuality of a thing is not due to any separate entity, but is explained by the reception of the form, i.e. the determinative principle of things, in the matter as the principle capable of being determined. This matter is predisposed to a certain quantity. It is matter as the basis of quantity receiving the form that thereby individualizes things. In this theory there is no place for the inscape because the form is not individual in virtue of its own essence, but only in virtue of its being joined with the quantified matter. But if we turn to Scotus's exposition of this problem we see how inscape falls directly into place in this theory; for inscape precisely covers what Scotus calls *haecceitas*; this statement as well as this term requires an explanation.

Scotus distinguishes in each object three 'formalities', that is to say, three entities that constitute an object, which, corresponding to the logical determinations in our mind, generic, specific, and individual, have each their own reality in the object. Thus in every object there is a generic form, a specific form and an individual form. One should be careful not to misunderstand Scotus here; he does not hold that these three forms are separate entities *in this sense* that they exclude one another and are placed in the thing one behind or on top of the other; they are on the contrary in one another as distinct features of one multi-potential thing. Now just as the specific form arises from the generic by the addition of the specific difference, so the individual form arises from the specific by the addition of an individualizing difference; and this perfection, which is the final determination of the being in its specific essence, is called by Scotus *haecceitas*, 'this-ness'. Thus while in the philosophy of Aristotle and St. Thomas there is no separate entity which limits the universal, determines and individualizes it, there is such a separate entity in the theory of Scotus: and inscape was for Hopkins its sensible manifestation. From this it follows that according to Scotus created things are immediately active in virtue of this separate entity, the individuating 'haecceity'; for this principle, being 'form', is active. In Aristotle and St. Thomas on the other hand

things are not so immediately active, because the individuating principle, *sc.* the matter, is a passive principle.   This theory of Scotus
again confirmed Hopkins's vision of things as ever active.

These are some points that show how Hopkins's theories found a
philosophical justification and confirmation in the system of Scotus.
This is a point that has been overlooked: when I speak of Scotist
influence on Hopkins, it should not be taken to mean that Scotus
shaped Hopkins's peculiar views about external reality; Hopkins was a
Scotist before he was aware of it; he practised Scotism, so to say, before
he knew the system of Scotus.   For all the instances I have given of
the use of 'inscape' and 'instress' in his diary and of his awareness of
an active principle in things date from before the time that he began
his thorough study of Scotus.   But in maintaining this I do not assert
that Scotus did not exercise a decided influence on Hopkins; for once
he had found out that his views fitted so well in Scotus's philosophy,
he adhered to it with confidence and spent more time and energy in
understanding it.

Where Hopkins was undoubtedly directly influenced by Scotus is
in his attitude towards his own self.   The study of Scotus made him
turn in upon himself and consider the essence of the individuating
principle in himself.   This reflection upon the make-up of his own
being, which gradually grew into a preoccupation with the inmost
depths of his self, his own nature, its origin and end, has unmistakably
left its marks upon his poetry.   I do not contend that it was the
influence of Scotus alone that aroused in Hopkins that peculiar inclination towards self-examination and self-analysis.   From his youth on-
wards there existed in him a tendency towards introspection; traces of
an intense self-awareness and of a vigorous control exercised over all
the affects of his heart and the thoughts of his mind are apparent in
his early diaries, only short fragments of which have been published.
That such self-control made for an acute consciousness of his self is
clear enough.   Add to this his susceptibility to the subtle influences of
nature and art, as evident from his published diary, and furthermore
the practice of examination of conscience as part of his daily duties as
a Jesuit, and we have the more important influences at work to inten-
sify the inclination towards self-analysis.   Yet the effect which his
study of Scotism had on him in this respect should not be minimized.
His habitual self-examination never extended to the fact of his self;
this was simply taken for granted until his Scotist studies made him
examine the essence of the ego, of 'that inmost self of mine which has
been said to be and to be felt to be, to taste, more distinctive than the

taste of clove or alum, the smell of walnutleaf or hart's horn, more distinctive, more selved, than all things else . . .' (*N.* 312). It is the reflection upon the fact that he exists as this individual, as this *self*, that made him see in this his own existence a proof of God's existence. I shall quote the fairly long introduction to this argument; it is very instructive as well as very typical:

We may learn that all things are created by consideration of the world without or of ourselves the world within. The former is the consideration commonly dwelt upon, but the latter takes on the mind more hold. I find myself both as a man and as myself something most determined and distinctive, at pitch, more distinctive and higher pitched than anything else I see; I find myself with my pleasures and pains, my powers and my experiences, my deserts and guilt, my shame and sense of beauty, my dangers, hopes, fears, and all my fate, more important to myself than anything I see. And when I ask where does all this throng and stack of being, so rich, so distinctive, so important, come from / nothing I see can answer me. And this whether I speak of human nature or of my individuality, my self being. For human nature, being more highly pitched, selved and distinctive than anything in the world, can have been developed, evolved, condensed, from the vastness of the world not anyhow or by the working of common powers but only by one of finer or higher pitch and determination than itself and certainly than any that elsewhere we see, for this power had to force forward the starting or stubborn elements to the one pitch required. And this is much more true when we consider the mind; when I consider my self being, my consciousness and feeling of myself, that taste of myself, of *I* and *me* above and in all things, which is more distinctive than the taste of ale or alum, more distinctive than the smell of walnutleaf or camphor, and is incommunicable by any means to another man (as when I was a child I used to ask myself: What must it be to be someone else?). Nothing else in nature comes near this unspeakable stress of pitch, distinctiveness, and selving, this self being of my own. Nothing explains it or resembles it, except so far as this, that other men to themselves have the same feeling. But this only multiplies the phenomena to be explained so far as the cases are like and do resemble. But to me there is no resemblance: searching nature I taste *self* but at one tankard, that of my own being. The development, refinement, condensation of nothing shews any sign of being able to match this to me or give me another taste of it, a taste even resembling it.
One may dwell on this further. We say that any two things, however unlike are in something like. This is the one exception: when I compare my self, my being-myself, with anything else whatever, all things alike, all in the same degree, rebuff me with blank unlikeness; so that my knowledge of it, which is so intense, is from itself alone, they in no way help me to understand it. And even those things with which I in some sort identify

myself, as my country or family, and those things which I own and call mine, as my clothes and so on, all presuppose the stricter sense of *self* and *me* and *mine* and are from that derivative (*N*. 309–10).

   This theoretical preoccupation with his self found its counterpart in the closest analysis of his complete being; and this can easily be traced in his poetry.   Hopkins was aware of his body as he was aware of his soul.   This awareness of his body, of the life of the senses, of the nature of his sensitive experience, explains the sensuous character of his poetry.   He reflected upon all his activities; all his senses were concerned in the perception of inscape, and he himself was very conscious of it.   It gives his poetry something hard and very precise, even a flatness and crudeness of diction, so often admired but often misunderstood by poets and critics.   In the intensity of bodily experience he could not be contented with vague indications; he is impelled to mention the very part of his body that is concerned in it: 'and the *midriff* astrain with leaning of, laced with fire of stress' (*Deutschland* st. 2), 'I have put my *lips* on pleas . . .' (*Poems* 23), 'I lift up *heart, eyes* . . .' (*Poems* 14), '*bones* built in me, *flesh* filled, *blood* brimmed the curse' [of being my own self] (*Poems* 45).   He speaks of his heart as being 'touched in your bower of *bone*' (*Deutschland* st. 18); when he is crushed under the weight of dire desolation he speaks of his 'bruised *bones*' (*Poems* 40); he feels God's *finger* and it is God's *right foot* that has been placed upon him (*Deutschland* st. 1 and *Poems* 40). Similarly in speaking of others: Christ's interest *eyes* man, Christ's *foot* follows kind (*Poems* 10). I return to this subject in another chapter (p. 124).

   More important than the awareness of his body is his intense consciousness of what took place in his soul.   In his poems and more particularly in the *Deutschland* and the 'terrible sonnets' he has carefully recorded the nature of the pains that had come over him.   He could not let sufferings just happen to him: he 'lived' his sorrows as intensely as his joys: he could never passively acquiesce in them.   He is ever asking himself what he suffers and why it is that he should suffer so much.   The answer he gives to this question in *Poems* 45 is worth consideration:

> God's most deep decree
> Bitter would have me taste: my taste was me;
> Bones built in me, flesh filled, blood brimmed the curse.
>   Selfyeast of spirit a dull dough sours.   I see
> The lost are like this, and their scourge to be
> As I am mine, their sweating selves; but worse.

He was then left to live his bare *self*; God had withdrawn His hand and had left him to his own resources, to his 'sweating self'. By God he had been raised through grace to a higher order of being and now this grace had been withdrawn and again he was his *self* and no more. It was precisely this problem of the way in which grace affects the will of man that had exercised a strange fascination on Hopkins. He had taken great pains in examining the workings of grace, the relation in man between will and intellect, the influence of grace on free will and so on, and through this thoroughgoing study he had come to know that without grace man is a bare *self*: and now he felt what it meant to be left a bare self. In his meditation on hell he had shown how the lost suffered just because they were 'their sweating selves',[16] and hence we can understand why 'terrible' is not too strong a word for the sufferings expressed in his sonnets. He had been acutely aware, since his study of Scotus especially, of his dependence on God's grace on the one hand and on the other of the war within between the spirit and the flesh, between the bare self and the self raised by grace:

> We hear our hearts grate on themselves: it kills
> To bruise them dearer. Yet the rebellious wills
> Of us we do bid God bend to him even so.   *Poems 46*

This aspect of the human self always creeps into his considerations of other men. His spiritual outlook on life turned his attention from the bare self to the 'complete' self, the self raised by grace; as a priest he could not help it. Struck as he is by the beauty of the portrait of brother and sister, he soon turns away from 'mortal beauty', and asks: 'Where lies your landmark, seamark, or soul's star?' (*Poems* 54); enthusiastic as he is about the gracious answer given him by his server at Mass and pleased with this boy so 'mannerly-hearted', he must express his anxiety about the boy's future:

> Only . . . O on that path you pace
> Run all your race, O brace sterner that strain!   *Poems 27*

The very same theme is introduced in *The Bugler's First Communion* (*Poems* 23); indeed, in spite of the fact that 'this child's drift seemed by a divine doom channelled', the poet has his misgivings; it is possible that the boy will not redeem the fair promise he gives now.

> Recorded only, I have put my lips on pleas
> Would brandle adamantine heaven with ride and jar, did
> Prayer go disregarded.

When he is affected by the foundering of the *Eurydice,* it is not the death of the seaman that causes him the greatest sorrow; no, but the possible loss of souls:

> These daredeaths, ay this crew, in
> Unchrist, all rolled in ruin—
> Deeply surely I need to deplore it . . . *Eurydice* st. 24–5

Similarly in *The Wreck of the Deutschland*: hardly has he begun the story of the shipwreck than his thoughts are irresistibly drawn to the fate of those who lost their lives, and we find the poet pathetically pleading with his God and Master for mercy on their souls:

> O Father, not under thy feathers nor ever as guessing
> The goal was a shoal, of a fourth the doom to be drowned;
> Yet did the dark side of the bay of thy blessing
> Not vault them, the millions of rounds of thy mercy not reeve even them in?
> (st. 12)

And in stanza 31, when the poet is at the height of joy and triumph and admiration of the 'master of the tides', he suddenly bids his heart weep and bleed for 'the comfortless unconfessed' among those who were drowned.

In truth he could pray: 'Complete thy creature dear' (*Poems* 16), for man was not complete unless man's self, his inmost self, was raised and Christ was in him:

And God *in forma servi* rests *in servo*, that is / Christ as a solid in his member as a hollow or shell, both things being the image of God; which can only be perfectly when the member is in all things conformed to Christ. This too best brings out the nature of the man himself, as the lettering on a sail or device upon a flag are best seen when it fills (*N.* 343).

The great concern of this unselfish man was to bring out the nature of man complete, man's completed self.

The conclusion to be drawn from this chapter is that this poet must be read with intense concentration of all the faculties. He is never satisfied unless he has caught the inscape of things and has felt their instress; and the eagerness to know the self of things is matched by the keen consciousness of his own self, a most acute self-awareness.

This chapter was then not written for the sake of biographical interest; it is intended to be the necessary introduction to, and the indispensable help for, the reading of Hopkins's poetry with that concentration and attention which his most sincere poetic confessions deserve: for Hopkins's poetry originates from the deepest and most earnest realization of his own rich self.

'INSCAPE' AND CANONS OF POETRY

IN the case of every poet who has brought innovations to the medium or the technique of poetry it is of great importance as well as of special interest to examine what reasons led him to deviate from the generally accepted practice in writing poetry. Most readers of very modern poetry would probably be grateful to its authors, if they gave them a short exposition of their poetic views and how these are realized in writing, because so many innovations can to all appearances only be valued when explained by their authors. With regard to the innovations of Hopkins, which are by no means so novel and original as has been thought, we are fortunate in that his correspondence with Bridges, Dixon and Patmore contains a wealth of information about his poetic theories. Even apart from their bearing upon Hopkins's own practice these theories are of great interest as literary criticism. For Hopkins was no mean critic: his judgement about the merits of his contemporaries Hardy and Stevenson has been confirmed by time; [1] the many quotations that will be given in the course of this chapter will bear testimony to the soundness of his critical sense.

His attitude towards criticism deserves our attention; as an undergraduate he wrote this significant passage:

A perfect critic is very rare, I know, Ruskin often goes astray . . . The most inveterate fault of critics is the tendency to cramp and hedge in by rules the free movements of genius, so that I should say, according to the Demosthenic and Catonic expression, the first requisite for a critic is liberality, and the second, liberality, and the third, liberality (III. 57).

All his life he firmly adhered to this view of criticism. He is ever liberal in his criticisms, always encouraging and always fair. Much as he dislikes Swinburne he has an open eye for the good qualities of his poetry; much as he loves to see Bridges placed among the classics of English literature his praise is as sincere as his fault-finding; he only hated to criticize bad poetry because he could not praise it (III. 31). Bridges and Dixon greatly respected Hopkins's critical views and acted on the corrections suggested by him; they changed lines or stanzas in their poems accordingly. The reverse can hardly be said to be the case.   Hopkins sent his poems almost exclusively to these two poets, he asked for their opinion, but more often than not he waived their suggestions aside under the plea that he could not think of changing anything, which, indeed, is a very weak plea.   It was not pride or over-confidence in his own talents that induced him to discard so often the criticisms of his friends.   It proceeded from the firm conviction that they had failed fully to understand his poetry.   He would never admit that he was obscure: the fact that he was again and again charged with obscurity was to him the best proof that his poetry was misunderstood.[2]

Patmore does not appear to have appreciated Hopkins's critical remarks very highly.   Indeed, he asked with insistence that Hopkins should give his opinions and he is very grateful for the trouble which Hopkins took in critically reading his poems and in suggesting, at great length, how and where they might be improved.   But having acknowledged these remarks, Patmore usually left it at that.   He granted the accuracy of what Hopkins suggested, but, mostly without any reason that we know of, he did not act accordingly.   The opinion expressed by Prof. Abbott in his introduction to the third volume of letters, where he says that Patmore recognized the tribute of Hopkins's criticism, the worth of the man who made it, and 'uses it most sensibly' (III. xxvii), is then to be taken with considerable restrictions.   Even Patmore's boast: 'I think I have acted on at least two-thirds of your hints, and have only not acted on the other third because they involved an amount of re-writing of wh. I am now not capable' (III. 221) should not be taken too literally.   Anyone who takes the trouble to go through the notes made by Prof. Abbott to the suggestions of Hopkins will be surprised at the great number of cases where 'unchanged' or 'unaltered' was the reply of Patmore to these suggestions (III. pp. 153–9, 166–70, 172–6, 192–201).   We must not be hard on the older man and conclude that he must have been insincere in his correspondence or had no confidence at all in the views of Hopkins; the burning of the *Sponsa Dei* quite disproves this.[3]   But Patmore held poetical opinions entirely different from those of Hopkins: that emendations suggested by Hopkins and admittedly excellent on Hopkins's own grounds could not be brought into agreement with Patmore's ideas about the function of poetry is only to be expected; it is likely that both poets realized this.   Hence the tone of criticism in his letters to Patmore is not nearly so authoritative as that in his correspondence with Bridges and Dixon.   It is as if Hopkins shrank from thorough criticism of Patmore's poetry: he is almost apologetic when Patmore confesses that he cannot change his poems and even goes to the length of defending Patmore:

I think I know very well what you mean when you speak of the danger and difficulty of making more than verbal alterations in works composed long ago and of a bygone mood not being to be recovered (III. 165).

Hopkins knew that there was no common ground on which his own theories and those of Patmore met. I shall return to this subject later.

Hopkins was a good and consistent critic because his critical theories were well thought out and logically built up into a complete system. The fundamental tenet of his literary views and more particularly of his poetical theories is that 'inscape is the aim of poetry'. It is not hard to see why Hopkins set himself the task of expressing the inscape of his own self in poetry and why he looked for inscape in the poetry of others. Everything expresses in its connatural activity its own individuality:

> Each mortal thing does one thing and the same:
> Deals out that being indoors each one dwells;
> Selves—goes itself; *Poems* 34

a fortiori this is true of man who is conscious of his actions. Above all it is verified in the poet whose peculiar activity concerns the very explicit expression of his own self. Of poetry it is most true:

> *myself* it speaks and spells. id.

Unless poetry therefore gives us a knowledge of the poet's inscape, that is, unless poetry bears out the individually distinctive characteristics of the poet and thus gives us an insight into the poet's individuality, poetry had better not be written at all. Through every line of poetry there should breathe the personality of the poet. One feels a certain awe if one enters into the deepest significance and the logical deductions of Hopkins's 'what I aim at is inscape'. It is the same awe that we feel in reading his poems, because he has so perfectly succeeded in giving us his inscape: we are almost taken too much into his confidence; the things he tells us are often too intimate. His poems could not have been written by anyone else, as Dixon very rightly remarks (II. 110, II. 44). In various places throughout his correspondence we come across passages that well illustrate the importance which Hopkins attached to the 'individualising touch': 'Poetry must have, down to its least separable part, an individualising touch',—so he wrote to Patmore (III. 155), with whom he agreed that

D

de Vere had 'all the gifts that make a poet excepting only that last degree of individuality which is the most essential of all' (II. 112).   In another letter to Patmore he thus criticizes the Irish poets as a body:

... full of feeling, high thoughts, flow of verse, point, often fine imagery and other virtues, but the essential and only lasting thing left out—what I call *inscape*, that is species or individually-distinctive beauty of style ... (III. 225).[4]

In the same strain he had written earlier to Bridges with reference to his play about Nero:

Every scene is good, every soliloquy beautiful to individuation.   (By the by the Irish, among whom I live, have no conception of this quality: their ambition is to say a thing as everybody says it, only louder) (I. 210).

Hopkins quarrelled about this point with Patmore when they discussed the merits of Barnes:

I scarcely understand you about reflected light: every true poet, I thought, must be original and originality a condition of poetic genius; so that each poet is like a species in nature (*not* an *individuum genericum* or *specificum*) and can never recur (III. 222).[5]

As long as this uniqueness was borne out in the poetry, the poet was a real, even if a faulty, poet.   His unbounded admiration for the music of Henry Purcell arose from the artist's inscape so well expressed in his music:

> It is the forgèd feature finds me; it is the rehearsal
> Of own, of abrupt self there so thrusts on, so throngs the ear.

Poems 21

   Hopkins has given us a fairly complete exposition, even though it is scattered up and down his letters, of how a poet is to achieve the only true end of poetry.   The means are necessarily directly imposed by the end, and hence from a right understanding of inscape, which to Hopkins is the end of poetry, the greater part of his opinions about the means can logically be deduced.   If a poet must express his inscape, he should, to begin with, be true to himself.   Freely he chooses to give voice to his emotions; he should then be sincere and earnest in relating them.   Any falling off in this respect will immediately betray itself and is fatal to poetry.   Repeatedly Hopkins insists on this fundamental quality of the poet and of his poetry:

And let me say, to take no higher ground, that without earnestness there is nothing sound and beautiful in character ... (I. 148).

This leads me to say that a kind of touchstone of the highest and most living art is seriousness; not gravity but the being in earnest with your subject—reality (I. 225).

... want of earnest I take to be the deepest fault a work of art can have (III. 212).

Earnestness, sincerity, honesty will safeguard any poet against false feeling or affectation and artificiality of expression, which are necessarily destructive of the poet's inscape. If he is true to his own self, he will express his humanity in an unaffected and unsophisticated way; he will safely steer between frigidity on the one side and mawkishness on the other. In his poetry he will instinctively strike the balance between matter and form, so essential to poetry; for there can be no sincerity and earnestness without adequate matter to be serious or earnest about. Hence it is that Hopkins looks for thought and insight as much as for ennobling emotion in all good poetry.[6] The combination of manliness and tenderness is in this respect very typical of Hopkins's criticisms, as it is of his own poetry.[7]

The various qualities mentioned formed for Hopkins the first standard by which poetry should be judged; they are fundamental and of far greater importance than fine imagery, melodiousness, apt rhythmical flow, &c. There can be no doubt about this point: with Hopkins a poem might possess all these accessory qualities; if it was not serious and 'human', it was valueless. And the reverse also held for him. A poem might lack imagery or melodiousness; as long as it was sincere and as long as pathos and feelings of humanity were expressed in it, the poem was worthy of great praise. The reason is evident enough: imagery, melodiousness and many other such-like qualities are to Hopkins merely ornamental unless they are woven into the canvas of the poet's inscape, which can only be expressed in sincerity and true feelings. In praising Bridges he explicitly deals with this point; without mincing matters he writes:

Since I must not flatter or exaggerate I do not claim that you have such a volume of imagery as Tennyson, Swinburne, or Morris, though the feeling for beauty you have seems to me pure and exquisite; but in point of character, of sincerity or earnestness, of manliness, of tenderness, of humour, melancholy, human feeling, you have what they have not and seem scarcely to think worth having (I. 96).

In fact Bridges's poetry is almost always praised for these essential qualities with hardly any reference to what we might call the secondary qualities. Thus a sonnet is liked because 'it breathes that earnestness

and tenderness which you have at command' (I. 90), and elsewhere
he writes that all the poems are beautiful, 'breathing a grave and feeling
genius' (I. 34), or as he says in another place, 'marked with character
throughout and human nature, not "arrangements in vowel sounds" '
(I. 72). If we bear these theories in mind we have no reason any
longer to be surprised that Hopkins could be almost extravagant in his
praise of the works of a third-rate poet such as Dixon is. We shall
never be able to comprehend this apparent lack of critical taste unless
we firmly fix our attention on what was to Hopkins the true end of
poetry. Hopkins did not mean to flatter his friend: when he opened
the correspondence with Dixon, he did not even know him; he only
knew that here was a poet who deserved more attention and more
praise than was given to him and this is what he told Dixon in that
first most remarkable letter. The Canon is praised for the same good
qualities that Hopkins appreciated so highly in Bridges's poetry. And
to Hopkins it is of no consequence whether his letter containing
words of praise of Dixon's poetry is addressed to the poet himself, or
to Bridges, or whether his praise will have to go into the manual of
English literature composed by Arnold. To Bridges he wrote:

. . . thought and feeling, in which he is always a master and never makes a
false note . . . But he is unequal and the inequality lies in execution . . .
His command of pathos is exquisite and he excels in all tragic feeling, and
that with an extreme purity, a directness of human nature, and absence of
affectation which is most rare (I. 139).

To Dixon himself:

A true humanity of spirit, neither mawkish on the one hand nor blustering
on the other, is the most precious of all qualities in style, and this I prize in
your poems, as I do in Bridges' (II. 74).

And the following remarks occur in his notice of Canon Dixon in
Arnold's manual:

In his poems we find a deep thoughtfulness and earnestness, and a mind
touched by a pathos of human life . . . noble but never highflown, sad
without noise and straining—everything as it most reaches and comes home
to man's heart. In particular he is a master of horror and pathos; of
pathos so much that here it would be hard to name his rival (II. 177).

These are only a few passages taken from a large collection, in which
Hopkins shows why he thought highly of the poetry of the good
Canon.[8] Inversely, where Hopkins cannot be enthusiastic about the
poems of his friends, it is because they lack these essential qualities.[9]

We are now in a position to understand why it was that Hopkins apparently never felt at ease in dealing with the poetry of Patmore. Indeed, he does praise the poetry of Patmore; thus he defends his *Unknown Eros* against the attacks made on it by Bridges:

By the by how can you speak of Patmore as you do? I read his *Unknown Eros* well before leaving Oxford. He shews a mastery of phrase, of the rhetoric of verse, which belongs to the tradition of Shakespeare and Milton and in which you could not find him a living equal nor perhaps a dead one either after them (I. 93).

And to Dixon he writes that Patmore's fame is far below his merit (II. 6). All this was written long before Hopkins got to know Patmore personally. When he is personally acquainted with him and Patmore sends him his poems to be criticized, Hopkins is at times quite enthusiastic: 'Your poems are a good deed done for the Catholic Church and another for England, for the British Empire . . .' (III. 218); he is unpleasantly surprised to find that Patmore was not placed among the best living poets of the day (III. 201). But on the whole we miss the whole-hearted praise that fell to Bridges and Dixon and we miss the zeal with which he set up propaganda for the muse of these two poets; he never encouraged people to study Patmore as a poet. Adverse criticism is not nearly so outspoken in the case of Patmore as in that of his other two poet-friends. Careful as he is not to condemn the poetry of Patmore, he entertained serious doubts about its value as poetry: Patmore lacked that warmth and humanity, that sincerity which impressed Hopkins so much. Patmore is frigid [10]— and frigidity destroys seriousness of style (III. 200)—because he adopts too much of an objective attitude towards what he expresses in his poetry. Frigidity is the worst fault of *The Unknown Eros* (I. 82) because 'the feeling does not fuse and flush the language'. Perhaps Hopkins would have hit the truth better if he had said that the feeling did not even fuse and flush the thought. This is the real point of divergence between these two poets: Hopkins was convinced that feeling could never be separated from thought in poetry; to Patmore poetry was a valuable means of expounding his ideas and of instructing others. Hence Patmore is too intellectual and even sour: 'the acuteness of the intelligence is in excess of the instress or feeling and gives them (*sc.* Patmore's early poems) a certain cold glitter' (III. 173). The following passage taken from one of Hopkins's letters to Patmore is most relevant to the deepest ground of divergence and at the same time shows why Hopkins would yet not condemn the practice of Patmore:

And when I read *Remembered Grace, The Child's Purchase, Legem Tuam Dilexi* and others of this volume I sigh to think that it is all one almost to be too full of meaning and to have none and to see very deep and not to see at all, for nothing so profound as these can be found in the poets of this age, scarcely of any; and yet they are but little known . . .   And so I used to feel of Duns Scotus when I used to read him with delight: he saw too far, he knew too much; his subtlety overshot his interests; a kind of feud arose between genius and talent . . . (III. 201).

We can see how the theories of the two men clashed: their view of the function of poetry differed entirely.   Patmore frequently chose poetry as the means to set forth his ideas and opinions; he might use prose as well, but then the care he would have to take of the stylistic qualities of prose would demand as much trouble and energy as the writing of poetry.   This is the gist of the following paragraph:

There are two reasons for my not attempting to make my prose what I know that prose might, and, on certain subjects, should be.   First there is no audience for such writing; secondly, I could work in verse, with little more difficulty, and much more effect (III. 235).

Patmore very likely never troubled himself whether the effect would be a poetical effect.   He appears to have wavered whether to write his *Sponsa Dei* in prose or verse.   He fixed his choice on prose because he did not think his notes 'would be more, or so impressive in verse.   They lend themselves as little to verse as the Epistles of St. Paul would do . . .' (III. 213).   *The Angel in the House* is enthusiastically praised by Hopkins, above all because 'it is in the highest degree instructive, it is a book of morals and in a field not before treated and yet loudly crying to be treated' (III. 215).

But Hopkins himself could never write poetry as Patmore did.   In his opinion the true end of poetry was inscape; if this could be reconciled with a treatise on nuptial love or some other subject, so much the better, but Hopkins did not see the way to it.   The battle that engaged these two poet-critics about the genius of Keats is a further illustration of their different conception of the function of poetry.   Hopkins could not agree with Patmore's view that Keats was a feminine genius and lacked all manliness.   To support his own opinion that Keats showed great promise of becoming a manly poet, Hopkins compared him with Shakespeare, who in his youth wrote sensuous poetry just as Keats did; like Shakespeare, Keats, if he had become older, would have outgrown the tendencies of his youth and his poetry would have assumed a more manly character (III. 233–4).   Patmore replied that the sensuality of the early Shakespeare was accidental to his *Lucrece* and *Venus and Adonis*, but that 'the intellect is immensely predominant' (III. 235). Clearly then, Hopkins had misunderstood Patmore's view that sensuality was an infallible indication of feminine genius; to Patmore a poet was manly if the intellect was predominant. It was now an issue about which Hopkins had no intention whatever of entering the lists.

One should not conclude from this paragraph about the different opinions of Hopkins and Patmore that the former in any way minimized the importance of thought and insight in poetry; his own poetry is remarkable both for its ennobling emotions and its originality and depth of thought. But in Hopkins 'feeling had fused the matter', while in Patmore the matter was more important than, and consequently severed from, the emotion which it awoke.

I now turn to some criticisms by Hopkins, scattered through his many letters, of the poetry or prose of the writers of the early nineteenth century and especially of his own day. Not that these criticisms will add anything new to what I have shown were Hopkins's canons of criticism; but besides confirming these canons they form an interesting background to his own practice and help us to understand what Hopkins thought was wrong with the literature of his own day.

A second-rate poet like William Barnes is highly appreciated because he was his own species (cf. p. 32). He had in him 'the soul of poetry' (I. 162). He is not at all at one with Bridges: 'I hold your contemptuous opinion an unhappy mistake: he is a perfect artist and of a most spontaneous inspiration' (I. 221). The spontaneous inspiration is described in some detail in a letter to Patmore: 'Still I grant in Barnes an unusual independence and originality, due partly to his circumstances. It is his naturalness that strikes me most; he is like an embodiment or incarnation or manmuse of the country, of Dorset, of rustic life and humanity' (III. 222).

Wordsworth's great *Ode on Intimations of Immortality* is passionately defended against attacks made on it by Dixon; both the subject and the poet's insight into it constitute the extreme value of the poem:

I feel now I am warm and my hand is in for my greater task, Wordsworth's ode; and here, my dear friend, I must earnestly remonstrate with you; must have it out with you. Is it possible that—but it is in black and white: you say the ode is not, for Wordsworth, good; and much less great. . . . The ode itself seems to me better than anything else I know of Wordsworth's, so much as to equal or outweigh everything else he wrote: to me it appears so. For Wordsworth was an imperfect artist, as you say: as his matter varied in importance and as he varied in insight . . . so does the value of his work vary. Now the interest and importance of the matter were here of the highest, his insight was at its very deepest and hence to my mind the extreme value of the poem (II. 147–8).

As soon as Hopkins is asked to give his opinion about the poets of his own day he grows indignant at the waste of talent that is evident in the lack of pathos and sincerity and in the abundance of artificiality, affectation, mawkishness, in the midst of many fine qualities of imagery and diction that could have gone to the making of great poetry. To Patmore he writes about the poems of Patmore's son Henry as follows:

But if the poems have a shortcoming beyond points of detail it would be in flow, in the poetical impetus, and also in richness of diction: they are strong where this age is weak—I mean Swinburne and the popular poets, and, I may say, Tennyson himself—, in thought and insight, but they are weak where the age is strong (III. 188–9).

The poets of his day failed because they had nothing to be serious about in their poetry; Tennyson's 'gift of utterance is truly golden, but go further home and you come to thoughts commonplace and wanting in nobility'; it is 'genius uninformed by character' (I. 95). Swinburne —plague of mankind (I. 39)—repeatedly comes off very badly. Indeed, his genius is astonishing (I. 79), he has at his command a music of words and a mastery of consistent and distinctive poetic diction which is extraordinary (II. 156), but 'words are only words'; everything he writes is 'rigmarole' (II. 135) for he does not express feeling, and much less character (I. 79). In his very last letter to Bridges Hopkins fulminates against him in a very typical paragraph; thus he writes:

Swinburne has a new volume out, which is reviewed in its own style: 'The rush and the rampage, the pause and the pull-up of these lustrous and lumpophorous lines'. It is all now a 'self-drawing web'; a perpetual functioning of genius without truth, feeling, or any adequate matter to be at function on (I. 304).

Swinburne was to Hopkins the most striking instance of a poet who had the gifts of great poetry, but who in his poetical activity had upset the right order of values: sincerity, earnestness, truth, humanity, feeling had to take second place after melody, word-music, flow of verse and so on. His criticism of Browning is hardly more flattering:

But Browning has, I think, many frigidities. Any untruth to nature, to human nature, is frigid. Now he has got a great deal of what came in with

Kingsley and the Broad Church school, a way of talking (and making his people talk) with the air and spirit of a man bouncing up from table with his mouth full of bread and cheese and saying that he meant to stand no blasted nonsense.   There is a whole volume of Kingsley's essays which is all a kind of munch and a not standing of any blasted nonsense from cover to cover. Do you know what I mean?   The *Flight of the Duchess* with the repetition of 'My friend', is in this vein . . . (II. 74).

Not less violent is his denunciation of Carlyle:

Your [*sc.* Dixon's] words surprised me '—of some genius': they would commonly be thought, and so they appear to me, too weak.   I do not like his pampered and affected style, I hate his principles, I burn most that he worships and worship most that he burns, I cannot respect (no one now can) his character, but the force of his genius seems to me gigantic.   He seems to me to have more humour than any writer of ours except Shakspere. I should have called him the greatest genius of Scotland.   And yet after all I could fancy your making a good case against him, especially bearing the rule in mind *nemo coronabitur nisi qui legitime certaverit*: always to be affected, always to be fooling, never to be in earnest (for as somebody said, he is terribly earnest but never serious—that is never *in* earnest) is not to fight fair in the field of fame (II. 59).

Dickens was too mawkish for Hopkins, he had no true command of pathos (II. 73); and in a letter to Bridges we find the following humorous paragraph about him:

With the other half of the same shilling I bought *The Old Curiosity Shop*; never read it before, am not going to give in to any nonsense about Little Nell (like, I believe, Lang I cannot stand Dickens's pathos; or rather I can stand it, keep a thoroughly dry eye and unwavering waistcoat), but admire Dick Swiveller and Kit and Quilp and that old couple with the pony (I. 279).

Having set forward what were Hopkins's main ideas about the function and the essential qualities of literature, and more especially of poetry, I shall deal with the question that suggests itself here: did Hopkins practise what he preached?   Can his own poetry stand the test of being criticized by his own standards?   Anyone who has seriously read the poems of Hopkins will agree that however baffling his singularity may appear, however perplexing at times his obscurity, he cannot be charged with insincerity or affectation or frigidity.   If anything, his poems are too sincere and too human.   They have, indeed, that intensity of feeling which Dixon has called 'terrible', an epithet now almost exclusively applied to the later sonnets, though Dixon used it to describe the outstanding quality of his early poetry (II. 80).

Hopkins never resented adverse criticism, but he angrily remonstrates with Bridges when he is charged with affectation:

As for affectation I do not believe I am guilty of it: you should point out instances, but as long as mere novelty and boldness strikes you as affectation your criticism strikes me as—as water of the Lower Isis (I. 54).

And in another letter he defends himself with indignation against the accusation of insincerity and want of earnestness:

When I reproached you for treating me as if I were not in earnest I meant, and I now mean, to open up no further question; it was only of the injustice to myself I was thinking then (I. 163).

Fearing that Bridges might misinterpret passages in *The Wreck of the Deutschland* he is anxious to point out that whatever happens in the poem is literally true; he acted in the way described there; 'nothing is added for poetical padding' (I. 47). If his friends, the only people who, up to a point, appreciated his rare and original talent—'up to a point', for remember that Bridges wanted to call *The Wreck of the Deutschland* 'presumptuous jugglery' (I. 46)—did not understand his poetry and almost implored him to change his poems so that they might become clearer, he always answered that he could not think of any important change; 'I cannot think of altering anything. Why shd. I? I do not write for the public. You are my public . . .' (I. 46), so he wrote to Bridges. There is in his poems an inevitability of expression which is final; they cannot be changed or altered without damaging the poetic experience that prompted this expression of itself. The mood is too intimately linked up with the diction; retouching the one would mean that the other was no longer the same. Hence he must have felt a shudder at the remark of Patmore quoted above that he could say things in poetry more easily than in prose; he thought it dreadful to say things in prose which he had said in poetry: 'It is dreadful to explain these things in cold blood' is the remark that accompanies his prose explanation of the sonnet *Walking by the Sea* (I. 164). And indignation speaks from this answer to Bridges, who had presumably accused him of writing plays by fragments: 'But how cd. you think such a thing of me as that I shd. in cold blood write "fragments of a dramatic poem"?—I of all men in the world' (I. 218). It is probably for the same reasons that he disavowed all his early poetry, long after he had burnt it.[11] Clever as these youthful efforts are, they miss the inscape of the poet; they are products of poetic fancy rather than expressions of the poet's self.

As regards his own poetry Hopkins was never greatly troubled about criticisms of obscurity or oddity; but he was worried by possible failings in sincerity and true feeling. At times he had doubts about the value of his poetry; it was always because he feared that they fell short in these essential indispensable qualities:

I hope you may approve what I have done, for it is worth doing and yet a task of great delicacy and hazard to write a patriotic song that shall breathe true feeling without spoon or brag. How I hate both! and yet I feel myself half blundering or sinking into them in several of my pieces, a thought that makes me not greatly regret their likelihood of perishing (I. 283).[12]

But how Hopkins strove after the expressing of his own inscape and how successful he was is best illustrated by the difference of tone and subject-matter in various groups of poems. The striking difference of tone and matter between poems of various groups can be accounted for only by considering the poems as directly expressive of his inscape, as affected and shaped at that particular period by these definite circumstances of time and place. His poetry falls into three very distinct groups, closely corresponding to three periods in his life, well marked off by the work he was engaged upon.

If for the present we leave out Hopkins's first poem *The Wreck of the Deutschland*, we notice how there follow various poems dealing with the beauty of nature and with God as ever present in nature. To this group belong *God's Grandeur*, *The Starlight Night*, his sonnet on *Spring*, *The Lantern out of Doors*, *The Sea and the Skylark*, *The Windhover*, *Pied Beauty*, *Hurrahing in Harvest*, *The Caged Skylark*, *In the Valley of the Elwy* and some fragments as *Ashboughs*, *The Woodlark*, *Moonrise*. These poems were all of them written in the years 1875–77, when Hopkins was studying theology in Wales, 'always to me a mother of Muses' (I. 227). It was the time of immediate preparation for the reception of the priesthood. He was happy at the time and the countryside buoyed him up. His study of Scotus deepened, as has been shown, his admiration and love of the inscapes of this world, which were to him news and word of God. With delight he turned to a fervent contemplation of nature and the poems of this group are alive with the joy and serenity which he experienced in his communication with her. In these poems the careful observer of nature, who for so long had patiently looked at the clouds and trees and painfully described them in great detail, was for the first time allowed to sing of them. Freed from the self-imposed shackles of poetic silence he naturally turned to those subjects which for so long had been nearest his heart and had so often carried him into ecstasy. No wonder that these poems contain many lines which remind one strongly of passages in his diary.[13] Any country sight urged his vein, as he once wrote to Bridges (I. 136); here he lived in the country and he enjoyed it so much that he dreaded the prospect of having to leave it (I. 43). (He had hardly left Wales and gone to Sheffield, when he complained that life was as dank as ditch-water (I. 47).) If at times there is a tone of sadness in these poems, it is always inspired by the sad thought that to all this beauty of nature 'the inmate does not correspond' (*Poems* 16), or 'the beholder [is] wanting' (*Poems* 14) and 'all is seared with trade; bleared, smeared with toil' (*Poems* 7). The inscapes 'go without notice, go unwitnessed', as he complained to Dixon (II. 7).

I have singled out *The Wreck of the Deutschland* as not belonging to this group. In subject matter it is akin to the poem on the foundering of the *Eurydice*, the first poem written after his Welsh days. These two poems reflect another aspect altogether of the poet's soul and clearly foreshadow the later Hopkins of the 'terrible sonnets'. Both these poems are inspired by his sorrow at the news of so many sailors meeting their sudden death unprepared; it is the problem of suffering that racked the mind of Hopkins, who wondered why it was that people should meet their end 'comfortless unconfessed'. This thought has stirred his emotions far more intensely than the death of the Franciscan nuns exiled from Germany, even granted that this was the original theme of *The Wreck of the Deutschland*. It is his anxiety about the spiritual well-being of the men that made him restless and caused him bitter pain; his very sensitive soul could not, as we have seen, be indifferent to the lot of his fellow men. But in the *Deutschland* there is more; its tone is more impetuous and more passionate than that of the *Eurydice*. The *Deutschland* is a more personal poem, because in it he struggles with the problem of his own sorrows and his own sufferings as well as with those of other men. Hopkins wrote this poem soon after he had, very probably for the first time in his life, experienced real hardship, which had left an indelible mark upon his mind. Logic and philosophy had been hard (III. 88); some years before he had been operated upon and for some time after was in low health; so much so that he complained about it in a letter to Cardinal Newman (III. 261). At the end of his year's teaching at Roehampton he wrote the following entry in his diary:

I was very tired and seemed deeply cast down till I had some kind words from the Provincial. Altogether perhaps my heart has never been so burdened and cast down as this year. The tax on my strength has been greater than I have felt before: at least now at Teignmouth I feel myself weak and can do little. But in all this our Lord goes His own way (*N.* 199).

He was at this time feeling the weariness of life and shed many tears, 'perhaps not wholly into the breast of God', for there was some unmanliness in them too (*N.* 210). This bitter experience was the subject of the opening stanzas of the *Deutschland* and gives the whole poem its very profound content.

The poems of the second group date from the years 1878 to 1881. It opens with two nature poems. As a parish priest at Oxford he composed *Binsey Poplars* and *Duns Scotus's Oxford* (*Poems* 19 and 20). Both poems contain descriptions of the beauty of nature round Oxford; but in tone they are altogether different from the nature poems of the first group. A note of disappointment has crept in; it is not so much admiration of the beauty of nature as its destruction that inspired him to write these poems. It is the 'wild and wanton work of men' (*Poems* 54), the wilful destruction of the inscapes of this world for the sake of profit, that pains him. Man

> To his own selfbent so bound, so tied to his turn,
> To thriftless reave both our rich round world bare
> And none reck of world after   *Poems* 35

—this was the subject with which he was to deal in this second group; and naturally so. For at this time Hopkins was active as a preacher in various parishes in London, Liverpool, Bedford Leigh, Oxford and Glasgow, and, as he says himself, in his professional experience he found a good deal to write upon (I. 86). Most of the poems are auto-biographical in this sense that they relate incidents of his priestly life in which he acted in the way described in them: the first communion of a soldier, the 'gracious answer' of the boy who had served his Mass, his best wishes for a married couple, the death of a blacksmith whom he assisted in his last hours, his meeting with a weeping child, the reaction of a boy at his younger brother's acting in a school play, and so forth. These poems of Hopkins are not his best. The impulse is wanting, he wrote to Bridges (I. 127); for in those dreadful great towns it is very hard to be in good spirits (I. 136); fatigue now easily comes over him (I. 84). He was too sensitive to be able to stand the strain of living in the midst of men who were habitual drunkards, degraded, and fallen from the high state of man; what this meant to Hopkins, I have shown in my first chapter. The dark shadows that cover the last years of his life can be seen to approach now. They

make sad reading, all those lines in which Hopkins confides his sufferings to his friends, always hoping that they would be transitory:
'Liverpool is very wearying to body and mind; there is merit in it but
little muse' (II. 33).   '. . . time and spirits (to write) are wanting; one
is so fagged, so harried and gallied up and down.   And the drunkards
go on drinking, the filthy, as the scripture says, are filthy still: human
nature is so inveterate.   Would that I had seen the last of it' (I. 110).
And to Dixon he complained that his parish work was very wearisome,
especially in Liverpool, of all places the most museless (II. 42): 'I feel
much jaded' . . .   The muse of music 'is the only Muse that does not
stifle in this horrible place' (I. 126–7).   Things improved slightly
when he was moved to Glasgow: 'Things are pleasanter here than at
Liverpool.   Wretched place too Glasgow is, like all our great towns;
still I get on better here, though bad is the best of my getting on'
(I. 135).   When it was all over, he thus wrote about his Liverpool
and Glasgow experience to Canon Dixon, with whom he could speak
more easily on such matters than with Bridges: 'My Liverpool and
Glasgow experience laid upon my mind a conviction, a truly crushing
conviction, of the misery of town life to the poor and more than to the
poor, of the misery of the poor in general, of the degradation even of
our race, of the hollowness of this century's civilisation: it made even
life a burden to me to have daily thrust upon me the things I saw'
(II. 97).   He had tasted of the terrible loathing that was to make life
almost unbearable some few years later.   Needless to say, this was no
state conducive to the writing of poetry.   To keep up his spirits he
broke into humorous verse (I. 114); at another time he makes the
resolution to write in prose first, thus to help on his spent poetic
powers (I. 98).   But inspiration would not come.   Hence it is that
expressions of these hardships did not find their way into the poetry
of this group; it was only when he was at Dublin that suffering forced
him to express the sorrows of his soul in poetry.   This is very likely
the reason why these poems are the least satisfactory of all; they miss
the quietly ecstatic tone of the first group; they also lack that intensity
of feeling of the last group.   They are not the outcome of a spontaneous inspiration and most of them bear the marks of a straining after
poetic expression of which in the circumstances he was incapable.
This explains the somewhat forced emotionality of *The Bugler's First
Communion*, *Felix Randal* and *The Handsome Heart* (*Poems* 23, 29
and 27); some might even find a certain frigidity and bitterness in *The
Candle Indoors*.[14]

   In September 1881 Hopkins went back to the Noviciate for ten months and during this time he gave up composition altogether. After this follows the last period of his life, that of the 'terrible' sonnets, his most personal, his best, and his most harassing poems.   A good deal has been written about this beautiful group of poems, and a good deal of misunderstanding exists about them.   Critics have related the conflict expressed in these poems to that between the poet and the priest.   Thus, for instance, Middleton Murry holds that the failure of Hopkins as a poet was due to the ' starvation of experience which his vocation imposed upon him' (cf. p. xi).   Professor Abbott, the editor of the three volumes of correspondence, speaks with as little understanding of the poet-priest.   He writes that 'the "quarrel" between the priest and the poet was never fully reconciled in his mind' (I. xviii). As time went on 'he seems to have felt increasingly the difficulty of reconciling the offices of priest and poet' (I. xxxi); 'Hopkins the poet was too severely tried by the discipline he thought necessary to Hopkins the priest to flourish freely'; and Professor Abbott's conclusion is that Hopkins 'suffered slow martyrdom as a poet' (I. xli). Leaving aside some unscholarly criticisms that are mainly inspired by an *a priori* dislike of the Society of Jesus,[15] I notice that even a scholar of Dr. Gardner's standing can write: 'The story of his life presents, from one angle, the tragic conflict of a man torn between two vocations . . .; from another angle it represents the heroic struggle of a man who is so completely dedicated to one profession that he deliberately sacrifices another possible and in some ways more exciting profession, because he is sure that God wills it to be so.'[16]

An unbiased reading of the correspondence of Hopkins will convince any one that there existed no such struggle.   Hopkins says himself that, though his life was liable to many mortifications, want of fame as a poet was the least of them (II. 28); yet this unselfish man implores and exhorts his two poet-friends to strive after poetic fame most strenuously (I. 231).   He again and again insists that poetry is unprofessional, 'but that is what I have said to myself, not others to me' (I. 197).   On this point his mind was quite made up and he would allow no one to interfere with this conviction and try to persuade him to spend more time on composition.   Dixon frequently pleaded with Hopkins to write more, and in reply, he once for all tried to silence Dixon by giving a very clear and precise exposition of his attitude towards poetry; the long quotation must find a place here because of its importance:

I am ashamed at the expressions of high regard which your last letter and others have contained, kind and touching as they are, and do not know whether I ought to reply to them or not. This I say: my vocation puts before me a standard so high that a higher can be found nowhere else. The question then for me is not whether I am willing (if I may guess what is in your mind) to make a sacrifice of hopes of fame (let us suppose), but whether I am not to undergo a severe judgment from God for the lothness I have shown in making it, for the reserves I may have in my heart made, for the backward glances I have given with my hand upon the plough, for the waste of time the very compositions you admire may have caused and their preoccupation of the mind which belonged to more sacred and more binding duties, for the disquiet and the thoughts of vainglory they have given rise to. A purpose may look smooth and perfect from without but be frayed and faltering from within. I have never wavered in my vocation, but I have not lived up to it. I destroyed the verse I had written when I entered the Society and meant to write no more; the *Deutschland* I began after a long interval at the chance suggestion of my superior, but that being done it is a question whether I did well to write anything else. However I shall, in my present mind, continue to compose, as occasion shall fairly allow, which I am afraid will be seldom and indeed for some years past has been scarcely ever, and let what I produce wait and take its chance; for a very spiritual man once told me that with things like composition the best sacrifice was not to destroy one's work but to leave it entirely to be disposed of by obedience. But I can scarcely fancy myself asking a superior to publish a volume of my verses and I own that humanly there is very little likelihood of that ever coming to pass. And to be sure if I chose to look at things on one side and not the other I could of course regret this bitterly. But there is more peace and it is the holier lot to be unknown than to be known (II. 88–9).

If someone were to print his poems, he said, he would be partly, but not altogether, glad (I. 66).

How to construe a tragic conflict from this determined state of mind is a thing I cannot understand. Indeed, if he looked at things from one side only, he could regret want of fame; but this poet-priest, so sincere and earnest, could never take such a one-sided view. The above letter is not the only document proving that Hopkins had reflected about the possible good that his poems might do by being published; thus we read among his unpublished retreat-notes for 1883:

Also in some meditation to-day I earnestly prayed our Lord to watch over my compositions, not to preserve them from being lost or coming to nothing for that I am very willing they should, but they might do me harm through the enmity or imprudence of any man or my own; that he could have them as his own and employ them or not employ them as he should see fit. And this I believe is heard.

He appears to have been convinced that the time for his poems would come (II. 95), even though he could hardly have guessed that that time would come thirty years after his death. In his letters to Bridges and Dixon there also occur passages confirming this very objective and unwavering attitude towards his poetry.[17] It is certainly curious to notice that never once does Hopkins relate his sufferings to his having made a mistake in becoming a priest and in freely imposing shackles on his poetic talent. His great anxiety was to live up to his vocation and to approach as far as was within his power the high ideal that of his own free will he had chosen :

> During this retreat I have much and earnestly asked that God will lift me above myself to a higher state of grace in which I have more union with him and free from sin. . . . In meditating on the crucifixion I understood how my asking to be raised to a higher degree of grace was also asking to be lifted on a higher cross.

These notes, written during his retreat in 1883, throw ridicule on a supposed 'suicidal struggle between the priest and the nature-loving poet'.[18] I do not hold that Hopkins never really felt the pain which resulted from his making poetry 'unprofessional'. If we read his letters we now and again come across passages in which he confesses that it is a burden to him that his vein shows no signs of ever flowing again (I. 178), that he cannot do anything with a fagged mind and a continual anxiety (II. 139); his mind was dull and museless and for years he had 'had no inspiration of longer jet than makes a sonnet' (I. 270). But the painful thing was not that as a priest he was not allowed in conscience to spend time on poetry; he never cared greatly for his own poetry, and would never take the trouble of making fair copies or correcting or preserving them from being lost. Bridges did all that for him (I. 304). Besides, he cared far more for his philosophical work than for his poems (II. 150). But the painful thing to this sensitive nature was to feel that you could do a thing but it was the power that failed you (I. 221, 252). Indeed, it was the physical power that failed him; it was the incapacity for *any* work that crippled him, it was the failure in which all his undertakings, as by a strange necessity, ended, that caused him great sorrow. All he endeavoured ended in disappointment (*Poems* 50); he was 'time's eunuch'; and he could 'not breed one work that wakes' (id.). This was a terrible strain on him; he tried his hand on many subjects about which he cared more than about his poetry and one after the other miscarried. Being a professor at Dublin University he felt it incumbent upon him

E

to write about the subject he taught; and so he desired to write on Sophocles (I. 277), on Homer (III. 111, 129, 265), on Greek negatives (I. 270), on the *Argei* (I. 303), on the Dorian Measure (III. 228), on the art of the choric parts in Greek Tragedy (I. 150).[19]   He had for a long time wished to work out his rhythmical theories, in which connexion he had made an extensive study of the rhythms of Milton (I. 38), which he desired to publish (III. 231).   He is writing a popular treatise on light and ether (II. 139); he thinks of publishing St. Patrick's 'Confession' (I. 195) and planned to write on Patmore's poems (III. 241).   In his letters he frequently refers to his tragedy of St. Winefred, which was meant to be 'intelligible'.   He worked at a commentary on the *Spiritual Exercises* of St. Ignatius.   At one time we find him writing on the subject of sacrifice (II. 102).   He finished an article on 'Statistics and Free Will'—'an obstruse subject—but very intelligible' (I. 292), but this was never published.

Indeed, this continual failure was bitter suffering; but again, that to ascribe his sufferings to the thwarting of *poetic* gifts and to *poetic* sterility is doing great injustice to this saintly priest.   'What becomes of my verses I care little', so he says himself with a clearness that leaves nothing to be desired and that cannot be misinterpreted, 'but about things like this, what I write or could write on philosophical matters, I do; and the reason of the difference is that the verses stand or fall by their simple selves and though by being read they might do good, by being unread they do no harm; but if the other things are unsaid right they will be said by somebody else wrong, and that is what will not let me rest' (II. 150).   In a letter to Bridges he calls the writing of poetry a luxury (I. 270); and in the same letter he confesses that to his sorrow he cannot produce anything at all and the greatest sorrow is that he cannot produce scientific works, 'the duties almost of my position' (I. 270); 'all impulse fails me . . .   Nothing comes: I am a eunuch—but it is for the kingdom of heaven's sake' (id.).

In his dealings with his fellow men he appears to have met with as little success.   With his whole heart he most ardently wished to see his father and mother, brothers and sisters brought nearer to Christ: but his prayers were to all outward appearances never answered; English to the core, he was yet considered as only half a patriot because of his religion, and this false charge hampered his work for the conversion of England.   Things became worse when he went to Ireland, where he was altogether in the wrong place; and never even the shadow of success fell across his life.   For the last six years of his life he was in very low health; 'always jaded', 'tired', 'weary in body and mind', 'incapable of anything', are the ever-recurring epithets in his letters. He lived in a coffin of weakness and dejection, without even the hope of change, as he said to Bridges in 1885 (I. 214–5). On top of this he underwent the direst desolation and aridity in his spiritual life, in which state he could only as a child subject himself to the will of God. But the sufferings were terrible; no wonder he speaks of a state of dilapidation (II. 265), of prostration of strength (II. 122, I. 193, 251), and a state of mind that made him fear madness (I. 222). All this for the kingdom of heaven's sake; he had earnestly prayed to be raised to a higher degree of grace and he had been lifted to a higher cross.

This is the background against which we should place his last sonnets. One of them was written 'in blood' (I. 219) and four came like 'inspirations unbidden and against my will' (I. 227). There is the closest correspondence between the emotional experience forced into expression in these poems and the expressions which he used in his letters to his friends. Nothing is added for the sake of poetical padding. How could he? As a group they stand out clearly in his *œuvre*; they are confessions, most intimate and most sincere. In these he realized and reached the aim he had set himself: they are the perfect expression of his inscape.[20]

I return to Hopkins's canons of poetry and stress again his anxiety to be sincere and tell the truth and the whole truth. It is well to realize this. Whatever Hopkins says should be taken as it stands and should never be explained as the playings of a poetic imagination. He cannot exaggerate, nor can he camouflage his own intentions. He has no secret from any man. He is as outspoken in his letters as he is in his poetry. Thus, for instance, Hopkins could never deny his profession. People might have wondered why this priest kept up his correspondence with Bridges and Dixon for so long and at such length. They were his good friends and being his friends he desired to do them good and the greatest good he could give them was their conversion to his own religion. This must have been a delicate point to write about: it would smack of proselytizing and any awkwardness in handling it might easily have put Bridges and Dixon on their guard. Hopkins never thought of feigning that it was only a common interest in matters poetical that induced him to write these long letters. When the opportunity is there the heart of the priest will out: 'if we care for fine verses how much more for a noble life' (I. 61). In his letters he frankly writes of his disappointment that his wish to see his friends converted is not fulfilled; and he blames Bridges for not giving thought to religious things.[21]

As for the presentation of *objective* truth, Hopkins is almost scrupulous. Half-truths or superficiality he abhorred. Everything in an object, every aspect of it, was relevant to its nature. This conviction made him often, as we may call it, exaggerate: he undoubtedly exaggerated, but he could not help it. But granted that he went too far, it is well to realize how Hopkins considered every word of what he had written. Some illustrations follow taken from his sermons, in which he punctiliously deals with every objection that might possibly occur to any member of his congregation but that could actually arise only in his own mind. The why and wherefore of every word of a text is given. He never leaves one side of the question to be solved by the congregation themselves. Thus in a sermon dealing with the fall of man he answers in great detail the question why Eve was alone when being tempted; and it is most likely that the people could not follow the reasoning of the preacher. In the same sermon (*N.* 277 ff.) he gives a minute description of how the serpent offered Eve the forbidden fruit, a detail cautiously introduced by 'we must suppose': 'We must suppose he offered her the fruit as though it were the homage and the tribute of the brute to man, of the subject to the queen, presented it with his mouth or swept it from the boughs before her feet.' In another sermon he has recourse to the Greek term λατρεία to explain to his very simple congregation in what the worship due to Christ essentially consists (*N.* 296). And again elsewhere he works out the comparison of the church to the mustard seed; and he carries it to ridiculous lengths when he compares the branches, boughs, twigs and leaves to national churches, dioceses, parishes, families and single individuals; even the birds of the air sitting in the mustard tree are not forgotten: they are the guardian angels waiting upon the church (unpublished; cf. *N.* 430 (x)). And yet the working out of the comparison in such a way is typical of Hopkins.

In his poetry we find this passion for truth mirrored in, for instance, the final stanza of the *Eurydice*. It was an afterthought; the sailors had died outside the Catholic Church; to console the relatives he had told them to pray to Christ the Saviour; here the poem ends, but the poet is quick to perceive that possibly the final stanza might be wrongly explained. To make the contents doctrinally safe he gives us some theological thoughts about the effect of prayer for those deceased.

> Not that hell knows redeeming,
> But for souls sunk in seeming
> Fresh, till doomfire burn all,
> Prayer shall fetch pity eternal.

The study of the relation between the first and the second quatrain of the sonnet on Purcell is to the point here. Hopkins was well aware that Purcell was a heretic, but having satisfied his conscience that in spite of his heresy Purcell is saved, he exclaims, 'Let him oh! with his air of angels then lift me . . .' (*Poems* 21). A most pathetic confirmation of his anxiety to state the exact truth is surely given in the following alteration occurring in *Poems* 45, where Hopkins first wrote

> God's most *just* decree
> Bitter would have me taste . . .

But he could not understand how it was *just*; its justice was beyond his grasp and so he wrote: 'God's most *deep* decree . . .'

This search for truth reveals itself further in his passion for detail: 'Thou knowest the walls, altar and hour and night . . .' (*Deutschland* st. 2); He entertains hopes 'somewhere of some day seeing' this boy as 'our day's God's own Galahad' (*Poems* 23). In the *Deutschland* it is curious to note how every detail is relevant to something or other: the place of the wreck: 'at our door'; the time: 'what was the feast followed the night . . . ?'; the name of the steamer: 'O Deutschland, double a desperate name'; the number of the drowned sisters:

> Five! the finding and sake
> And cipher of suffering Christ; [22]

—the day of the sailing is given, a Saturday; destination, America, and so on. At great detail he examines the words of the nuns and the effect upon the other passengers and the crew. In the *Eurydice* we are told the number of her crew, her cargo, what kind of ship it was, the season, the weather, &c. &c. This instinctive passion to tell the whole truth well explains his anxiety to put in whatever thought is suggested to him at any moment. We are then not surprised at the sudden transition of thought between octet and sestet in many of his sonnets, which at a first reading, because of its suddenness, appears strangely abrupt, as is the case in *The Candle Indoors*, where the poet jumps from the picture of a house to that of the heart because in both burns a candle, albeit that in the heart there burns a 'vital candle' (*Poems* 26). It explains the rapid succession of thoughts in his poetry, the best example of which is found in the *Deutschland* (st. 29), where

the nun's confession of Him who 'has the words of eternal life' at once
reminds the poet of St. Peter's confession and this irresistibly urges
him to work out the suggestion and compare the sister to a rock like
St. Peter:

> . . . to the blast
> Tarpeian-fast . . .

Hopkins goes very far in his passion for the exact truth: he is fastidious
where he writes to Dixon that he can never become reconciled to the
latter's calling men and women 'angels', even though he grants that
it is commonly done (II. 65).   With Patmore he waged a veritable
battle about 'women should be vain', a line occurring in *The Angel
in the House* (Book II, Canto vi), which Patmore left unaltered in
spite of the serious objections made against it by Hopkins (III. 159–61).

In his criticisms there often occurs a rather ingenious analysis of
the imagery of some poem, which was prompted by his desire for
objective truth and his abhorrence of poetic fancies.   He cannot stand
false perspective in an image, because to him this could only come
from frigid fancy.   He thus criticizes Dixon for obscurity of imagery
and gives a 'glaring instance' of false perspective in an image of
Browning.

In his *Instans Tyrannus* he makes the tyrant say that he found the just man
his victim on a sudden shielded from him by the vault of the sky spreading
itself like a great targe over him, 'with the sun's disk for a visible boss'.
This is monstrous.   The vault of heaven is a vault, hollow, concave towards
us, convex upwards; it therefore could only defend man on earth against
enemies above it, an angry Olympus for instance.   And the tyrant himself
is inside it, under it, just as much as his victim.   The boss is seen from
behind, like the small stud of a sleevelink (II. 56).

This instance must suffice here.[23]

If faulty imagery made Hopkins uncomfortable and if he was ever
on the alert to detect any defect however small, we may well ask why
he was so zealous to find the truth and nothing but the truth even in
the representation of an image.   Hopkins would have objected to the
use of *even* in the foregoing sentence, as if imagery were something
of a luxury in which reality and truth did not matter so much because
they were accidental illustrations of some fact or other.   Hopkins
could not look upon imagery as something imposed upon the poetry.
Indeed, he had often discovered that imagery was little more than
ornament and more or less superfluous illustration, as for instance
in Swinburne and Tennyson.   But we have seen how severely he

criticized and condemned such poetry.   To him imagery was inseparable from the true poetic experience; the image was given with the
emotion, and flushed by it; and thus an image is embodied in the poem
as a living part.   The importance of this view of imagery should not
be underestimated, since Hopkins's poetry must necessarily be read
with that concentration of mind and passion for truth in imagery which
was his own.   One must read the poetry of Hopkins as he was wont
to read the poetry of others.   I therefore turn, to conclude this section,
to the way in which Hopkins read his Homer.   There exist some notes
on the *Iliad*, dating from his Dublin period.   I shall have to say more
about these notes in another connexion in later chapters; I shall now
deal with them as far as they bear out Hopkins's way of entering into
detail of imagery.   I single out three examples.[24]

The first passage occurs in Book IV, 422–5:

> Ὡς δ' ὅτ' ἐν αἰγιαλῷ πολυηχέϊ κῦμα θαλάσσης
> ὄρνυτ' ἐπασσύτερον Ζεφύρου ὕπο κινήσαντος·
> πόντῳ μέν τε πρῶτα κορύσσεται, αὐτὰρ ἔπειτα
> χέρσῳ ῥηγνύμενον μεγάλα βρέμει . . .

As when on the echoing beach the sea-wave lifteth up itself in close array
before the driving of the west wind; out on the deep doth it first raise its
head, and then breaketh upon the land and belloweth aloud . . .

Hopkins's commentary reads:

In the breaker-image the 'combing' answers to the Greeks arming, the
breaking on the shore to the battle before Troy gates,—

> . . . ἀμφὶ δέ τ' ἄκρας
> κυρτὸν ἐὸν κορυφοῦται, ἀποπτύει δ' ἁλὸς ἄχνην

(and goes with arching crest about the promontories, and speweth the foam-
ing brine afar) to the surging against Troy walls and javelin throwing on
both sides.

The second example is taken from Hopkins's notes on the fifth
book; it is very simple but again well shows how he worked out every
image for himself and drew parallels between it and the event it was
meant to illustrate; V, 87–91:

> θῦνε γὰρ ἂμ πεδίον ποταμῷ πλήθοντι ἐοικὼς
> χειμάρρῳ, ὅς τ' ὦκα ῥέων ἐκέδασσε γεφύρας·
> τόν δ' οὔτ' ἄρ τε γέφυραι ἐεργμέναι ἰσχανόωσιν,
> οὔτ' ἄρα ἕρκεα ἴσχει ἀλωάων ἐριθηλέων
> ἐλθόντ' ἐξαπίνης, ὅτ' ἐπιβρίσῃ Διὸς ὄμβρος·

(For he stormed across the plain like a winter torrent at the full, that in swift course scattereth the causeys; neither can the long lines of causeys hold it in, nor the fences of fruitful orchards stay its sudden coming when the rain of heaven driveth it.)

Hopkins remarks: 'The γέφυραι / embankments are the ranks, φάλαγγες; the ἕρκεα ἀλωάων / *globi*, the throngs.'
The last instance occurs in Book V, 615 ff.

> τὸν ῥα κατὰ ζωστῆρα βάλεν Τελαμώνιος Αἴας,
> νειαίρῃ δ' ἐν γαστρὶ πάγη δολιχόσκιον ἔγχος,
> δούπησεν δὲ πεσών· ὁ δ' ἐπέδραμε φαίδιμος Αἴας
> τεύχεα συλήσων· Τρῶες δ' ἐπὶ δούρατ' ἔχευαν
> ὀξέα παμφανόωντα· σάκος δ' ἀνεδέξατο πολλά.
> αὐτὰρ ὁ λὰξ προσβὰς ἐκ νεκροῦ χάλκεον ἔγχος
> ἐσπάσατ'· οὐδ' ἄρ' ἔτ' ἄλλα δυνήσατο τεύχεα καλὰ
> ὤμοιιν ἀφελέσθαι· ἐπείγετο γὰρ βελέεσσι.

Him Telamonian Aias smote upon the belt, and in his nether belly the far-shadowing spear stuck and he fell with a crash. Then glorious Aias ran at him to strip him of his armour, and the Trojans rained on him keen javelins glittering, and his shield caught many thereof. But he set his heel upon the corpse and plucked forth the spear of bronze; only he could not strip from his shoulders all the fair armour therewith, being overwhelmed with spears.

Hopkins has visualized this scene very clearly and omitted no detail; he solves the difficulty why it is that the javelin, which has been called φαεινός (611), is here called δολιχόσκιος: 'the javelin had its warning light and warning shadow, here the shadow follows the light'. He then goes on to point out how 'φαίδιμος, ὀξέα παμφανόωντα and τεύχεα καλά keep up the thought of lightning spokes on both sides, but χάλκεον ἔγχος is the plain serviceable metal.'

But even Homer is charged with employing 'pure unreflecting imagery'; one example must suffice.

And on the other side the two Aiantes and Odysseus and Diomedes stirred the Danaans to fight; yet these of themselves feared neither the Trojans' violence nor assaults, but stood like mists that Kronos' son setteth in windless air on the mountain tops, at peace, while the might of the north wind sleepeth and of all the violent winds that blow with keen breath and scatter apart the shadowing clouds (*Iliad* V. 519–526).[24]

To this passage Hopkins appends this note:

The simile of the clouds motionless covering the mountaintops is curious in this that in making the Greeks the clouds it suggests the Trojans are the wind and will scatter them, but they do not. It is therefore pure unreflecting imagery.

Having set forth what was Hopkins's aim of poetry and by what means he tried to achieve it, I now propose to examine the relation between this and the medium employed.   Its importance is obvious; to its neglect are due the many misunderstandings about Hopkins's poetic technique.

The language used by the poet must have the same individualizing touch as the matter of his poetry, matter and form being for Hopkins one and inseparable.   The poetic experience, no matter how distinctive and how 'selved', will lose its individuality if it is to be expressed in conventional forms.

In his writings there occur many significant passages bearing on the subject of poetic language; all of them are directly inspired by his zeal for inscape, for the individualizing touch, even in the expression of the poetic experience.   As early as 1864 Hopkins noted down some theories about the medium properly belonging to poetry (*N*. 29–30). Though barely twenty at the time he showed an unusual ripeness of judgement in these matters.   In a letter to Baillie, written at about the same time, the same views are expounded.   I shall quote at some length from this letter, because the views expressed in it were never abandoned by the poet:

I think then the language of verse may be divided into three kinds.   The first and highest is poetry proper, the language of inspiration.   The word inspiration need cause no difficulty.   I mean by it a mood of great, abnormal in fact, mental acuteness, either energetic or receptive, according as the thoughts which arise in it seem generated by a stress and action of the brain, or to strike into it unasked.   This mood arises from various causes, physical generally, as good health or state of the air or, prosaic as it is, length of time after a meal.   But I need not go into this; all that it is needful to mark is, that the poetry of inspiration can only be written in this mood of mind, even if it only last a minute, by poets themselves.   Everybody of course has like moods, but not being poets what they then produce is not poetry.   The second kind I call *Parnassian*.   It can only be spoken by poets, but is not in the highest sense poetry.   It does not require the mood of mind in which the poetry of inspiration is written.   It is spoken *on and from the level* of a poet's mind, not, as in the other case, when the inspiration which is the gift of genius, raises him above himself.   For I think it is the case with genius that it is not when quiescent so very much above mediocrity as the difference between the two might lead us to think, but that it has the power and privilege of rising from that level to a height utterly far from mediocrity: in other words that its greatness is *that it can be* so great.   You will understand.   *Parnassian* then is that language which genius speaks as fitted to its exaltation, and place among other genius, but does not sing (I have been

betrayed into the whole hog of a metaphor) in its flights.   Great men, poets
I mean, have each their own dialect as it were of Parnassian, formed generally
as they go on writing, and at last,—this is the point to be marked,—they can
see things in this Parnassian way and describe them in this Parnassian tongue,
without further effort of inspiration.   In a poet's peculiar kind of Parnassian
lies most of his style, of his manner, of his mannerism if you like. . . .
Now it is a mark of Parnassian that one could conceive oneself writing it if
one were a poet.   Do not say that *if* you were Shakespear you can imagine
yourself writing Hamlet, because that is just what you can*not* conceive.   In
a fine piece of inspiration every beauty takes you as it were by surprise, not
of course that you did not think the writer could be so great, for that is not
it,—indeed I think it is a mistake to speak of people admiring Shakespear
more and more as they live, for when the judgement is ripe and you have read
a good deal of any writer including his best things, and carefully, then, I
think, however high the place you give him, that you must have rated him
equally with his merits however great they be; so that all after admiration
cannot increase but keep alive this estimate, make his greatness stare into
your eyes and din it into your ears, as it were, but not make it greater,—
but to go on with the broken sentence, every fresh beauty could not in any
way be predicted or accounted for by what one has already read.   But in
Parnassian pieces you feel that if you were the poet you could have gone on
as he has done, you see yourself doing it, only with the difference that if you
actually try you find you cannot write his Parnassian. . . .   I believe that
when a poet palls on us it is because of his Parnassian.   We seem to have
found out his secret.   Now in fact we have not found out more than this,
that when he is not inspired and in his flights, his poetry does run in an
intelligibly laid down path.   Well, it is notorious that Shakespear does not
pall, and this because he uses, I believe, so little Parnassian.   Now judging
from my own experience I should say no author palls so much as Wordsworth; this is because he writes such an 'intolerable deal of' Parnassian. . . .

Just to end what I was saying about poetry.   There is a higher sort of
Parnassian which I call *Castalian*, or it may be thought the lowest kind of
inspiration.   Beautiful poems may be written wholly in it.   Its peculiarity
is that though you can hardly conceive yourself having written in it, if in
the poet's place, yet it is too characteristic of the poet, too so-and-so-all-
over-ish, to be quite inspiration. . . .   The third kind is merely the language
of verse as distinct from that of prose, Delphic, the tongue of the Sacred
Plain, used in common by poet and poetaster.   Poetry when spoken is
spoken in it, but to speak it is not necessarily to speak poetry.   I may add
there is also *Olympian*.   This is the language of strange masculine genius
which suddenly, as it were, forces its way into the domain of poetry, without
naturally having a right there.   Milman's poetry is of this kind I think, and
Rossetti's *Blessed Damozel* (III. 69–73).

It should be noted that the basis of this threefold division is not a clearly marked technique evident in each of them, but the kind or degree of inspiration. I need not work out this point, as this view of Hopkins is the logical deduction from his high appreciation of earnestness and sincerity as the only ends by which the poet can ensure the true expression of his inscape. The most typical phrase in the long extract given is to my mind: 'one could conceive oneself writing it'; that condemns Parnassian. As soon as a poet can conceive himself writing in the same manner as another poet, that poet's language is according to Hopkins no longer its own species; it misses that last touch of individuality which is the ultimate revelation of one's own 'I', which in every person is something different. Parnassian has lost the stamp of the self and is only recognizable as belonging to this poet by mannerisms of style. Seventeen years after he had thus written at length about the poetic medium, he writes to Dixon that Wordsworth fails as a great poet because of his use of Parnassian—just as he had written to Baillie—'Parnassian, that is the language and style of poetry mastered and at command, but employed without any fresh inspiration' (II. 72); and Bridges was criticized for using this language in some passages of his *Prometheus the Firegiver* (I. 159). Used without fresh inspiration, as an instrument well at command, Parnassian was the language which could easily be employed to drape prose thought, to give common thought a poetic colour. Hopkins could never defend this language, because it showed that there was no fusion of matter and form.

If on the one hand in Hopkins's opinion a poet should be very careful not to master a peculiar poetic language to such an extent that he can use it at will, irrespective of the contents of the poems, he should on the other hand not go to the other extreme and rely upon the guidance of some master of language solely. For not to have any language of one's own at all is as bad as, if not worse than, to borrow blindly from another poet. With regard to his own practice he said that he greatly admired the masters of poetry, but that the effect of this admiration was that it made him do otherwise (I. 291). Naturally —for every poet has his own language, in its actual existence necessarily dependent on the poet's own inspiration. Consequently Hopkins considered the idea of schools of poetry a very dangerous one in literary appreciation. It is doubtful praise to belong to a school (II. 98); it implies that personal emotions are adapted to some conventional form, a personal experience is uttered in the voice and tongue of a group of people; and successfully to mount one's own form on top of such a conventional form is no easy matter. His abhorrence of echoes in literature is almost comic. 'The echos are a disease of education, literature is full of them; but they remain a disease, an evil' (I. 206).

We can now understand why Hopkins never managed to finish his tragedy on St. Winefred, at which he worked off and on for some eight years. It was his main ambition; he would not dream of giving it up. What remains of it promises well; *The Leaden Echo and the Golden Echo* (*Poems* 36) has received universal praise; the soliloquy of Caradoc (*Poems* 58, pp. 75–8), in which occur what to Hopkins were the strongest lines he had ever written (I. 212), deserves far more attention than has been paid to it. It has been argued that Hopkins failed to finish this tragedy because aridity of soul, bad health and mental fatigue prevented him from seeing it to a successful end. These factors undoubtedly damped his inspiration, and hampered the poet badly; but I am by no means certain whether under more favourable circumstances Hopkins would have succeeded in his ambitious undertaking. For as early as 1879, five years before the bleakest and blackest period of his life began, he wrote to Bridges: 'I have a greater undertaking on hand than any yet . . . I seem to find myself, after some experiment, equal to the more stirring and critical parts of the action, which are in themselves the more important, but about the filling in and minor parts I am not sure how far my powers will go . . .' (I. 92). The 'filling in and minor parts' did not afford scope for feeling; they were the structural links, and in the bare construction of a play only perfect handling of the situation, and complete mastery of dramatic technique and language, can make up for want of inspiration, which is necessarily at its lowest in these parts. The danger was that he should lapse into Parnassian, 'the language of poetry draping prose thought'; Hopkins did not wish to give in, but he lacked the talent of writing these parts in the language of true poetic inspiration; thus far Hopkins failed to be a great dramatic poet.

From these theories about the poetic medium results Hopkins's violent denunciation of the use of archaisms and of a complete archaic language. It is not that an archaic language is not a good language; with reference to Elizabethan English he remarked: 'No one admires, regrets, despairs over the death of the style, the living masculine native rhetoric of that age, more than I do; but " 'tis gone, 'tis gone, 'tis gone" ' (I. 284). But any archaic language, in spite of its excellence, is unfit as a poetical language because it is out of time, it is not the language of the poet emotionally moved, who in simplicity of heart and passionately-loved sincerity is inspired to write about his own self. It is affectation to write in an obsolete language (I. 284, 290) and affectation is incompatible with poetry.

> I hold that by archaism a thing is sicklied o'er as by blight. Some little flavours, but much spoils, and always for the same reason—it destroys earnest: we do not speak that way; therefore if a man speaks that way he is not serious . . . (I. 218).

Surely this quotation speaks for itself; it sums up Hopkins's poetic theories on more than one essential point. More than once he warns Bridges and Dixon not to fall into this defect. He never felt quite comfortable when poets used a language which they did not speak; 'for it seems to me', so he wrote to Bridges, 'that the poetical language of an age shd. be the current language heightened, to any degree heightened and unlike itself, but not (I mean normally: passing freaks and graces are another thing) an obsolete one' (I. 89). In the following chapter I shall examine what is implied in *current language heightened*; a right conception of it will dispel most of Hopkins's oddity and obscurity.

I have been explaining at great length the full implications of 'what I aim at is inscape'. Simple as it may sound, Hopkins had not made poetry easy for himself. Poetry became very arduous and not a luxury for leisure time; it demanded one's entire personality. Probably the canons drawn up by Hopkins are too severe. He asked too much of his energy; poetry became a burden. It imposed a strain on mind and soul which made him confess that he made verse too laborious a thing (I. 66). It partly explains his very small output; the intensity of his poetic experience made the costs too high for most of his poems. Unlike other poets Hopkins could never adopt an objective matter-of-fact attitude towards his poems. He was not the patient artist trying to make a perfect word-picture, putting in a touch here and adding a slight correction there. He was no craftsman chiselling his words and gradually building up an edifice. Hopkins could only write 'hot on the anvil' (I. 263). The expression was always clamoured for by each poetic experience; there was an absolute and final connexion and interdependence between the two. And so one should be careful in speaking of Hopkins as a technical innovator, a theorist or an experimentalist, as is often done. One does not experiment with one's own self and to Hopkins poetry was very much part of his self. 'Experimentalist' has a bad sound in so far as it suggests that greater importance is attached to the form than to the matter, more attention paid to the rhythm, sound, music, in general the technique, than to the poetic emotion itself. It may even suggest that the poem is written for the sake of a new technique only. But in any case experimenting unconsciously posits a separation between matter and form and a denial of the inevitable oneness of these two elements, while for Hopkins the experience precisely demanded its own and only expression. Hence one cannot be careful enough in speaking of Hopkins as a theorist; no one should expect any practical rules that guided his writing in his peculiar way. All the theory that Hopkins left in his writings I have given in this chapter; more theory there is not.

I do not maintain that Hopkins was no good craftsman and was a poet, so to speak, by accident. He never neglected to gain complete acquaintance with the art of poetry. He was always interested in the technique of poetry; his remarks on the sonnets prove this beyond a doubt (II. 85–7). Technically he was well schooled; but he never wrote poetry merely to try a new technique on.

Simple and straightforward as Hopkins's canons are, there lurked a great danger in them. It is the virtue of inscape to be distinctive, but it is the vice of distinctiveness to become queer. This Hopkins knew very well and he was also aware that he had not escaped this vice of queerness and oddity (I. 66). He refers to his singularity in various places (I. 291, III. 222), but he considered it as more or less inevitable; once the reader has become weathered to these 'snags' in his style (I. 159) they begin to tell in the poem and no longer have a disturbing effect—*so he thought*. He confesses himself that the *Eurydice* was at first sight repulsive (I. 79); at another time he appears to have made the firm resolution of becoming more intelligible, because he thought he had gone far enough, as Bridges and Dixon never tired of telling him (I. 250, 272). But, it should be remembered, he rarely wrote for a public; and when he did write for a public he aimed at a style 'smoother, more intelligent'; he tried it, but failed, in his tragedy on St. Winefred (I. 291).

A second danger was obscurity; it was another point about which Bridges and Dixon did not mince matters. But his obscurity cannot be related to his zeal for inscape in the same way as his oddity. There is no reason why a poet should be obscure in expressing his own inscape. Hence it is that Hopkins would never admit that there was truth in the charge of obscurity. Though repeatedly he stumbles over, and is vexed at, the obscurity of his friends—an obscurity by no comparison so awkward as his own—if that charge was brought against him, he brushed it aside. If he was thought obscure, he must have been read in the wrong way; and that was the end of it. I shall show later how and why he so firmly adhered to this view. I close this chapter with a very illuminating quotation showing what Hopkins thought of his own obscurity in the *Deutschland*: the remarks he makes are worth remembering.

I must tell you I am sorry you never read the Deutschland again. Granted that it needs study and is obscure, for indeed I was not over-desirous that the meaning of it all should be quite clear, at least unmistakeable, you might, without the effort that to make it all out would seem to have required, have nevertheless read it so that lines and stanzas should be left in the memory and superficial impressions deepened, and have liked some without exhausting all. I am sure I have read and enjoyed pages of poetry that way. Why, sometimes one enjoys and admires the very lines one cannot understand, as for instance 'If it were done when 'tis done' sqq., which is all obscure and disputed, though how fine it is everybody sees and nobody disputes . . . Besides you would have got more weathered to the style and its features— not really odd. Now they say that vessels sailing from the port of London will take (perhaps it should be / used once to take) Thames water for the voyage: it was foul and stunk at first as the ship worked but by degrees casting its filth was in a few days very pure and sweet and wholesomer and better than any water in the world. However that maybe, it is true to my purpose. When a new thing, such as my ventures in the Deutschland are, is presented us our first criticisms are not our truest, best, most homefelt, or most lasting but what come easiest on the instant. They are barbarous and like what the ignorant and the ruck say. This was so with you. The Deutschland on her first run worked very much and unsettled you, thickening and clouding your mind with vulgar mudbottom and common sewage (I see that I am going it with the image) and just then you unhappily *drew off* your criticisms all stinking and bilgy, whereas if you had let your thoughts cast themselves they would have been clearer in themselves and more to my taste too. I did not heed them therefore, perceiving they were a first drawing-off. Same of the Eurydice—which being short and easy please read more than once (I. 50–1).

'CURRENT LANGUAGE HEIGHTENED'

IN the foregoing chapter I have shown how, according to Hopkins's poetic theories, the poet has, strictly speaking, no choice of medium in which to express the inscape of his self; for the perfect poetic language and the perfect poetic style is 'of its age' (II. 99). If a poet is serious and takes his poetic experience in earnest, he is bound according to Hopkins to use the current language of his day. This living language the poet has thrust upon him; if he conforms with this necessity, his poetry will bear the mark of that inevitability of expression which is characteristic of all great poetry and makes one feel that in no other way could this experience have been so well expressed. The employment of an archaic language or a distinctly poetic jargon argues for Hopkins deliberate choice of medium and thus denies any inherent necessary relation between the matter and the form of the poem; matter and form are then no longer one and this cannot but damage a faithful rendering of the poet's inscape.

Current language is the language spoken by ordinary people in their everyday lives. As the only proper medium of poetry it is opposed to any kind of archaic language; this is logical enough, but it is also opposed to any artificial language because artificiality was to Hopkins affectation, and affectation was an untruth and therefore incompatible with the expression of his inscape. Yet current language is not always free from the stain of artificiality, at any rate current Victorian language was not free from it; and Hopkins is very careful not to let those pedantic artificialities intrude into his writings. In a letter to Bridges he once wrote: '. . . this Victorian English is a bad business. They say "It goes without saying" (and I wish it did) and instead of "There is no such thing" they say a thing is "non-existent" and *in* for *at* and *altruistic* and a lot more' (I. 284). In his reaction Hopkins swings perhaps too far in the opposite direction and tends to become a purist: 'Disillusion is a bad word; you mean Disenchantment. It is as bad as Or-de-al and Preventative and Standpoint and the other barbarisms' (I. 113). This saying had apparently but slight effect on the future poet laureate, for Hopkins returned to the subject some months later: ' "Disillusion" does exist, as typhus exists and the Protestant religion.

The same "brutes" say "disillusion" as say "standpoint" and "pre-ventative" and "equally as well" and "to whomsoever shall ask"'
(I. 121).

Even more emphatically Hopkins objected to the distinctly poetic diction of his time.   Indeed, the Romantic Movement of the beginning of the nineteenth century had wished once for all to do away with the 'poetic diction' of the neo-classics, but it fell into another diction as 'poetic'.   And in the course of the century poetry developed a jargon as artificial and conventional as that of the eighteenth century.   Hopkins could not stand it: that language could never be the medium of poetry for the simple reason that 'we do not speak that way' (I. 218). Bridges is criticized for making use of this poetic diction in his poem entitled *The Dead Child*:

But indeed, 'wise, sad head' and 'firm, pale hands' do not strike me as severe at all, nor yet exquisite.   Rather they belong to a familiar commonplace about 'Reader, have you never hung over the pillow of . . . pallid cheeks, clammy brow . . . long, long night-watches . . . surely, Sir Josiah Bicker-staff, there is *some* hope!   O say not all is over.   It cannot be.'   You know (I. 122).

And in another letter to Bridges he wrote:

So also I cut myself off from the use of *ere, o'er, wellnigh, what time, say not* (for *do not say*), because, though dignified, they neither belong to nor ever cd. arise from, or be the elevation of, ordinary modern speech (I. 89).

Hopkins might have added that he also cut himself off from the use of 'drave' and 'spake', and 'as lief' and a host of other words and expressions styled 'poetical' by the *Concise Oxford Dictionary*.   It is worthy of note that as early as 1867 Hopkins attacks this distinctly poetic diction where he confesses that he cannot appreciate Swinburne's *Atalanta* because 'it is too full of *untos* and *thereafters* and *-eths*' (III. 82).

Inversion is a figure of speech that often belongs to the same category; what he thought about it we shall see below (p. 88).   And though he does not unconditionally condemn the use of 'do' and 'did' followed by the verbal stem, he entertains serious doubts about its effect in poetry; it is an easy way to fill up the line for one thing, and, even where effective, 'do' and 'did' belong to that half-archaic style which even at its best is a blight (I. 211 and III. 148).[1]   These are some elements of Victorian poetic diction to which Hopkins could never become reconciled.

Even a superficial reading of his poetry will convince anyone that

Hopkins avoided the pitfalls of this poetic diction. His language and his style impress one as straightforward, vigorous, manly and even sober, in spite of their oddities and intricacies. His vocabulary is Saxon to the marrow. Latin words are extremely rare; where they are used, they are never stuck on like rich jewellery but are placed in the line with a singular felicity.[2] Hopkins has never been charged with indulging in the use of an artificial poetic cant, but some one might make out a good case against him for employing a language as archaic and as obsolete as that ever used by Dixon or Bridges. For does Hopkins not overdo his search for the Saxon word? Does not his eagerness to dig up and re-instate old obsolete words injure his poetry? Is his preference of the Saxon word to the well-adapted Latin word not as clear a sign of affectation as the writing in a language entirely archaic? 'Degrees of comparison' is surely good English; why then regret that we do not call them 'pitches of suchness'? (I. 163). Hopkins wrote 'angel-warder', but 'guardian angel' is undoubtedly good 'current language'; the old-fashioned 'hie' is preferred to 'haste', 'ghost' to 'spirit', 'thew' and 'brawn' to 'muscle', 'lade' to 'load', 'brine' to 'sea' and so on. 'Fettle', 'pash', 'mammock', 'rivel', 'rive', 'reeve', 'wend', 'heft', 'sillion', 'shive', 'barrow', 'bole', 'tuck', 'burl' and 'buck' are all of them good Saxon words, but they can hardly be said to belong any longer to the ordinary modern language of Victorian days. Hopkins once jokingly told Dixon that to understand the latter's poetry a 'Dixon-ary' was needed; many readers would have been grateful to Hopkins if he had composed some such dictionary to be used when reading his own poems.[3]

Yet we must be careful not to judge and condemn too rashly the practice of Hopkins. If we rigidly apply his own standard 'we do not speak that way', Hopkins stands condemned and on his own theories his poetry must be admitted to be a failure. If, nevertheless, his poetry is a success, either it is in spite of his theory, or we have mis-interpreted this theory. And indeed, the application of Hopkins's own standard requires an important qualification. The poet used the plural 'we': '*we* do not speak that way'; he should have used the singular; and this is not an over-subtle or ingenious distinction that can hardly claim serious attention. The language that any man uses is intimately bound up with his own being. It is the connatural means of expressing himself; every man uses his own language; and although it is true that the fact of communication requires a close parallelism and even similarity of expression between men, it nevertheless remains a fact that the means of expression are individual. Every man has his own intonation, pitch, inflection of voice, gestures, facial expression, all elements of language. Every man has his own pronunciation—and to this fact Hopkins referred in his letters (III. 165)—and every man has his own vocabulary and his own constructions, individual within a body of words and constructions that belong to the language as a system of communication. In a man like Hopkins this individuality of language was greater than in other men. The harmony of his being, begotten from constant self-analysis and self-control, extended to the relation between the expressed self and the expression. With his intense reflection on everything that touched his self, he was conscious of the balance he must strike between his thoughts and feelings and the material in which he had to express them. He was aware of the heterogeneous elements that in time had found their way into the English language. He felt that this heterogeneity was in reality an imperfection; a pure language seemed to him a finer thing than a mixed language, until the mixture had become imperceptible (I. 166); but in the English of his day the mixture was very clearly perceptible and the mixing still continued. As an artist of words he was capable of completing what the language lacked in perfection. His keen interest in English etymology (the notes on this subject printed by House are only a small portion of a large collection) and his constant care to pick and choose the right word in both prose and poetry made him most sensitive to the 'naked thew and sinew' (I. 267) of the English language. And so in his own language he gradually achieved the desired equilibrium between the original source and the added extraneous elements. His whole being became delicately attuned to the Anglo-Saxon element of the English language and that is why this Anglo-Saxon element is so predominant in the language of all his writings. It is here of interest to observe that not until 1882 did Hopkins take up the study of Old English; and though we might consequently expect that the archaic element would be more pronounced in the writings dated after this year, yet there is no marked difference at all between his language before and after this date; the language of his diary is as Saxon as that of his latest poetry.

The Anglo-Saxon element in Hopkins's writings, and more especially in his poetry, does not show itself in the use of Saxon words only. I need only remind readers of his sprung rhythm, of which he said that it existed in full force and great beauty in Anglo-Saxon (I. 156), and of his alliterations; even the structure of his sentences and many word-formations show a curious likeness to those of Anglo-Saxon.

Our conclusion then should be, not that he failed to conform to the standard which he set up for poetic language in general: 'we do not speak that way', but that this standard must be interpreted aright. It was precisely his sincerity and earnestness and anxiety faithfully to render his inscape that necessitated his employment of this peculiar Saxon language, a thing as he said himself, 'vastly superior to what we have now' (I. 163). Alas, it was gone; but this too we must understand correctly; it was gone and lost to the living language as the social means of communication; but it could be, and in fact was recovered, to a certain extent at least, by this poet, without it becoming either archaic or artificial. For he did not impose this Anglo-Saxon element on the language from without as something accidental to it; but through force of the exigencies of his own being he could not help having recourse to these elements, which were of the essence of his own individuated language. To Hopkins the Anglo-Saxon words and expressions were not added ornament that well suited the tone or atmosphere of his poetry; they were part of the expression of his own inscape. And that is the reason why, in spite of its Anglo-Saxon character, the language of Hopkins is modern, and not archaic or artificial. Those queer words mentioned above, and so many analogous formations, about which I shall speak in the last chapter, are part and parcel of his poetic medium. They never stand out as isolated relics from an antique period; they are never forced into the poem, but unobtrusively take their place. Hence it is that we never get the impression that Hopkins is after striking words for which, as it would seem, the whole line, or even the whole stanza, were written, a fault which infects and vitiates a good deal of modern poetry where 'every line, nay every word, looks full in our face, and asks and begs for praise', as Coleridge (in *Anima Poetae*) remarked of the modern poetry of his day.

From the foregoing it will be clear why Hopkins was not unsympathetic towards the attempt of Barnes to renew the English language, yet considered it as necessarily doomed to failure.

... the Rev. Wm. Barnes, good soul, ... has published a 'Speech craft of English Speech' = English Grammar, written in an unknown tongue, a sort of modern Anglosaxon, beyond all that Furnival in his wildest Forewords ever dreamed. He does not see the utter hopelessness of the thing. It makes one weep to think what English might have been; for in spite of all that Shakspere and Milton have done with the compound I cannot doubt that no beauty in a language can make up for want of purity ... But the madness of an almost unknown man trying to do what the three estates of the realm together could never accomplish! He calls degrees of comparison pitches of suchness: we *ought* to call them so, but alas! (I. 162–3).

Barnes was trying to graft a dead language on a living one.

So far we have studied the notion of current language; but Hopkins held that the only proper medium of poetry was current language *heightened*. What then is current language *heightened*?

I had best begin this enquiry by drawing the reader's attention to a most important and very fundamental distinction, *sc.* that between so-called 'logical' and 'affective' language.[4] *Logic* and *affect* lie outside the scope of this modest study of linguistics; I merely observe that there exists a manner of speaking and writing in which the grammatical and syntactical rules of a given language determine the form which language is to take, in which a system, logically built up, lies at the basis of its structure: this I call logical language. Secondly, we know from our own experience that there exists a manner of speaking and writing in which those rules and that system no longer determine the form of the language but have disappeared so that we only retain the lexical elements proper to this language; I then speak of affective language. If a true poet uses this language, he charms by a perhaps provocative, yet most felicitous, manner of using his words in a quite unsystematic way. There exists even a third manner of speaking and writing. Implying the second, it discards even the 'logic', the system, of these lexical elements themselves. The very structure of the words appears to have been uncovered, laid bare, with the natural result that in now being employed by the poet they have new life instilled into them; they are lifted, raised, 'heightened' to a level of meaning and suggestiveness quite above that which is normal when used by common folk.

When and why does a poet fix his choice on any one of these three forms of language as the most suitable for the expression of his poetic experience? Language always informs us about something. In the greater number of cases this information is cast into a systematic form of language. The use of this logical language implies that the form of the language is in accordance with the systematic rules, and therefore it argues that he who fixes his choice on this form is in mind and heart at least so calm and composed that he can with deliberation adapt the expression of his vision to this system of rules and let it be governed by it. Furthermore, the use of this form implies that the manner of speaking and thinking of both the speaker and the listener in no way infringes on the given possibilities of this language of presenting the words themselves with the meaning they normally convey in systematic use.   A few well-known lines will make clear what is meant:

> My heart aches, and a drowsy numbness pains
> My sense . . .

> Heard melodies are sweet, but those unheard
> Are sweeter . . .

> My heart leaps up when I behold
> A rainbow in the sky.

Syntactical and grammatical rules are all of them observed; the poet adapts the expression of his experience to the system of the language; the words are all of them used with their normal meaning; all the lines are written in logical language.

But not always is the poet so composed and master of his thoughts and affects that he can quietly adapt the expression to these rules.   At times the emotive tension is so high that his language cannot take on this systematic form; he has recourse to affective language.   At such moments of impetuous inspiration the poet frees himself from the rules that govern the ordinary composition of his utterances.   He is too hurried and too flurried to check the onrush of his thoughts and feelings and express them in a form intelligently preordained; he shakes off the shackles of strict systematic language, he cannot think of adapting the structure of his expression to a given system.   If a poet is thus forced to use this form of language, the reader is continually faced with grammatical and syntactical irregularities or distortions, which often cause great obscurity.

We should note that this affective language need not, and very often is not, more poetic or more effective than logical language; I recall here the great soliloquies in *Macbeth*, *Hamlet* or *Othello*, in which the language is mainly conformed to the system of logical language.

In this affective language the meaning of the words themselves is left intact; the words are not changed, are not strung together, are not conglomerated in such a fashion that at first sight one is bewildered and left gasping as if a baffling upheaval in the realm of meaning had taken place.   In this affective language there are, if one likes to call them so, grammatical and syntactical shortcomings, but as to the employment and composition of significant words, 'logic' reigns supreme.

When using the third form of language, in which the very system of the lexical elements gives way, the poet is overwhelmed by his emotions.   This ecstasy, or intense suffering, this superb state of inspiration makes it too difficult, if not impossible, for him to adapt his expression to any system at all: the common language in its every element is heightened and elevated, till often it grows most unlike itself.

It is this second form, and in many poems the third form, of language that makes the beauty of the poetry of Hopkins. Of course, Hopkins *informs* us and in so far as he informs, *logic*, the logical adaptation of the expression to the systematic rules, is maintained, even there where the expression clearly bears the mark of his personality. But often the logic of grammar and syntax and even of the lexical elements is fully sacrificed—if a sacrifice it may be called by which so much beauty is gained—to that most earnest and sincere and most direct expression of his self, which was prompted by his undoubtedly visionary manner of seeing things and living with them, as beings 'charged with love, charged with God'.

But this peculiar Hopkins-heightening of the language imposed a heavy burden on the technical resources of expression. It is easy enough to point out that at times Hopkins could not help doing away with rules of grammar and syntax; but it should be realized that thereby he necessarily drops the ordinary method of laying down in writing the current of his thoughts and the sequence of his feelings. If he cannot employ the *systematic* normal way of indicating the relation between parts of phrases and between phrases within a sentence, what other means can he resort to in order to express this relation? In affective speech this relation is largely brought out by intonation, pitch, loudness of voice, gestures and other elements essential to it; but the written line cannot contain the representation of these elements of affective language. There is no system to register the rise and fall of the voice, accelerations and slowing-downs, facial expression and gestures, and so on. How is he to mark in his poems the intonation, how to fix in writing the speed and the pitch of diction, how to express all those elements which are the very life of affective speech and make clear its meaning? Rules of grammar and syntax are entirely useless to him—a totally different notation is needed. Hopkins was very much alive to this difficulty. He felt the need for marks acutely and he used them freely in his first poem *The Wreck of the Deutschland*, so freely that they 'could not but dismay an editor's eye' (II. 15). But it was a hopeless undertaking: 'You were right to leave out the marks: they are not consistent for one thing and are always offensive. Still there must be some. Either I must invent a notation applied throughout as in music or else I must only mark where the reader is likely to mistake . . .', so he wrote to Bridges

(I. 189).   He returned to this subject in a later letter: 'This is my difficulty, what marks to use and when to use them: they are so much
needed and yet so objectionable' (I. 215).   Some eighteen months
before his death he once again dealt with it and at some length this
time:

> I do myself think, I may say, that it would be an immense advance
> in notation (so to call it) in writing as the record of speech, to distinguish
> the subject, verb, object, and in general to express the construction to the
> eye; as is done partly in punctuation by everybody, partly in capitals by
> the Germans, more fully in accentuation by the Hebrews.   And I daresay
> it will come.   But it would, I think, not do for me: it seems a confession of
> unintelligibility.   And yet I don't know.   At all events there is a difference.
> My meaning surely *ought* to appear of itself; but in a language like English,
> and in an age of it like the present, written words are really matter open and
> indifferent to the receiving of different and alternative verse-forms, some of
> which the reader cannot possibly be sure are meant unless they are marked
> for him.   Besides metrical marks are meant for the performer and such
> marks are proper in every art.   Though indeed one might say syntactical
> marks are for the performer too (I. 265).

Given the fact that Hopkins had no workable system that could
register all the essential elements of affective language, we understand
how again and again he points to the only possible way of understanding his poetry.   Repeatedly and most insistently he implores and
pleads with his friends to read and reread his verse and read it aloud,
read it with the ear, declaim it.   'My verse is less to be read than
heard, as I have told you before,' he writes to Bridges (I. 46).   When
he sends his poem *Spelt from Sibyl's Leaves* to Bridges he accompanies
it with the following warning:

> Of this long sonnet above all remember what applies to all my verse, that
> it is, as living art should be, made for performance and that its performance
> is not reading with the eye but loud, leisurely, poetical (not rhetorical)
> recitation, with long rests, long dwells on the rhyme and other marked
> syllables, and so on (I. 246).

The success of the *Eurydice* depends entirely on the correct reading:
'To do the Eurydice any kind of justice you must not slovenly read it
with the eyes but with your ears, as if the paper were declaiming it at
you' (I. 51–2).   Bridges had said that the *Deutschland* was obscure
and Hopkins answered that the obscurity arose from the reader, not
from the poet: his friend did not read it with the ear.   Hence he warns
Bridges beforehand to give the *Eurydice* a better chance: ' . . . take
breath and read it with the ears, as I always wish to be read, and my

verse becomes all right' (I. 79). *Harry Ploughman* is 'altogether for recital, not for perusal' (I. 263). If the good Canon and Bridges are completely baffled by the obscurity and oddity of *Tom's Garland* and cannot make out its meaning, Hopkins, somewhat disappointed in this, points out that 'declaimed, the strange constructions would be dramatic and effective' (I. 272). Unless read and read aloud his rhymes can hardly be defended; some of them Hopkins himself regretted, but most of them were 'rigidly good—to the ear' (I. 44).

It is only by reading them in the right way that the poems of Hopkins can be understood correctly. Only then can the essential elements of affective speech, which cannot be expressed in writing, become functional and bear out the meaning of the line. The rest of this chapter and the chapters following will prove that, if Hopkins is read aloud and if it is remembered that he employs affective language, his obscurity dwindles considerably because, to use his own metaphor, the meaning 'explodes' (I. 98, 125).

In this connexion I must add a few words about the invention of sprung rhythm. It was not in the first place dissatisfaction with the rhythm of the poetry of his day that drove Hopkins to explore other possibilities: sprung rhythm is a natural result of his theory of inscape as the aim and end of poetry. For just as the ultimate choice of medium did not lie with the poet, so the proper rhythmical form was no question of choice. The medium was thrust upon the poet in the form of current living language; similarly the rhythm was dictated by living individuated speech. As there could be no adaptation of the expression to a systematic language when the poet was in the second or third state of inspiration described above, so could there be no adaptation of this peculiar form of language to a prearranged system of rhythm. The emotion clamours for its own form. 'Why do I employ sprung rhythm at all?' he asks himself in one of his letters to Bridges. 'Because it is the nearest to the rhythm of prose, that is the native and natural rhythm of *speech*, the least forced, the most rhetorical and emphatic of all possible rhythms...' (I. 46; italics mine). Extending the application of one of Hopkins's own sayings, we might almost maintain that he used sprung rhythm because 'we speak that way'. Sprung rhythm is the rhythm of affective speech, is 'current rhythm heightened, intensified, elevated'.

The most striking characteristic of that peculiar form of language which I have called affective language is its directness of expression. This directness of speech has been marked as one of the most important contributions of Hopkins to the technique of poetry; it is one of the reasons why modern poets are eager to be taught by him. In reading modern poetry one is aware, in fact often too much aware, that the poets are striving after a directness which would have startled Hopkins himself. They have a passion for current language which degenerates into a passion for the flat prosaic word. The mistake that is made is that these poets adopt an attitude towards the poetic medium without accounting for it intelligibly or even giving it a reasoned basis of existence. They take it as an absolute something, while in the case of Hopkins it naturally proceeded from his attitude towards the function and aim of poetry. If one studies Hopkins's directness of diction without its bearings on his whole theory of poetry, one must come to wrong conclusions, just as one must come, and many have come, to pitiable results when this directness of diction is blindly imitated. It is easy enough to talk of grammatical and syntactical distortions, torture of meaning and torture of words and so on,[5] but such expressions betray, or if not that, might lead to, a serious misunderstanding of Hopkins's technique; they easily suggest, perhaps are meant to suggest, that Hopkins took a certain wilful, even childish, delight in destroying the system of the living language. It has been said that 'with Hopkins language was a servant, to be bullied and coerced into as immediate contact with the thought as possible. The rules of grammar and syntax were not allowed to stand in the way; if they affected the immediacy of the expression they were ignored'.[6] The objections I have to make to this way of presenting and explaining Hopkins's most direct form of language is that here a standard is applied which properly only fits the language whose primary function is mere information; it is only when we deny that language can take on different forms, each with an independent existence, that we can speak of distortions, where we should speak of affective language.

After this condensed theoretical exposition of various forms of language, I turn to Hopkins's poems to study how he actually heightened the language of his day. This investigation lends itself to an obvious division into three sections, based on the three forms of language described above. Thus I intend to take my starting point from *logical language* and propose to show how, while adapting his mode of expression to the system of the language and observing the rules of grammar and syntax, he yet manages to heighten this informative, logical language. I need hardly point out that rhyme and rhythm and the apt choice of words also have a very marked heightening effect, but these factors do not concern us now. I shall only examine various grammatical and syntactical figures that raise the language to a higher level of expressiveness and which the poet turns to with predilection and cannot help using repeatedly. In the second section I shall show how, as the emotive tension grows and increases, logical language gradually loses its usefulness till finally it succumbs and has to give way under the strain of the poetic emotion; I shall be careful to attend to the fact that never are the rules of grammar and syntax set aside for reasons unworthy of a true artist. In the case of Hopkins there was a necessity from which he could not escape that drove him to employ another system altogether. The closing remarks of this chapter and the whole of the following will be devoted to this aspect of Hopkins's poetic medium. In the final chapter I shall deal with the subject of the breakdown of the system of the lexical elements themselves.

I shall be brief in dealing with those means that heighten logical language and consequently do not inflict any irregularity upon the normal form of informative language. They are not typical of Hopkins except for their frequency; they cause no difficulty, but this does not mean that they are never misinterpreted. In the first place I mention the very frequent use of the interjection. The poems of Hopkins are studded with 'oh's, 'ah's and 'O's, so that at a first reading one is slightly bewildered, overwhelmed by the lavishness with which these monosyllables are strewn through the poems. The poet appears too impetuous and too vehement in trying to convince us by every means how deeply stirred he is by this thing or event. And yet Hopkins never uses them to fill up a line; invariably they strike a note of true feeling. A subdued enthusiasm or quietly ecstatic joyousness is well suggested by the interjection in these lines:*

> And though the last lights off the black West went
>   *Oh*, morning, at the brown brink eastward, springs—
> Because the Holy Ghost over the bent
>   World broods with warm breast and with *ah!* bright wings.
> *Poems* 7

> Brute beauty and valour and act, *oh*, air, pride, plume, here
>   Buckle! AND the fire that breaks from thee then, a billion
> Times told lovelier, more dangerous, *O* my chevalier!
>   No wonder of it. . .
>   . . . and blue-bleak embers, *ah* my dear,
> Fall, gall themselves, and gash gold-vermilion.   *id.* 12

---

* In all the following quotations the italics have been added.

At other times they emphasize the 'terrible pathos' and strike us as cries of utter hopelessness:

> But *ah*, but *O* thou terrible, why wouldst thou rude on me
> Thy wring-world right foot rock? . . .   *Poems* 40

> What hours, *O* what black hours we have spent . . .   id. 45

> *O* the mind, mind has mountains; cliffs of fall . . .   id. 41

An atmosphere of 'pity and indignation' is suggested by their use in:

> England, whose honour *O* all my heart woos . . .   id. 44

> *O* then if in my lagging lines you miss
> The roll, the rise, the carol, the creation . . .   id. 51

> *O* I admire and sorrow! The heart's eye grieves
> Discovering you, dark tramplers, tyrant years.   id. 54

Wherever they are used, they are prompted by inspiration and that is why they always sound true: they always bear out his sincerity and seriousness:

> On Saturday sailed from Bremen . . .
> *O* Father, not under thy feathers nor ever as guessing
> The goal was a shoal . . .   *Deutschland* st. 12

> She was first of a five and came
> Of a coifèd sisterhood.
> (*O* Deutschland, double a desperate name!
> *O* world wide of its good!)   id. st. 20

I have only given a very small selection but large enough I hope to give an idea of Hopkins's practice.

Immediately connected with the use of this inarticulate cry is Hopkins's predilection for the exclamatory phrase; its affective value is evident enough. And although the logic of the system is zealously guarded, with a play upon the word logic, the logic of the contents is gone. The poet no longer argues, he no longer attempts to make his point clear by means of a logical argument. To impress us with the beauty of the moonlit night and to make us share his enthusiasm, he makes no appeal whatever to the intellect through a reasoned exposition of how and why he is himself so moved by this beauty in nature; he endeavours to infect us with his own joy, so he button-holes the reader:

> *Look* at the stars! *look, look* up at the skies!
> *O look* at all the fire-folk sitting in the air! . . .

> Look, look: a May-mess, like on orchard boughs!
> Look! March-bloom . . .   Poems 8

What description he gives is often cast in the form of exclamations of admiration or of disappointment and sorrow:

> What the heart is! which, like carriers let fly . . .   id. 27

> Summer ends now; now, barbarous in beauty, the stooks arise
> Around; up above, what wind-walks! what lovely behaviour
> Of silk-sack clouds! has wilder, wilful-wavier
> Meal-drift ever moulded and melted across skies?   id. 14

> How lovely the elder brother's
> Life all laced in the other's,
> Love-laced!   id. 30

And then there is that outburst of admiration at the sight of the hawk on the hover:

> . . . the achieve of, the mastery of the thing!   id. 12

This same lack of logical argument is evident in the repeated questionings of the poet's mind. Some instances have already been given in the lines quoted above, and unless we consciously attend to them, we can hardly believe that they are so numerous as in fact they are. It serves no purpose to give a complete list here: I shall only give some instances to show that these questions are no mere empty rhetorical figures in Hopkins's poetry: they are questionings of the poet's heart, more often than not questionings to which the poet was at a loss to find an answer. Notice the terror and fear expressed in:

> And after it almost unmade, what with dread,
> Thy doing: and dost thou touch me afresh?
>   Deutschland st. 1

There is that hopeless question in the third stanza of the Deutschland:

> The frown of his face
> Before me, the hurtle of hell
> Behind, where, where was a, where was a place?

His 'terrible sonnets' above all contain many questions: how sincere they are is clear to everybody:

> . . . why wouldst thou rude on me
> Thy wring-world right foot rock? lay a lionlimb against me? scan
> . . . my bruised bones? and fan,
> O in turns of tempest, me heaped there . . .?   Poems 40

> Comforter, where, where is your comforting?
> Mary, mother of us, where is your relief?   *Poems* 41

> Why do sinners' ways prosper? and why must
> Disappointment all I endeavour end?.
>   Wert thou my enemy, O thou my friend,
> How wouldst thou worse, I wonder, than thou dost
> Defeat, thwart me?   id. 50

In lines like these we instinctively feel that Hopkins is writing, as it
were, on the verge of logical language. We sense how the system
still holds him, but how he is ready to fly off into the use of affective
language proper at any moment. This impression is, no doubt, partly
brought about by the form of address used in the lines; and indeed, in
the very frequent occurrence of this form throughout his poetry,
Hopkins approaches affective speech very closely. For even if in
addressing a person the system of the logical language is left intact, one
must admit that the system imposes certain limits on the frequency
of its employment: where such uses thickly follow each other, they
tend to obscure and push into the background the nature of logical
language. I give a brief selection, in addition to instances already
given, to show how common and effective they are in Hopkins's
poetry. The *Deutschland* starts with a cry to God:

>   Thou mastering me
>   God . . .
> Thou hast bound bones and veins in me, fastened me flesh.

He continues in this strain:

>   Thou heardst me truer than tongue confess
>   Thy terror, O Christ, O God . . .   st. 2

Later on he addresses St. Francis (st. 23), the drowned sisters (st. 35)
and again Christ and God (st. 30, 32, 33, 34). The *Eurydice* begins
in the same fashion:

>   The Eurydice—it concerned thee, O Lord . . .

and farther on the poet addresses and consoles the mothers and wives
of the drowned sailors. As we expect, the terrible sonnets are full of
these forms:

>   Mine, O thou lord of life, send my roots rain.   *Poems* 50

>   Thou art indeed just, Lord, if I contend
>   With thee . . .   id.

>   Not, I'll not, carrion comfort, Despair, not feast on thee.   id. 40

From this last example it is clear that it matters little whether the individual addressed is a person proper or personified object: thus he similarly addresses Peace:

> When will you ever, Peace, wild wooddove, shy wings shut,
> Your round me roaming end, and under be my boughs?
>
> *Poems* 22

and Fancy in the *Deutschland*:

> But how shall I . . . make me room there:
> Reach me a . . . Fancy, come faster—   st. 28

And here is another example, taken from the *Eurydice*:

> And you were a liar, O blue March day . . .   st. 6

He freely communicates with his own heart: thus for instance he writes in the *Deutschland*:

> My heart, but you were dovewinged, I can tell
>   Carrier-witted, I am bold to boast . . .   st. 3

>   Ah, touched in your bower of bone
>   Are you! turned for an exquisite smart,
> Have you! make words break from me here all alone,
>   Do you!—mother of being in me, heart.
> O unteachably after evil, but uttering truth. . . .   st. 18

And in *Poems* 14 he writes:

> And, eyes, heart, what looks, what lips yet gave you a
> Rapturous love's greeting of realer, of rounder replies?

And another very fine instance from one of the terrible sonnets:

> What hours, O what black hours we have spent
> This night! what sights you, heart, saw; ways you went!
>
> *Poems* 45

And as a last example of how Hopkins is ever addressing the object he contemplates, I quote the following lines from *The Windhover* (*Poems* 12):

> Brute beauty and valour and act, oh, air, pride, plume, here
> Buckle! AND the fire that breaks from thee then. . . .

These examples must suffice; I have already spoken about this subject in the first chapter.

The interjection, the exclamatory phrase and the form of address are some of the more obvious means by which Hopkins heightened the logical language of mere information. Before paying attention to other means that heighten logical language, it is well to make some more remarks about its use in poetry. I have said above that logical language implies that the user is so composed and undisturbed that he can adjust the expression of his experience to the system of the language. This holds good of both poet and prose-writer; the very fact, however, that we can put poet and prose-writer on a par, makes us suspect, and suspect very rightly, that as there are evidently degrees of mental composure, so there will be degrees in the adjustment of the expression to the system. The more composed a writer is, the more concerned to present his experience in as objective a manner as possible, the more complete will be his adaptation of expression to fixed syntactical and grammatical rules. But in the case of an inspired poet, even where he employs logical language, he will adapt his expression to the system precisely in so far as it is compatible with his emotional attitude towards the experience to be expressed. A poet does not often build up periods, he discards the intricacies of the system of logical language, he is satisfied with the bare essentials of the system. In this case want of grammatical and syntactical clarity will be compensated for by, for example, those elements of affective language mentioned above.

This is also well demonstrated by the manner in which, in this simplified logical language, the clauses within a sentence are joined together, or rather are not joined together. Complete logical language is a language of subordination, but the logical language used by Hopkins as well as by other poets is a language of co-ordination. Logical language proper adapts even the expression of the relation between two clauses to a systematic link; in Hopkins co-ordination is the rule. The relation between the clauses is not expressly indicated in a structure whereby what goes before is necessarily related to what follows by means of a syntactical link. Hopkins observes and places facts side by side; the relation is apprehended in the juxtaposition itself. If the verse is correctly read aloud, if it is declaimed, the nature of the relation becomes amply evident. But in writing Hopkins was up against an old difficulty: the written line loses the very serviceable pliability and suppleness of the spoken line. As we have seen, no consistent system of marks could overcome this difficulty and remedy this defect inherent in written language, but some marks, generally recognized, were useful and indispensable and these Hopkins

eagerly employed.   Thus to indicate that there exists a relation between two co-ordinated sentences Hopkins has recourse to the colon.
The colon precisely introduces the dependent, though co-ordinated,
sentence; it signals the reader to attend to what immediately follows.
This reading-sign one cannot afford to overlook with impunity; in
Hopkins it is always functional and it illuminates lines that would
otherwise be obscure.   I shall give a good number of instances and
indicate the relation that exists, according to my interpretation,
between the co-ordinated parts.

The relation may be one of temporal succession as in:

> She drove in the dark to leeward,
> She struck—not a reef or a rock
> But the combs of a smother of sand: night drew her
> Dead to the Kentish Knock;
> And she beat the banks down with her bows and the ride of her keel:
> The breakers rolled on her beams with ruinous shock;
>
> *Deutschland* st. 14

> Thou knowest the walls, altar and hour and night:
> The swoon of a heart that the sweep and the hurl of thee trod
> Hard down with a horrow of height. . . .   id. st.2

> . . . then off, off forth on swing,
> As a skate's heel sweeps smooth on a bow-bend: the hurl and gliding
> Rebuffed the big wind.   *Poems* 12

That the succession is slightly tinged by a relation of result will not
be denied by anyone.   Often the colon introduces the explanation of
the first sentence and thus almost replaces the co-ordinating conjunction *for*; thus in the following lines:

> No wonder of it: sheer plod makes plough down sillion
> Shine . . .   id. 12

> Father and fondler of heart thou hast wrung:
> Hast thy dark descending and most art merciful then.
>
> *Deutschland* st. 9

> The Eurydice—it concerned thee, O Lord:
> Three hundred souls, O alas! on board. . . .
>
> *Eurydice* st. 1

> And yet you will weep and know why.
> Now no matter, child, the name:
> Sorrow's springs are the same.   *Poems* 31

> Here! creep,
> Wretch, under a comfort serves in a whirlwind: all
> Life death does end and each day dies with sleep.   *Poems* 41

There is perhaps no easier way to understand what Hopkins meant by heightening current spoken language and to undergo its poetic effect to the full than by tasting the stridency of expression which is lost by the introduction of the syntactical link expressed by a conjunction.

It is only when we realize the function of the colon, that it is possible to make out the meaning of this crammed and broken language:

> Happy the father, mother of these!   Too fast:
> Not that, but thus far, all with frailty, blest
> In one fair fall . . .   id. 54

Contrast is expressed by the colon in:

> Then let the march tread our ears:
> I to him turn with tears . . .   id. 28

> Not mood in him nor meaning, proud fire or sacred fear,
> Or love or pity or all that sweet notes not his might nursle:
> It is the forgèd feature finds me . . .   id. 21

> Flesh fade . . .
> . . . world's wildfire, leave but ash:
> In a flash, at a trumpet crash,
> I am all at once what Christ is . . .   id. 48

More pathetic is this line from a terrible sonnet:

> I am gall, I am heartburn.   God's most deep decree
> Bitter would have me taste: my taste was me.   id. 45

At other times the colon stresses a relation of concession:

> . . . Low be it: lustily he his low lot . . .
>   . . . swings though   id. 42

> The glass-blue days are those
> When every colour glows,
> Each shape and shadow shows.
> Blue be it: this blue heaven
> The seven or seven times seven
> Hued sunbeam will transmit
> Perfect, not alter it.   id. 37, l. 83

This set of examples should suffice and we now turn to another reading-sign, favourite with Hopkins, the dash.   It marks a complete break in the structure of the sentence, which increases the effect of the bluntest juxtaposition. Its function does not essentially differ from that of the colon. It signals attention to the contrast between two sentences in such lines as:

> Never ask if meaning it, wanting it, warned of it—men go.
> *Deutschland* st. 8

We can see the poet here, making his gestures, curt and decisive; and the reader cannot argue with the poet so 'in earnest'.

> One stirred from the rigging to save
> The wild woman-kind below,
> With a rope's end round the man, handy and brave—
> He was pitched to his death at a blow. **id. 16**

Often the dash introduces an afterthought or the correction of the foregoing statement:

> Heart, go and bleed at a bitterer vein for the
> Comfortless unconfessed of them—
> No not uncomforted: lovely-felicitous Providence . . . **id. 31**

> Marcus Hare, high her captain,
> Kept to her— . . . would follow his charge . . .
> *Eurydice* st. 12

> As a dare-gale skylark scanted in a dull cage
> Man's mounting spirit in his bone-house, mean house, dwells—
> That bird beyond the remembering his free fells;
> This in drudgery . . . *Poems* 15

> She had come from a cruise, training seamen—
> Men, boldboys soon to be men: *Eurydice* st. 4

The colon and the dash are very frequently used by Hopkins: in the *Deutschland* alone I have counted twenty-one colons and twenty-four dashes, not to mention the numerous exclamation marks, which are also valuable reading-signs in affective language.

If the colon and the dash mark in the structure of the sentence at least some sort of dependence between two clauses, even this slight sign is often omitted and we have complete syntactical co-ordination. If a reader of Hopkins's poetry takes this syntactical co-ordination to run parallel with co-ordination of thought or mere succession of experiences, he will often fail to understand it completely. Indeed, one fact is reported together with another, they are joined by the conjunction 'and'; but this syntactical parity does not stand for a corre-

sponding parity in the poet's mind.   Thus there is nothing less than
disparity, or contrast, expressed in the following lines (italics inserted):

> Thou art lightning *and* love, I found it, a winter *and* warm; . . .
> Hast thy dark descending *and* most art merciful then.
>
> *Deutschland* st. 9

> Away in the loveable west . . .
> I was under a roof here, I was at rest,
>   *And* they the prey of the gales   id. st. 24

Again, express the co-ordination by a subordinate conjunction, and
we notice how the language is 'lowered'.   The terror of these lines is
mainly conveyed by the cold-blooded juxtaposition of two extremes.
Notice further the relation of temporal succession implied by the
conjunction 'and ' in:

> she rears herself to divine
> Ears, *and* the call of the tall nun
> To the men in the tops and the tackle rode over the storm's brawling.
>
> *Deutschland* st. 19

> Hope had grown grey hairs . . .
> Hope was twelve hours gone;
> *And* frightful a nightfall folded rueful a day   id. st. 15

How strident the bare observation of the ringing bells in:

> . . . One stroke
> Felled and furled them, the hearts of oak!
> *And* flockbells off the aerial
> Downs' forefalls beat to the burial.   *Eurydice* st. 2

How dramatic the phrasing in the following lines:

> They fought with God's cold—
> *And* they could not *and* fell to the deck . . .
>
> *Deutschland* st. 17

> Do what you may do, what, do what you may,
> *And* wisdom is early to despair.   *Poems* 36

How rich in meaning that simplest of all words 'and' here is!

Often the co-ordination is not even indicated by a colon, a dash or
a simple 'and'.   One fact is placed after the other and in the language
dependence is not even hinted at; it makes for an abruptness of diction
which is very often dramatic:

> She drove in the dark to leeward,
> She struck—not a reef or a rock . . .   *Deutschland* 14

> And lives at last were washing away:
> To the shrouds they took,—they shook in the hurling and horrible airs.
>
> Deutschland 15

> Flesh falls within sight of us, we, though our flower the same,
>   Wave with the meadow, forget that there must . . .   id. 11

After so many examples of co-ordination it is not hard to understand why Hopkins so often comes forward all of a sudden with a
comparison, not introduced, not even properly worked out, but placed
side by side with the fact it illustrates.   Unless one bears in mind that
the language of Hopkins is one of co-ordination and of co-ordination
necessarily sustained throughout, one is often taken entirely by surprise by these comparisons.   The 'lush-kept, plush-capped sloe' comparison of the *Deutschland* (st. 8) belongs to this group, but no one
can miss this illustration.   More concealed and more easily overlooked
is the comparison in the following lines, where it has been embodied
in the expression of the experience itself:

> No wonder of it: sheer plod makes plough down sillion
> Shine. . . .   *Poems* 12

>   we, though our flower the same,
>   Wave with the meadow, forget that there must
>   The sour scythe cringe, and the blear share come.
>
> Deutschland st. 11

> Man's spirit will be flesh-bound when found at best,
> But uncumbered: meadow-down is not distressed
>   For a rainbow footing it nor he for his bones risen.
>
> Poems 15

> O I admire and sorrow!   The heart's eye grieves
> Discovering you, dark tramplers, tyrant years.
> A juice rides rich through bluebells, in vine leaves,
> And beauty's dearest veriest vein is tears.   id. 54

Unless one attends to these transitions from reality to illustration
the poetry is often very obscure.

Another natural result of Hopkins's predilection for co-ordination
is the startling suddenness of the recoil of thought in the sestet of
many sonnets.   Thus, for example, the poet switches over from
spring in nature to spring and May-day in boy and girl, with not a
trace of a 'like' or 'as' (*Poems* 9).   Notice the abruptness with which
the explanation follows the observation of facts, as in the *Deutschland*

st. 20, where Hopkins states that 'Gertrude, lily, and Luther are two of a town' and then bluntly continues:

> From life's dawn it is drawn down,
> Abel is Cain's brother and breasts they have sucked the same.

Hopkins appears to have been fond of these sudden transitions of thought.   Or, better and more accurate: these sudden transitions were almost second nature to the poet, so swift was the onrush of thoughts and images, so 'fused', as he would say himself.   In the poem entitled *The Lantern out of Doors* (*Poems*, 10) the poet describes how a lantern 'moving along the night' set him musing: 'Who goes there? . . . where from and bound, I wonder, where?'   He then continues:

> So men go by me whom either beauty bright . . .

but in his final draft of the poem he has dropped the conjunction 'so'; an omission rather relevant to Hopkins's practice.

The connexion between the halves of the sestet of his poem on Patience (*Poems* 46) is not very obvious; some may even have found it very obscure.   Having described the costs at which he can be patient:

> Natural heart's ivy, Patience masks
> Our ruins of wrecked past purpose. . . .

the poet in the first three lines of the sestet gives voice to his firm resolution to be patient: it may be true that he has to inflict severe pain on his own heart, yet this cannot detain him from praying God to bend his will to him.

> We hear our hearts grate on themselves: it kills
> To bruise them dearer.   Yet the rebellious wills
> Of us we do bid God bend to him even so.
>   And where is he who more and more distils
> Delicious kindness?—He is patient.   Patience fills
> His crisp combs, and that comes those ways we know.

Hopkins could never take a one-sided view of things; and so in the closing lines of this poem he is considering not the sorrow and pain implied by being patient, but its great advantage and power to do good. For the fruit of patience is kindness; he who has suffered in patience himself, and thus knows what it means to suffer, will be kind to all those who now need patience in order to be able to bear their own sorrows.

It will be noticed how these last lines of the poem contain a slight nuance in the meaning of 'patience' and 'patient'.   So far these words had referred to the poet's endurance of his own pains; now they refer to his sympathy (in its original Greek sense of 'fellow-suffering') with others.

If a poet is obscure, there is always the danger that people will begin to look too far for the solution of any difficulty, or maybe they will even suspect obscurity where in fact the text is quite easy to interpret. I shall give one instance here, where to my mind the thought is logically worked out by Hopkins, where there is no sudden transition in the sequence of his ideas, and which has yet been the cause of controversy and worse among critics.

> Brute beauty and valour and act, oh, air, pride, plume, here
>   Buckle! AND the fire that breaks from thee then, a billion
> Times told lovelier, more dangerous, O my chevalier!
>
>   No wonder of it: sheer plod makes plough down sillion
> Shine, and blue-bleak embers, ah my dear,
>   Fall, gall themselves, and gash gold-vermilion.   *Poems* 12

This is the sestet of Hopkins's sonnet *The Windhover*.   There is in my opinion nothing very obscure about the thought of these lines. The poet's ecstasy reaches a climax when he inscapes the bird displaying all its majestic splendours in its flight; it is the bird in action that strikes the poet as ever so much more beautiful than the bird just hanging on the wing.   In the last three lines he exemplifies whence this increase in beauty comes by means of two very fine images. There is no need to enter into this sestet in greater detail here, because I have already referred to it in the two foregoing chapters and I shall have occasion to deal with it in the two chapters following.   It is hardly believable that these lines could have given rise to speculations most astonishing in their far-fetchedness.   Critics have overlooked what must appear to be the meaning intended by Hopkins himself and have chosen their own way of interpreting these lines: the chevalier refers to Christ;[7] the expression 'gash gold-vermilion' calls up the 'symbol of the climax of Christ's task' and thus suggests the crucifixion; the exclamation 'ah my dear' is addressed to Christ,[8] etc.   Now Hopkins dedicated this sonnet to Christ Our Lord and at this hint critics have set to work to discover why it was that Hopkins dedicated this poem to Christ.   They forget that it was the best thing he ever wrote (I. 85) and that is the only reason why he gave this, his best, to Christ.   Obvious as this explanation is, it cannot satisfy many critics; they think there must have been other reasons, preferably subconscious ones. I leave them alone; be it only remembered that Hopkins did not dedicate this poem to Christ until some six years after he had written it! When he sent the poem to Bridges and Dixon, it bore as yet no dedication; Bridges then copied it with other poems into the book called by himself the 'A' MS. This book was sent to Hopkins in 1883. It is this transcription of *The Windhover* that bears the dedication in question; consequently it cannot have been written before 1883. But this is very likely not an argument that will shake those critics, some of whom try to find in Hopkins's poetry a confirmation of Freudian theories. How anyone can believe the *fire* in this sestet to refer to the burning of Hopkins's early poetry, how one can even believe that any such connexion can exist, is past my understanding.[9] Hopkins is at times obscure enough; why try to make him obscure even there where he is quite clear? But to return to the subject from which we have somewhat deviated.

Hopkins used the language of co-ordination. To set off the frequency of this peculiar form of marshalling the phrases side by side without properly joining them together, we should note how very rare subordination is in his poetry. I have counted only about fifteen lines in which Hopkins uses a subordinating conjunction.[10]

Thus far I have examined how Hopkins heightened his language by various technical devices that were compatible with a systematic use of the given language. I shall now make some remarks about that form of language in which now more, now less, the rules of grammar and syntax are abandoned, according as they hamper more or less the perfect expression of the poetic experience. Deviations from the system are found on every page of Hopkins's poetry and are easy enough to find: we are up against them continually. There is no need to point them out, but one should try to account for these grammatical and syntactical irregularities.

If a poet turns to affective language as the medium of his poetry, he is no longer capable, as I have shown above, of adapting the expression to the logic of the system. He now adjusts the expression to the logic of his *experience*, so to speak; and the fundamental rule of this logic is that what first presents itself to the poet's mind is expressed first. This rule is observed both within the sentence or clause and within the word-group. Its effect on the complete sentence will be studied first.

The Eurydice—it concerned thee, O Lord   *Eurydice* st. 1

The Majesty! what did she mean?   *Deutschland* st. 25

> But the Lady Month, May,
> > Why fasten that upon her, . . .? *Poems* 18
>
> Felix Randal the farrier, O he is dead then? . . . id. 29

We are all familiar enough with this usage of what is called the psychological subject of the sentence.[11] In affective speech this turn is very frequent. The psychological subject of the phrase is by no means always the same as the logical subject; where this is not so, we necessarily must come across some sort of syntactical irregularity; as a rule, however, it is not difficult to disentangle the construction, provided we remember to read it with the ear:

> Sweet fire the sire of muse, my soul needs this; . . . id. 51
>
> Mine, O thou lord of life, send my roots rain. id. 50
>
> Come then, your ways and airs and looks, . . .
> Resign them, sign them, seal them . . . id. 36
>
> This darksome burn, horseback brown,
> *His* rollrock highroad roaring down,
> In coop and in comb the fleece of *his* foam
> Flutes and low to the lake falls home. id. 33

Even in this last instance it is not difficult to see that syntactically *this darksome burn* is a genitive as is shown by the use of the pronoun *his*. The inverse order also occurs in Hopkins:

> Must it, worst weather,
> > Blast bole and bloom together? *Eurydice* st. 4
>
> Wondering why my master bore it,
> > The riving off that race . . . id. st. 25
>
> A bugler boy from barrack . . .
> Came, I say, this day to it—to a first Communion. *Poems* 23
>
> > One stroke
> Felled and furled them, the hearts of oak! *Eurydice* st. 2
>
> > Into the snows she sweeps,
> > Hurling the haven behind,
> > The Deutschland, on Sunday. . . .
> > > *Deutschland* st. 13
>
> > I see
> The lost are like this, and their scourge to be
> As I am mine, their sweating selves; *Poems* 45

Examples of this type are so frequent in all poetry that they need not detain us.   Be it only noted that taken strictly they deviate from the systematic use of the language.

The prominent position given to an idea in this last set of examples cannot of course be due to the application of the rule that whatever is first in the poet's mind is first in the expression, because it is not expressed first, but last.   Yet there is a certain similarity; for here, just as in the examples on the previous page, the poet sunders part of the syntactical unit, so that in his meditative mood he may the longer dwell on it and prevent it from being levelled with other parts of the sentence: and that is after all the intended effect achieved by the front position of the psychological subject as well.

What has been shown to take place within the sentence, also occurs within the word-group.   Expressions as 'whole my heart' and 'wide the world' well illustrate the occurrence of the psychological subject within the group.   A word takes pride of place not from any pre-meditated search after startling poetic effects but from the instinctive urge towards the most impelling directness of expression.   Thus Hopkins speaks of 'wisest my heart', 'far with fonder a care', 'idle a being', 'wide the world's weal'.[12]   Hence the inversion in:

> Hast thy dark descending and *most* art merciful then.
>
> > *Deutschland* st. 9

> Let me though see no more of him, and not disappointment
> Those sweet hopes quell whose *least* me quickenings lift. . . .
>
> > *Poems* 23

Fundamentally the same cause accounts for constructions as: 'frightful a nightfall . . . rueful a day', 'mighty a master', &c.; but to this construction I return in the following chapter (p. 114).

I am thus led to speak of the many inversions in the poetry of Hopkins.   I do not maintain that every inversion was always dictated by his anxiety to place the more important words in the sentence at the beginning: at times rhythm and rhyme undoubtedly tempted him to deviate from the logical word-order, a temptation that, as undoubtedly, Hopkins did not always resist.   In spite of what he once wrote to Bridges, that he avoided inversions because they destroy the earnestness of utterance, we might almost say that inversion is more frequent than the normal order of words.   But in most cases Hopkins had good reasons for inversion.   As a rule where he inverts the order of words, the verb is placed at the end of the sentence, and the object and subject are found in close proximity.   This is easy to explain if we bear in mind the context; the mere juxtaposition of two terms will often clearly indicate the nature of the relation existing between them.   Hence the verb appears to be entirely redundant, as it would express a relation already implicitly indicated in the juxtaposition of the two terms. This state of affairs sufficiently accounts for position of the verb at the end of the phrase, but there is more in Hopkins.   First some instances: an almost haphazard collection follows:

> . . . why wouldst thou rude on me
> Thy wring-world right foot rock?   *Poems* 40

> . . . lustily he his low lot . . . swings though.   id. 42

> . . . his eye no cliff, or coast or
> Mark makes in the rivelling snow-storm.   *Eurydice* st. 17

> . . . God's most deep decree
> Bitter would have me taste . . .   *Poems* 45

> . . . earth her being has unbound. . . .   id. 32

> . . . I can
> Kind love both give and get   id. 44

> Selfyeast of spirit a dull dough sours.   id. 45

> Let . . . not disappointment
> Those sweet hopes quell . . .   id. 23

> Yet the rebellious wills
> Of us we do bid God bend to him even so.   id. 46

> Patience who asks . . .   id. 46

> Earth . . . heaven that dost appeal
> To   id. 35

> all
> Life death does end . . .   id. 41

The reader will now have some idea of Hopkins's practice.   I wish to point out the working of contrast in these inversions; 'earth— heaven', 'life—death', 'disappointment—hopes', all in the closest possible proximity: they are neighbours in the sentence.   This well confirms the view that the terms so closely related in the mind are projected together into writing.   But let us look at what happens to the verb in such instances.   Where the relation is clearly enough indicated by placing the terms side by side in the sentence, the verb has become a luxury, or at least is no longer strictly needed.   Hopkins, sensitive artist as he was, is aware of it and acts accordingly.   The expression of the verb already suggested by the terms of the relation entails a falling off in terseness. To prevent the sentence petering out in an insignificant and almost superfluous verb, the verb closing the sentence has to be given a certain prop, and this is done by expressing the already suggested relation between the terms preceding the verb in a more pregnant way; the verb one expects is happily left out. Let us look at some of the lines quoted: 'rock', 'swings', 'makes', 'give and get', 'quell' well replace the flat words that are suggested by the lines: it is this final flick in the use of a fresh expression that preserves the balance of the sentence.

More complicated is the inversion in the following lines:

> . . . rare gold, bold steel, bare
> In both;   *Poems* 42

But in this quotation matters are obscured by the omission of a good many words; the inversion concerns us here. The two terms are stated side by side: whether you take the gold of the few comfortable rich people, or the steel of the working classes, 'bare in both', the outcasts of this world possess neither. Here the system of logical language has succumbed altogether; a line like this not only requires right intonation, it asks for gestures too. Words rush forward, and there is hardly any system to check them. At times words that normally serve to channel the onrush of ideas and see the construction of a sentence to a safe end, are discarded. Notice, for example, the exclamatory sentence complete in one word:

> But we dream we are rooted in earth—*Dust!*
>   *Deutschland* st. 11

> This, by Despair, bred Hangdog dull; by Rage,
> Manwolf, *worse*; . . .   *Poems* 42

This is the best place to add a few words about the many omissions and gather together those irregularities that do not easily lend themselves to a more systematic treatment. Words that are not strictly wanted are left out; there is no place for them in the speed of the poem. The omission of the conjunction *that* is the rule in Hopkins as it is the rule of affective speech.[13] Other conjunctions are very rare, first because Hopkins's language is one of co-ordination, and secondly because he prefers the subjunctive mood to the conjunction:

> *Wert* thou my enemy, O thou my friend . . .   id. 50

> [England] would neither hear
> Me, *were* I pleading . . .   id. 44

> . . . I have put my lips on pleas
> Would brandle adamantine heaven with ride and jar, *did*
>   Prayer go disregarded . . .   *Poems* 23

> But *quench* her . . . dearest to her . . . spark,
>   Man, how fast his firedint . . . is gone . . .   id. 48

> But *be* the war within . . .   id. 49

> Whereas *did* air not make
> This bath of blue . . .
>   . . . the sun would shake   id. 37

> Low *be* it: lustily he his low lot . . . swings though . . .   id. 42

> Flesh *fade*, and mortal trash
> *Fall* to the residuary worm; world's wildfire, *leave* but ash:
>   In a flash, at a trumpet crash,
> I am all at once what Christ is . . .   id. 48

Sometimes the preposition is left out: 'Look, foot to forelock, how all things suit!' (*Eurydice* st. 20). Yet note the peculiar effect which the omission has. The poet does not describe the sailor boy: at a stroke he places the picture before us, he wants us to visualize it at once: 'Look, *foot to forelock*. . . .' An exactly similar instance occurs in these lines:

> Natural heart's ivy, Patience masks
> Our ruins of wrecked past purpose. There she basks
> *Purple eyes* and *seas of liquid leaves* all day.   *Poems* 46

The insertion of the preposition 'with' before *purple* and *seas* would certainly save many readers some difficulty in understanding the lines. But now that we have grasped the meaning and now that we know why Hopkins left out the preposition, we willingly dispense with it. The picture is better as it stands: the picture of the ivy as *purple eyes*, referring to the berries, and *seas of liquid leaves* is complete in itself. The preposition *at* is left out before *unforeseen times* in *Poems* 47. Further, Hopkins writes: 'I wish day come' (*Poems* 40) and 'were I come o'er again' (*Poems* 39), where the preposition *to* is omitted. It is, however, incorrect to say that before expressions as 'what time', 'that spell' the preposition is merely omitted; there are other reasons that explain these expressions than mere speed of diction. More is said about these in the final chapter.

The verb is frequently omitted and this often leads to obscurity; but a distinction must be made between the verb expressed but not repeated, and the verb not expressed at all. Hopkins with his strong

mind, which could handle strings of thoughts and images without
confusing them or becoming entangled in them, never felt the need to
repeat a verb to bring his line of thought to a safe conclusion:

> what sights you, heart, saw; ways you went!
> And more must, in yet longer light's delay.   *Poems* 45

> I cast for comfort I can no more get
> By groping round my comfortless, than blind
> Eyes in their dark can day or thirst can find
> Thirst's all-in-all in all a world of wet.   id. 47

Here *get* is not repeated after *can* in the third line.

> I was under a roof here, I was at rest,
> And they the prey of the gales;
> *Deutschland* st. 24

where the poet could not spare room for the form 'they were'.
In the following instances I have bracketed the omitted form of the
verb:

> Feasts, when we shall fall asleep,
> Shrewsbury may see others keep;
> None but you [keep] this her true,
> This her Silver Jubilee.   *Poems* 6

> Man's spirit will be flesh-bound when found at best,
> But uncumbered: meadow-down is not distressed
> For a rainbow footing it nor [is] he [distressed] for his bones risen.
> id. 15

> Left hand, off land, I hear the lark ascend,
> [I hear] His rash-fresh re-winded new-skeinèd score
> In crisps of curl off wild winch whirl . . .   id. 11

> This, by Despair, bred Hangdog dull; by Rage [this bred]
> Manwolf, worse. . . .   id. 42

> God with honour hang your head,
> Groom, and grace you, bride, [grace] your bed
> With lissome scions . . .   id. 28

> Then though I should tread tufts of consolation
> Days after, so I in a sort deserve to [tread]   id. 23

> These things, these things were here, and but the beholder
> [was] Wanting . . .   id. 14

In these and similar instances that abound in Hopkins's poetry the

verb is expressed though not repeated; it is partly or altogether
left out in sentences, as, for example:

>   Recorded only, I have put, . . .   *Poems* 23
>   My aspens dear, . . . all felled . . . not spared, not one . . .   id. 19
>   . . . self in self steeped and pashed. . . .   id. 32
>   Loathed for a love men knew in them. . . .
>   *Deutschland* st. 21
>   O Father . . . of a fourth the doom to be drowned;   id. 12
>   What by your measure is the heaven of desire,
> The treasure never eyesight got, nor was ever guessed what for the hearing?
>   id. 26

This last instance shows that not only the verb is at times omitted;
subject and object and other parts of the sentence are often looked for
in vain.   Hopkins did not feel the need of expressing the verb twice
over, any more than he felt inclined to spare room for a repeated
subject or object, though at times we may greatly wish that Hopkins
had expressed it twice or even three times:

> Delightfully the bright wind boisterous ropes, wrestles, beats earth bare
> Of yestertempest's creases; in pool and rut peel parches
> Squandering ooze to squeezed dough, crust, dust; stanches, starches
> Squadroned masks and manmarks. . . .   *Poems* 48

It is not at first sight clear which is the subject that goes with 'parches';
the verb is used transitively or intransitively; fortunately the verbs
'stanches' and 'starches' help us here and I take 'the bright wind' as
subject of the three clauses.

>   This to hoard unheard,
>   Heard unheeded, leaves me a lonely began.   id. 44

Leaving the tail-end of this sentence out of consideration, we notice
that the line would have gained in *clarity at first sight* if Hopkins had
written: 'to hoard this unheard, or if heard, to hoard this unheeded,
leaves me,' &c . . . but that would have been the end of poetry.

>   But no way sped,
>   Nor mind nor mainstrength; . . .   id. 42

This complete sentence is closely packed: here the poet, infuriated by
the misery of the poor and the heartlessness of those in comfort and
ease, had neither time nor space to spend on verb or subject; bare
essentials, and no more: 'But think of those that have in no way sped,
that have neither mind nor mainstrength' appears to be the shortest

paraphrase of this packed sentence. But I return to this line in the following chapter.

The closing lines of *Poems* 43 are by no means clear and here we wish that Hopkins had found room for a repetition of 'them' and 'under'; I place them between brackets:

—broad in bluffhide his frowning feet lashed! raced
With [them], along them, cragiron under and [under] cold furls—

And even as the lines now stand, they are certainly not clear at first sight. If we take 'them' to refer to the cragiron and the furls, this clarifies matters.

An example of merely apparent omission occurs in my opinion in this line:

Your feast of; that most in you earnest eye
May but call on your banes to more carouse.　　*Poems* 54

Readers will have tried to complete the phrase in italics, perhaps have made ingenious guesses, but they cannot boast of a reasonable success. It should be remembered that the poem is a fragment; it is only when we know the other drafts of the poem that we can make a guess what was in Hopkins's mind. I shall do no more than give the readings of two other drafts: the reader will then easily find the solution to this unfinished phrase.

Your feast of youth and that most earnest eye . . .
Your lovely youth and that most earnest eye . . .

Hopkins was never afraid that in expressing a complex thought he would lose the way somewhere. I do not say, to continue the metaphor, that he never strayed; for at times he did stray, but only to cut off roundabout ways. Hopkins might have thought of the reader, however, and here or there left a footprint or other mark to show which way he had gone. The reader himself will have had the experience that in some poems it is hard to discover whither the poet has gone in his constructions and in his thoughts; I shall briefly discuss three examples. In st. 25 of the *Deutschland* the poet meditates on the words of the sister: 'O Christ! Christ, come quickly'; he asks himself:

The majesty! what did she mean?

He considers many possible solutions: 'Is it love in her of the being as her lover had been?' 'Or is it that she cried for the crown then . . . ?' These solutions are weighed and both of them found wanting; but the second alternative:

> is it that she cried for the crown then,
> The keener to come at the comfort for feeling the combating keen?

takes up a complete stanza before it is set aside as unsatisfactory, before the poet concludes that the sister did not eagerly call on Christ to come quickly because she saw how the weather was improving and consequently how the chances of rescue became more probable. Stanza 27 then continues the same strain of thought, begun two stanzas before: 'No, but it was not these . . .' Even in this stanza he does not give the ultimate reason of the nun's request to Christ; he closes the stanza thus:

> Other, I gather, in measure her mind's
> Burden, in wind's burly and beat of endragonèd seas.

When he is about to set forth his solution of the problem, he breaks down under the strain of emotion that it calls up in him:

> But how shall I . . . make me room there: . . .

till some few lines farther the only reason why the sister prayed as she did, is flung out and thrown at the reader as it were:

> Strike you the sight of it? look at it loom there,
> Thing that she . . . there then! the Master,
> *Ipse*, the only one, Christ, King, Head:

The nun had been allowed some glimpse of the vision of Christ and that was enough to make her cry that she might be with Him at once. In the stanza following this point is more or less doctrinally explained. The poet says that she was allowed this vision because she was 'heart right . . . single eye'. Meanwhile the explanation of those simple words of the sister, 'Christ, come quickly', has taken no less than five stanzas.

Here is another example from the *Deutschland*; he thus writes about the 'master of the tides':

> . . . past all
> Grasp God, throned behind
> Death *with a sovereignty* that heeds but hides, bodes but abides;

> *With a mercy* that outrides
> The all of water, an ark
> For the listener; for the lingerer *with a love* glides
> Lower than death and the dark;
> A vein for the visiting of the past-prayer, pent in prison,
> The last-breath penitent spirits—the uttermost mark . . .   st. 33

H

The expressions in italics are like mileposts clearly showing the way.
God's mastery over Death is described first in itself: 'with a sovereignty
that heeds but hides, bodes but abides'; then in its consequences for
man: to him who listens to God's voice death has become a mercy,
to him who lingers and is afraid to turn to his God, God's love will
in the end prevail over the bitterness of death so that neither death
nor dark will go undefeated.   The word-groups, 'with a mercy', 'with
a love', 'an ark for the listener', &c. do not just hang in the air.   On
the contrary, the thought is here so intricate and compressed that
Hopkins is very careful not to disregard any rules of grammar and
syntax with the one exception of the omission of the relative pronoun;
but otherwise the grammatical and syntactical structure of the phrase
is correct.   This can hardly be said of such a phrase as:

>   . . . gold go garlanded
> With, perilous, O no . . .   *Poems* 42

A line like this can only be understood if read aloud and declaimed,
complete with gestures.   It is very hard to translate into a logical
language: 'do you perhaps think they are going about garlanded with
gold?   That is perilous.   O no, you are wrong there.'   The reader
can work out for himself what is omitted here!   The last instance:

> Happy the father, mother of these!   Too fast:
> Not that, but thus far, all with frailty, blest
> In one fair fall; but, for time's aftercast,
> Creatures all heft, hope, hazard, interest.   *id.* 54

This staccato speech is truly affective speech; here logical language
leads us nowhere.   Let us see how the stanza is pieced together; for
so it is.   The poet contemplates the portrait of the twin brother and
sister.   His impulsive admiration makes him exclaim 'happy the
father, mother of these'.   But hardly have these words been spoken
when he checks himself and with sorrow he remembers that the
parents can only be called happy when it is certain that these children
will not fall victims to the 'wild and wanton work of men' (final
stanza).   Hence it is that, after the exclamation of admiration 'Happy
&c.', he suddenly stops short with a 'Too fast'; this is further explained
in the divided phrasing of the second line: 'not that', i.e., I cannot call
them happy without any restrictions, but 'thus far': they may be called
happy up to the present moment, because they have been blest with
these twins, granted that they are still frail.   The 'thus far' is further
explained: we do not know what the future will have in store for them
and thus they will be the object of the parents' hope and interest.

Hopkins may have had this type of line in mind when again and again he insisted on his friends reading his poetry aloud; these lines cannot be understood otherwise, because so much is left out that no structure, grammatical or syntactical, to speak of, is left.

After this digression I return to the study of the implications of that dominating principle of affective speech: what is first in the poet's mind clamours for direct and immediate expression. I have shown how this principle affected the building up of phrases and single sentences. We now look at its effect on the *compound* sentence. Logically one expects that in accordance with this rule that clause should come first which is first in the poet's mind; this is easy enough and need not be dealt with here. What is worthy of notice is that the second clause does not always follow in the form demanded by the structure of the first. It is as if in the very act of seeing the compound sentence to a successful end, another clause suddenly broke in upon the poet and presented itself with such emphasis that it ousted the second clause demanded by the first, which is then never seen or heard of again. Needless to say that the result is, according to the rules of logical language, a muddle.

> Pitched past pitch of grief,
> More pangs will, schooled at forepangs, wilder wring.
>
> *Poems* 41

Why is there no subject in the absolute construction? Because the main clause was originally shaped to contain a personal subject 'I', of which this participial construction was predicated.

Notice how the following lines are twisted:

> . . . so some great stormfowl, whenever he has walked his while
> The thunder-purple seabeach plumèd purple-of-thunder,
> If a wuthering of his palmy snow-pinions scatter a colossal smile
> Off him, *but meaning motion* fans fresh our wits with wonder.
>
> id. 21

Had Hopkins written 'though meaning motion' the sentence would still have been involved, but syntactically correct. It is as if he built up this sentence whilst actually writing it. Let us look at another instance:

> Though grief yield them no good
> Yet shed what tears sad truelove should.
>
> *Eurydice st.* 27

Notice the sudden transition: 'them—you'. From being merely an interested observer in the event, the poet suddenly takes an active part in it by addressing the mother and the sweetheart.

> They could tell him for hours, dandled the to and fro
> Through the cobbled foam-fleece, what could he do . . .?
>
> *Deutschland* st. 16

Here we have a similar instance of change in attitude: the poet describes in the first clause; but all of a sudden he is a spectator himself very much concerned with what is happening and starts asking questions. Notice a similar change in construction in the following instances:

> Though no high-hung bells or din
> Of braggart bugles cry it in—
> What is sound? . . .   *Poems* 6

> How to keep—is there any any, is there none such. . . .
>
> id. 36

> Though felt before, though in high flood yet—
> What none would have known of it, only the heart, being hard at bay,
> Is out with it.   *Deutschland* st. 7–8

> O unteachably after evil, but uttering truth,
> Why, tears! is it? tears; . . .   id. st. 18

This last example well illustrates the use of 'affective speech' in poetry. Hopkins takes no care to finish his sentences.   Notice how various clauses clash in the last line of this stanza:

> Recorded only, I have put my lips on pleas
> Would brandle adamantine heaven with ride and jar, did
> Prayer go disregarded:
> *Forward-like, but however, and like favourable heaven heard these.*
>
> *Poems* 23

Many thoughts clamoured for expression simultaneously; Hopkins could not check them.   An extreme example of how thoughts hurried onward without the poet being able to keep pace with them in expression is given in these lines from the *Deutschland*:

> But how shall I . . . make me room there:
> Reach me a . . .   Fancy, come faster—
> Strike you the sight of it? look at it loom there,
> Thing that she . . . there then! the Master, . . .   st. 28

There is another type of construction that deserves our attention here:

> And frightful a nightfall folded rueful a day
> *Nor* rescue, only rocket and lightship, shone.
>
> id. st. 15

> Though this child's drift
> Seems by a divine doom channelled, *nor* do I cry
> Disaster there . . .   *Poems* 23

> Hold them cheap
> May who ne'er hung there. *Nor* does long our small
> Durance deal with that steep or deep.   id. 41

In these quotations we expect a negative clause to precede the *nor* clause. This 'contortion' is not so hard to explain, as it must be confessed to be quite in harmony with Hopkins's whole attitude towards language. Hopkins intensely 'lived' the experience expressed in the first clause; after the first two chapters this will need no argument here. Reflecting on this experience as already fixed in writing, and fixed in the form as already given to it, he transcends this peculiar form of expression whether positive or negative, being only conscious that a negation is clearly implied. As illustration I take the first quotation: 'Frightful a nightfall folded rueful a day' expresses in the form of a positive statement the denial of light. Now in fastening upon this image of the night folding the day, Hopkins never lost sight of the negation it implied; that is why he continues: '*nor* rescue',—that is no more than moon or stars—'shone'. */59318/*

If at times two syntactical structures stumbled over each other owing to the rush of thoughts, it is not surprising that a similar mishap—for such it is to those who expect logical language in poetry as well as in prose—takes place where two grammatical constructions collide.

> O surely, reaving Peace, my Lord should leave in lieu
> Some good! And so he *does leave* Patience exquisite, . . .
>   *Poems* 22

Hopkins hated *do* and *did* as mere expletives; so we cannot in good faith explain the italicized construction in this way. Mere emphasis will not account for it, because there is no reason whatever to stress 'leave'; 'exquisite' appears to be the word that would need a stronger stress. I always read the construction as the combination of 'so he does', and 'he leaves Patience exquisite'. This is logical and entirely fits the context; and that Hopkins was undoubtedly aware of this peculiar nuance of 'so he does' in the complete expression 'so he does leave', will be proved in the final chapter dealing with Hopkins's most sensitive word-consciousness. Again, consider the following line:

> To man, that needs would worship block or barren stone,
> Our law says . . .   *Poems* 38

The normal expression is 'needs must'. The alteration reads like a

last-minute correction; the poet-priest well knew that to say that man
'*needs must* worship block or barrren stone' was untenable doctrine.
Hopkins uses the expression 'look at it loom there' in the passage of
the *Deutschland* where he almost stammers when he is coming forward
with the fact that the sister saw Christ on the waters (st. 28).   To me
there is here a clear contraction of two phrases: 'look at it', and 'see it
loom there'.   I do not hold that these two phrases were both complete
before him; but once he had written 'look at it' he was well aware
that there is little to choose between 'look' and 'see'; that 'see' was
required to make the phrase correct logical language never worried
him.   There are more of these contractions:

> Each limb's barrowy brawn . . .
> . . . features, in flesh, what deed *he each* must do—   *Poems* 43

In logical language one of the two: 'what deed *they each* must do', or,
'what deed *each of them* must do'; but Hopkins created a third possibility.   It is either: 'country is honour enough in *us all*,' or, 'country
is honour enough in *all of us*', but Hopkins wrote: 'Country is honour
enough *in all us*' (*Poems* 42).   In the *Deutschland* occurs the line:
'but pity of the rest of them', which to me appears to be a compromise
between 'pity the rest of them' and 'have pity of the rest of them'
(st. 31).   Another instance is given by Dr. Gardner, though in a
different connexion: in 'hard at bay' we find a mixture of 'hard pressed'
and 'at bay'.[14]

> Nothing else is like it, no, not all so strains
> Us . . .   *Poems* 23

Even here the wording is not quite in agreement with logical language;
there is a strong suggestion here of 'nothing at all', which has been cut
into two.

Such strange combinations do not cause any difficulty to speak of;
I have given them a place because they well show what happened
when Hopkins was writing 'hot on the anvil'.   But I pursue this
subject still further; not only do two syntactical and two grammatical
constructions collide so that they become involved in each other; at
times two words arise almost simultaneously in the poet's mind.

> Heart, go and *bleed at a bitterer vein* for the·
> Comfortless unconfessed of them—
>   *Deutschland* st. 31

Over-subtle criticism would point out that one cannot bleed at a
bitter vein any more than at a sweet vein, &c.; but such criticism and

such dissection of metaphorical language is of very little help to any-
body.　What is worthy of our attention is the use of the preposition
'at': the normal preposition is 'in': we do a thing 'in a certain vein';
the adjective 'bitterer' assures us beyond any doubt that this expression
was in the poet's mind.　Why then did he write 'at'?　The answer
seems to be quite obvious: because we 'bleed at' a vein.　Having
explained the use of the preposition satisfactorily, we are faced by
another difficulty, for 'bitterer' has now become a very strange epithet:
if 'vein' is to all appearances to be taken in its most literal sense, what
is then the meaning of a 'bitterer vein'?　The solution is that here
Hopkins mixed up two expressions; the one, clearly called up by
'bitterer vein' is: 'Go, heart, and *weep* in a bitterer vein'.　But the
connexion 'heart—vein' could never escape the attention of Hopkins
(see the final chapter); it irresistibly called up the bleeding, an idea well
fitting the context.　The result is a somewhat curious but poetically
very fine line.　It is hard to make out which thought and which
expression was first in Hopkins's mind; but it is a point of no importance.　It suffices to notice that logical language was incapable of
stemming the onrush of words.

Let us study one more example of how two thoughts meet in one
expression.

And flockbells off the aerial
Downs' forefalls beat to the burial.　　　*Eurydice* st. 2

Why, we may ask, 'beat' and why not 'pealed' or some other word
properly predicable of bells?　Bells do not beat nor are they beaten;
a drum is beaten to give solemnity to a funeral.　Notice the connexion
'beat to the *burial*'!　This then is the solution: the bells of the sheep
ringing from the downs far off were to Hopkins as the deathdrum
that was beaten for the burial of these men drowned in the waves.
But this image of the beating of the deathdrum did not come as an
afterthought, nor as an illustration merely; it posted itself in Hopkins's
mind with the thought itself; hence the image is not expressed in a
separate grammatical structure or construction.　Hopkins heightened
the language: so the object and its image became fused both in the
poet's apprehension and in his expression of it.　'Pealed' was ousted
by the image of the beating drums.

This instance leads me to say a few words about the fusion of
object and its image.　In Hopkins's poetry one finds that qualities
properly belonging to the image only are bluntly predicated of the
object and vice versa; grammatical or syntactical or logical confusion

is the result, and yet the very confusion is poetic.   In the *Deutschland*
Hopkins describes the Galilee of Christ:

> *Warm-laid grave* of a womb-life grey.   st. 7

'Warm-laid grave'!—a strange combination.   The context makes us
here suspect 'bed' instead of 'grave'; so much is clear to everybody.
But the poet is picturing in the stanza the hiddenness of Christ and His
humility in terms of very concrete things: the manger, maiden's knee,
and let us add, the bed, lovingly made by His mother.   This humility
and hiddenness made him fasten on the image of the grave.   There
is no time to sift the object in his mind from the image called up; the
image becomes one with the object: 'warm-laid grave'.

Look carefully at this quatrain and see how it contains a veritable
muddle of imagery:

> The fine delight fathers thought; the strong
> Spur, live and lancing like the blowpipe flame,
> Breaths once and, quenchèd faster than it came,
> Leaves yet the mind a mother of immortal song.   *Poems* 51

The inspiration of the poet is compared to a father, to a spur, to a flame,
and to a breath; syntactically it is the strong spur that is quenched
and that breathes and that leaves the mind a mother.   And yet the
way in which this fourfold comparison is handled is completely
successful.   This example well bears out how to Hopkins there was
no separation of the object and its image.

While on this point I had better continue this subject now, though
there might be reasons for including it in the following chapter; for
the factor of Hopkins's very peculiar mode of apprehending and
perceiving things tells here.   The likeness of any object to another
was of the essence of that object; was consequently not something
imposed on it from without.   If then Hopkins inscaped the object,
its likeness with other objects was part and parcel of its individuality.
No 'like' or 'as' were of any use, because these words suggest the
illustrative accidental character of the likeness.[15]   That is why Hopkins coined words as 'rose-flakes', 'lily-locks', 'flake-doves', 'wolfsnow', &c. &c.   That is why he suddenly springs a comparison on
us, not introduced, nor worked out:

> Night roared, with the heart-break hearing a heart-broke rabble,
>   Till *a lioness arose* breasting the babble . . .
>   *Deutschland* st. 17

With a mercy that outrides
The all of water, *an ark* . . . *Deutschland* st. 33

. . . and not disappointment
Those sweet hopes quell . . .
In scarlet or somewhere of some day seeing
That brow and bead of being,
An our day's God's own Galahad. *Poems* 23

Here! creep
Wretch, *under a comfort* serves *in a whirlwind* . . . id. 41

I do not claim that this practice is peculiar to Hopkins; it has been pointed out, for instance, how Shakespeare also passed through this stage of working out his imagery.[16]   And indeed in the case of any truly inspired poet, the mind will overleap the logical connexion between the object and its image; the relation is directly apprehended, and prompted by this intuition of the connexion the poet feels no need to present it in a reasoned form.   With Hopkins image and object were given simultaneously and became absorbed in one poetic experience. The image was no longer illustration; it became one with the object, both in the poet's mind and in the expression in language.   The poet had no longer any option to omit it or insert it.   The conclusion and logical deduction is of importance: because the image and the object have grown into one, the function of the image is not confined to the comparison of the object with itself here and now; it extends itself as far as the influence of the object itself reaches.   This remark throws some light on what I have said above with reference to Hopkins's eagerness to detect false perspective in imagery.   But its real import is well illustrated in what is called run-on imagery; the term explains itself.   Hopkins has noted down one very clear and very fine example in his annotations of Homer.   In the *Iliad*, Bk. IV, 457, Echepolos is called κορυστής, wearing a helm with a crest and therefore 'marked out, catching the eye'; and later when he is thrown from the wagon and killed, he falls ὡς πύργος, like a tower.   To Hopkins this comparison was suggested by the rising crest.   But a few lines lower down Simoeisios is struck by the javelin and he falls αἴγειρος ὡς (482), like a poplar.   Hopkins remarks about the appropriateness of this comparison, because some lines higher up this youth had been called θαλερός, blooming, and had thus been implicitly compared to a tree. It is not the question here whether this run-on imagery was intentional, or whether the original image 'ran on' in the poet's subconsciousness. In the case of Hopkins himself I incline to believe that he was often well aware of it, for it was a subject about which he had made some discoveries himself:

My thought is that in any lyric passage of the tragic poets (perhaps not so much in Euripides as the others) there are—usually; I will not say always, it is not likely—two strains of thought running together and like counter-pointed; the overthought that which everybody, editors, see (when one does see anything— . . .) and which might for instance be abridged or para-phrased in square marginal blocks as in some books carefully written; the other, the underthought, conveyed chiefly in the choice of metaphors etc. used and often only half realised by the poet himself, not necessarily having any connection with the subject in hand but usually having a connection and suggested by some circumstance of the scene or of the story. I cannot prove that this is really so except by a large induction of examples and perhaps not irrefragably even then nor without examples can I even make my meaning plain. . . . Perhaps what I ought to say is that the underthought is com-monly an echo or shadow of the overthought, something like canons and repetitions in music, treated in a different manner, but that sometimes it may be independent of it. I find this same principle of composition in St. James' and St. Peter's and St. Jude's Epistles, an undercurrent of thought governing the choice of images used (III. 105–6).

This passage strongly reminds us of the latest contributions made to the study of Shakespeare's imagery by C. Spurgeon; it seems fairly certain that Hopkins suspected the presence of run-on imagery in all great poetry. We must be careful to distinguish between the over-thought and underthought in a tragedy and in a simple lyric; but the difference appears to be one of degree and not one of essence. In *Poems* 35 Hopkins contrasts the river Ribble with man, the former ever appealing to Heaven though 'with no tongue to plead, no heart to feel', the latter

> . . . tied to his turn,
> To thriftless reave both our rich round world bare
> And none reck of world after . . .

The poet describes man in terms that fit the river as well:

> Ah, the heir
> To his own self*bent* so *bound*, so *tied* to *his turn*, . . .

In *Poems* 32 the night sky is apprehended as a curtain against which the dark boughs stand sharply out. The image returns again where Hopkins speaks of 'life's skeined stained veined variety', which will be wound upon two spools. In the *Eurydice* the sailors are called 'hearts of oak'; this comparison makes him later refer to them as 'bole, and 'bloom'; 'bole' is the sailor weathered to his profession, 'bloom' is the 'boldboy' 'soon to be man'.   And the image is continued some twenty stanzas further where the poet laments the death of 'this *wildworth blown* so sweet'.   Examples of this type might be multiplied almost indefinitely; but there is a very clear instance where we can properly speak of underthought running through the whole poem, where an image is sustained throughout.   Hopkins thought very highly of *The Windhover* (*Poems* 12); it is in this sonnet that over-thought and underthought can be easily distinguished though they are interwoven into one strand of thought.   He compares the windhover to a chevalier; but it is better and more accurate to say that in his ecstatic vision the windhover, the hawk on the wing, *is* a chevalier. This is very clear from the sestet in which the poet addresses the bird and calls it chevalier:

> AND the fire that breaks from thee then, a billion
> Times told lovelier, more dangerous, *O my chevalier!*

It is confirmed by the fact that the bird 'rides' the steady air and is 'drawn', or carried by 'the dapple dawn', which I take to refer to the morning air.   But the chevalier is of royal blood: and this aspect is never lost sight of.   The opening line proves it:

> I caught this morning morning's minion, king-
> dom of daylight's *dauphin* . . .

It recurs in this line:

> how he rung upon the *rein* of a wimpling wing . . .

I have already referred to the meaning of 'rung' in the first chapter; here I add that it calls up the ringing bells with which the reins are adorned, as befits a royal charger.   But *rein* is a homophone of *reign*, and this recalls once again that the hawk is a dauphin, is a prince.[17] That we are allowed to take the two meanings of this homophone will be shown in our final chapter.   Note incidentally how the spelling 'reign' accounts for the choice of the preposition 'upon'.   In this line we thus have a very fine expression of the prince-chevalier holding his horse in ringing triumph.

> AND the fire that breaks from thee then . . .

following immediately upon the poet's bidding the bird to fly forth, calls up the galloping horse striking sparks from its hoofs.   And the ringing of the bells that adorn the reins of the dauphin's horse is heard in the line following 'a billion times *tolled* lovelier, more dangerous'. It will now be clear why Hopkins was driven to use the word 'buckle' in:

> Brute beauty and valour and act, oh, air, pride, plume, here
>   *Buckle.*

It is the image of the chevalier and the dauphin that demands this word and no other: the bird about to go off, 'forth on swing', is like the dauphin preparing to ride and gallop.   It is this weaving of the image into the canvas of the experience itself that gives the sonnet its beauty.[18]

Many quotations have been given in the course of this chapter, proving how Hopkins 'scorned' grammatical and syntactical rules and cared little for strict logic.   In this chapter the starting point was the existence of a logical form of language from which Hopkins deviated, now more, now less; in the following chapter I do not intend to study primarily how far Hopkins discards the system of logical language, but I shall show how affective language as used by Hopkins contains within itself a system entirely dependent on, and demanded by, his most personal apprehension of external reality.   This new factor affected the system of logical language on points that were left intact by Hopkins's attitude towards the medium of poetry.

4

PERCEPTION AND EXPRESSION OF INSCAPE

D IXON once praised the poems of Hopkins in these words:

I have read them many times with the greatest admiration: in the power of forcibly & delicately giving the essence of things in nature, & of carrying one out of one's self with healing, these poems are unmatched (II. 32).

Short as it is, this criticism is most accurate and contains high praise of Hopkins's poetry. Had Dixon been acquainted with the term 'inscape'—the word occurs only once in the correspondence between these two friends and that in one of Hopkins's last letters to Dixon (II. 135)—he might have written that the poems of Hopkins are unmatched in the power both of giving the poet's inscape and of most precisely expressing the inscape of external things: for this is the gist of the above criticism. It is now our object to examine how this new factor, the expression of the inscapes of this world, affected the systematic use of language. In this chapter an order different from that of the third chapter will be followed; while there the language itself and its very manifold deviations from its systematic use was taken as the starting point, here the order will be reversed. Proceeding now from cause to effect, we start from Hopkins's peculiar perception of external objects and study how its precise expression necessitated the employment of this peculiar form of language.

Hopkins strove after the most accurate expression of the inscapes he had contemplated; but it was no easy task that the poet set himself. He was faced with a difficulty at first sight insurmountable; and the trouble arose from the very nature of systematic language. Inscape is *individually distinctive* and unique, and as such it cannot be expressed in words which, with the exception of proper names, by their very essence as lexical elements of the given language, are *universal* terms. How is he to express the individual in terms which are representative of universals? The obvious and only solution was impracticable: the inscape of a given object being individual and unique can only be successfully expressed by a proper name, because a proper name is not applicable to anything else besides a definite inscape. But this solution was no solution, because Hopkins would have to use a language that others would never understand. Yet there are traces that he instinctively felt that the only completely successful solution would have been the use of a proper name for every inscape. In a letter to Patmore he bluntly states the fact that he has invented a number of words because he cannot do without them (III. 231). And to Bridges he writes about this difficulty as follows: 'This seems in English a point craved for and insisted on, that words shall be single and specific marks for things, whether self-significant or not . . .' (I. 165). It is important to note that Hopkins adds 'whether self-significant or not'; it would, however, have been disastrous if he had invented for every inscape a word that was not self-significant; his poetry would have been utterly incomprehensible. In the same quotation Hopkins has indicated the way in which he solved the problem: he is contented as long as words are *specific* marks of things, that is, as long as words indicate the *species* to which the individual whose inscape is perceived belongs.

Words as symbols of universals were of no use to Hopkins. He could not describe an object by indicating the genus to which it belongs and then limiting this genus to a species by the addition of a specific difference: 'an oaken chest'. For such a description indicates the universal nature of the object, and its specific essence, but gives no direct information whatever about its individual essence, and this is precisely what Hopkins is so anxious to express in words. I have pointed out in the first chapter how Hopkins did not attend to what this object had in common with others, but to what it did not, and could never, share with others. Hence to express an object in terms indicating the properties which it shared with others was a method altogether unfit for Hopkins. Inscape is the denial of universality and consequently description by way of limiting the universal was useless. The same objections may be made against the use of the words that are specific marks of things; but with a difference: for the specific has this one great advantage that it stands closer to the individual than the generic. To make this clear by a simple example: 'teapot' is a word that has become a specific mark; the limiting or restrictive function of 'tea' with regard to the generic term 'pot' has by use weakened to such an extent that a new word has gradually arisen which no longer calls up the original genus; the specific essence is now directly given. Words that are specific marks are the nearest approach possible to a satisfactory expression of inscape. The reason is obvious: the 'thisness' itself can only be expressed by a proper name; this being non-existent, one has recourse to its nearest species, which besides has this advantage above a proper name that it is self-significant and at least indicates the specific essence of the individual. Hopkins, then, adopted this way of describing the inscape of things: he made new compounds, being *specific marks* for things.

The corollary of this paragraph is as obvious as it is of vital importance for the correct understanding of the poet: Hopkins had as a rule no use for the restrictive adjective or noun, followed by a universal term or word that the poet might have called a 'generic mark'. There are in his inspired poetry no 'restrictive adjective—generic noun' combinations. He could not speak of the silver moonlight as *white beam* if he wished to express its inscape, or if that was strictly speaking impossible, at least its specific essence. He did not perceive a beam that happened to be white and was distinguished from other beams by its whiteness: quality and substance were inseparable in his perception and bound together in unity of essence: he perceived '*whitebeam*'.[1]

I must at once point to other very important corollaries. If the combination of restrictive adjective and generic noun is impossible in Hopkins's inspired poetry, it follows that where we *do* come across the combination adjective—generic noun, the function of the adjective cannot be restrictive but must be *descriptive*, that is, indicative of a quality not contained, either implicitly or explicitly, in the comprehension of the noun described by this adjective. Such an adjective occurring in Hopkins's poems adds to the noun following a quality non-essential to what the noun stands for. Thus we are led to conclude that an adjective in normal position in his poetry always expresses an added non-essential relation between it and the noun. In 'wind-beat whitebeam' (*Poems* 8) there is no sub-species created within the species whitebeam, as if there possibly existed also rain-beat or storm-beat whitebeams, which had to be carefully excluded here; no, the adjective adds an accidental relation between the moonlight and the wind.

To this rule: an adjective followed by a noun fulfils a descriptive function in the poems of Hopkins, there is one exception: the rule does not hold good when the noun following the adjective is a proper name or a noun used as such. This is only logical and what we should expect. Hopkins need form no compound with a proper name; this would be ludicrous and altogether impossible. For a proper name cannot be restricted in its extension; the extension comprises one individual only. Consequently, in his poetry, an adjective preceding a proper name or a noun used as such, is either descriptive or—and here the contradiction with the foregoing sentence is only apparent—restrictive; restrictive, that is, of the *comprehension* of this proper name.   One should therefore be very careful to distinguish these two applications of the term 'restrictive'; a word is restrictive of the extension of the word following it, if this word is a universal term; a word can be restrictive of the comprehension of the word following if this word is a proper name or a noun used as such.   The comprehension of a proper name can be restricted in such a way that the restrictive adjective singles out one aspect or one quality of the individual to which, consequently, our attention is drawn as the most striking and the most typical and hence very often as the one which is most expressive of the inscape.

Let us look at some examples; in the *Deutschland* Hopkins addresses God as follows: 'Thou mastering me God!' (st. 1) and 'past all grasp God' (st. 32).   The third instance is taken from *The Windhover* (*Poems* 12), where the hawk is described as 'dapple-dawn-drawn Falcon' (notice the capital).   Why, we ask, these monstrous adjectival groups in front-position?   Why should the ordinary rules of grammar be discarded, why this impatience with normal *systematic* expression? The answer is that here the adjectival group fulfils a restrictive function, while the normal post-position would necessarily give it a descriptive function.   In other words, the adjectival expression does not add a non-essential relation or quality to the noun qualified; it restricts the comprehension of the proper name or, as in the third case, of the common noun used as a proper name, in such a way that it singles out one aspect and posits the closest connexion between this outstanding quality and the individual essence as it is here and now contemplated by the poet.   In a phrase like 'Thou, God, mastering me' the full comprehension of *God* is placed before the reader and this comprehension is neither limited nor strictly added to by the adjectival group following: the only addition is the indication of a relation accidental to the essence of God.   Similarly in 'God past all grasp' there is lacking the close connexion between the essence of God and the quality singled out, that exists when the adjectival group occupies the front-position; in the stanza there is question of God precisely in so far as He is past our understanding.   Similarly in my third instance, the Falcon is contemplated as drawn or carried by the dapple dawn; it is the vision of the Falcon riding the dawn as his charger that inspired the poet; the fact that it is the dawn that *draws* the Falcon is an essential element of the poet's vision.   We clearly see how in these instances the system of logical language is set aside, how the language is heightened by the poet's clinging to an elementary and fundamental logic of expression that is not governed by any such system.

To continue: I have given three examples in which the noun stood unmistakably for an individual. But what I have said about the restrictive function of the adjectival group with regard to a proper name also holds good with regard to a specific noun, provided the specific noun can, in the given circumstances, point only to one individual, where, therefore, the specific noun is the mark of a species to which actually only one individual belongs. This category contains words like earth, moon, sun, heaven, air, &c. Thus Hopkins employs the adjectival groups in a restrictive function in the following expressions: 'fire-featuring heaven' (*Poems* 32), 'world-mothering air' (id. 37), 'the dappled-with-damson west' (*Deutschland* st. 5), 'the down-dugged ground-hugged grey' (id. st. 26). The adjective is no luxury; it is in this position that it brings out the inscape of the object as perceived by the poet. We might perhaps go even further; where an object is already clearly individualized through the context, where consequently it is no longer likely that the universal is called up to the mind, we find an adjective or adjectival expression in its restrictive function, restrictive, that is, with regard to its comprehension. (There is no contradiction here with what we have said above, *sc.* that the adjective followed by a generic noun can never be restrictive: there, be it remembered, we took restrictive as bearing upon the extension of a generic noun.) But it will be clear enough that often it is difficult to decide whether in a certain instance such an adjective is descriptive or restrictive of the comprehension of the following noun: something is left to the personal interpretation of the reader. The following lines contain, according to my interpretation, such a restrictive adjectival group:

> . . . why wouldst thou rude on me
> Thy *wring-world* right foot rock?   *Poems* 40

> Time's tasking, it is fathers that asking for ease
> Of the *sodden-with-its-sorrowing* heart . . .
>   *Deutschland* st. 27

> And the azurous hung hills are his *world-wielding* shoulder
>   *Poems* 14

> . . . that *most in you earnest* eye
> May but call on your banes to more carouse.   id. 54

I

Here we have four examples in which the noun qualified, each time standing for part of the body, is so individualized by the context that the mind is no longer referred to it as to a universal term. It is not easy, if not absolutely impossible, to prove that the adjectival group restricts the comprehension of these 'individual' terms, but the position given to these heavy adjectival groups is strongly in favour of the opinion that here the function of the adjective is to stress the close connexion between the qualitative word and the head noun: the inscape of the object is most intimately bound up with this characteristic expressed by the adjective.

A few words must be said about the descriptive adjective in the poetry of Hopkins. We should be on our guard against misinterpreting the specific Hopkinsian relation between it and the noun following. For even in his descriptive adjectives the connexion between quality and substance is closer than is the case with most poets. Even if a quality was not directly part of the object's inscape, that is, even if any one quality did not strike the poet as individually characteristic of this object, yet the fact that it was *in* the object meant to Hopkins that it was also *of* it; hence even a descriptive adjective adds to the true and faithful expression of an object's inscape.

It is this awareness of the close connexion between quality and substance that accounts for another curious practice of Hopkins that clashes with the systematic use of language. If the poet has his attention drawn to more than one quality of a given object and these qualities affect the individual alike, there is no reason why he should not deal with them alike in his poetry. Hence one adjective following, and another preceding the noun was an impossible word-order for Hopkins if the two adjectives fulfilled similar functions with reference to the noun. Front-position and post-position, attribution and predication, supposes a difference in the perception of the qualities, but where there is likeness of perception, there should be likeness of expression. It may be unfortunate that the English language does not contain those adjectives expressing relations of time and space that the poet needs: but in that case he will make them:

> Or if there does some soft,
> *On things aloof, aloft,*
> Bloom breathe . . .   *Poems* 37, l. 90

In his perception the quality of softness stands on a par with that of place, *on things aloof, aloft*; to Hopkins no system of language could be allowed to destroy this parity of perception by disparity of expression.   Another instance:

> Fresh, *till doomfire burn all,*
> Prayer shall fetch pity eternal.
>
> *Eurydice,* final st.

Why this temporal clause squashed in between an adjective and its defining noun?   The freshness of the prayer and the 'so-long-ness' are two qualities that functionally affect the noun alike.   No matter that one quality could be expressed by a simple adjective and that the other needed a complete clause with subject, verb and object: they are both expressed in attributive position.   Notice the attributive position of the adjective in:

> Each limb's barrowy brawn . . .
>
> . . . finds his, *as at a roll-call,* rank   *Poems* 43
>
> . . . With, *all down darkness wide,* his wading light.   id. 10

The same reason underlies the curious and intricate grouping in the following lines:

> I steady as a water in a well, to a poise, to a pane,
> But roped with, *always, all the way down from the tall*
> *Fells or flanks of the voel,* a vein . . .   *Deutschland* st. 4

This instance is somewhat different from the foregoing in that here the expressions in italics are not adjectival but adverbial.   They define the nature of the roping and that is why they are sandwiched in the group 'roped with a vein'.   'Brim, in a flash, full' (*Deutschland* st. 8), might also be quoted here, but I shall have more to say about the function and the place of the adverb or adverbial expression towards the end of this chapter.

So far I have studied the various ways in which Hopkins expressed the inscape of objects by means of special reference to one or more sensible qualities that in his perception best brought out what was individually distinctive of the object.   The more or less complete identification, in Hopkins's perception, of an outstanding quality with the essence of the individual, was mirrored, as I have shown, in the use of compound word, restrictive or descriptive adjective.   But it is not unthinkable that at times the inscape of an object was one with the most complete realization of the comprehension of the noun: no one quality stands out as most characteristic, but only concentrated attention on every aspect yields a satisfactory knowledge of its inscape.

Proof that Hopkins then had recourse to his own peculiar way of expressing the inscape of things is given in his fairly frequent preference of the adjective as a predicate to the attributive adjective. In attribution the reader is always asked to fix his attention on the second word and relate the adjectival expression directly to this second word; the application of the complete expression, adjective-noun, to the thing represented takes place with the second word as starting point, but this second word taken as defined by the first. In a simple expression as 'a good man' we do not immediately apply 'good' to goodness, but relate 'good' to man and then apply the group, with 'man' as its kernel, to this man. If on the other hand we predicate, we are primarily asked to realize the comprehension of the words separately and each by itself. In predication the words are used each with their full comprehension; they do not limit each other in any way, but stand side by side in complete identification. Thus where Hopkins aims at the expression of inscape not by means of this limitation, he turns to predication. Let us make this clear by studying an example.

No one will find much difficulty in discovering that there exists a great difference between 'a frightful nightfall' and 'frightful a nightfall':

> And frightful a nightfall folded rueful a day.
>
> *Deutschland* st. 15

Predication expresses the inscape of that dreadful night very stridently; its terror can be felt; this is because 'frightful' is not immediately referred to the nightfall; but with its complete meaning and all its suggestiveness it falls upon the reader's mind before being referred to the following noun. Similarly, 'nightfall' is allowed to assert itself with its full suggestive force; the retarded rhythm of the line gives the reader time to identify the two notions very consciously. Other instances need not detain us. The reader can find out for himself the difference between predication and attribution by changing the construction of the group. Thus Hopkins speaks of God as 'mighty a master' (*Poems* 16); further he writes 'high her captain' (*Eurydice* st. 12), 'treacherous the tainting of the earth's air' (*Poems* 36). Predication is one of those devices so easily overlooked and often not understood, that yet pack the poet's lines with meaning.

Post-position of the adjective has precisely the same effect: 'darkness wide' (*Poems* 10), 'cliffs of fall frightful, sheer, no-man-fathomed' (id. 41), (her wild hollow hoarlight hung to the) 'height waste' (id. 32), 'womb-life grey' (*Deutschland* st. 7), 'Hangdog dull' (*Poems* 42). Further: 'comfort kind', (*Poems* 28), 'mansex fine', (id. 23), flake-leaves light' (id. 72), &c., where the effect is not so emphatic and where possibly the rhythm of the line accounts for the inversion, as it certainly often does in Hopkins's popular poetry.

From what has been said so far it is abundantly evident how important it is for the understanding of Hopkins's poetry to realize that the immediate expression of the inscapes of external objects affected the system of the language as much as the poet's peculiar attitude towards the medium of poetry. If we come across irregularities, grammatical or syntactical, in his poetry, we should remember that such irregularities have their *raison d'être* in an artist and scholar so conscientious as Hopkins.

I now return to the compound word in Hopkins's poetry. I have already indicated why Hopkins employed them. It would serve no purpose to draw up catalogues of all the compounds occurring in his poems, because most of them are plain and easy enough. I shall single out for special treatment those groups which the reader may find confusing, but which are yet the more characteristic because in them Hopkins's aim to express the inscapes as accurately as possible is easily discernible.

The first group of compounds comprises those composed of adjective and noun, of the same type as 'whitebeam' discussed on page 109. This formation is very common in Hopkins: witness the numerous examples: 'gaygear', 'gaygangs', 'wanwood', 'boldboys', 'barebill', 'sweet-fowl', 'bluffhide', 'silk-ash', 'greenworld', 'Goldengrove', 'silk-sack', 'fineflower', 'gaylink', 'silk-beech', 'grimstones', 'dimwoods'.[2] These instances are clear enough and need no further comment because here analogy has hardly, if at all, played a part. The same cannot be maintained with regard to other groups of compounds about which I shall speak presently. Clearly analogical formations are 'quickgold' (*Poems* 8), formed on the analogy of quicksilver, and 'mainstrength' (*Poems* 42), which is formed after such compounds as 'mainspring', 'mainstay', &c.

A noun as well as an adjective, as the first element of the compound word, can make a generic term into a specific mark for things. The noun—noun compound occurs on every page of Hopkins's poetry and often more than once. I would be the last to maintain that every compound of this type originated from the poet's anxiety to express the inscape of the object. That here analogy played a very important part will not be doubted. It is impossible to give a complete list of the noun-noun compounds for the simple reason that it is often very hard to recognize the compound: but this is a subject which I shall treat when I make some remarks about Hopkins's erratic use of the hyphen (pages 118–19). I can do no more than point out certain types within this mass of compounds; the relation between the two nouns is a suitable basis for subdivision.

Thus there is a group of compounds in which the first noun is indicative of the same relation as its corresponding adjective would have been: Hopkins uses: 'heaven-handling', 'neighbour-nature', 'winter world', 'wonder wedlock', 'hoarlight', 'couple-colour', 'favour-make', 'gold-wisp', 'gold-dew', 'goldnails', &c.[3] In a second group the first noun replaces a genitive construction: a genitive possessive as in 'flockbells', 'manmarks', 'girlgrace', 'manshape', 'beechbole', 'day-spring', 'meadow-down'; a subjective genitive as in 'wind-walk', 'sea-swill', 'lipmusic', 'limbdance', 'bloomfall'; an objective genitive as in 'gospel proffer', &c.[4]

One may perhaps feel inclined to take this compound-formation as the result of a preference for terseness and crispness of diction to a certain dilatoriness necessarily connected with long genitive groups. This explanation may be correct in the case of words like 'beechbole' or 'dayspring', but to extend this view to all the instances given is to miss the exact shade of meaning of many compounds. Let the reader place side by side 'lipmusic' and 'music of lips', 'flockbells' and 'bells of flocks' and he will find out for himself what difference exists. It is again the difference between attribution and predication. To study one instance: 'flockbells' is a new specific mark; but in 'bells of flocks' we are forced to take in the entire meaning of both words. Notice how in this example a genitive group could only weaken the poetic expression:

> One stroke
> Felled and furled them, the hearts of oak!
> And flockbells off the aerial
> Downs' forefalls beat to the burial.   *Eurydice* st. 2

The flocks are neither seen nor heard nor in any way perceived by the senses: how superfluous then to ask the reader to bring them before his mind. As 'flockbells' is a new specific mark, the explicit reference to 'flocks' is happily dispensed with: the inscape of the ringing bells 'off the aerial downs' forefalls' is precisely and succinctly expressed by 'flockbells'.

The effect of compound-formation is again well illustrated by those compounds in which the first noun indicates the material of which the object, represented by the second noun, consists: 'foam-fleece', 'meal-drift', 'raindrop-roundels', 'lily showers', 'bone-house', 'shadow-tackle', 'fire-folk', 'hailropes'.[5] The connexion between the nouns is here very much closer than in a genitive combination: it will not be necessary to work out the difference between 'showers of lilies' and 'lily showers', between 'ropes of hail', and 'hailropes'. This way of placing side by side a compound word and its corresponding genitive group is often an excellent means of realizing why Hopkins in expressing the inscape of objects chose the compound in preference to the genitive combination.

There is another clearly marked group of compounds that deserves attention. At the end of the foregoing chapter I have pointed out how the image was given with the object and how they grew into one. If Hopkins is going to describe the individually distinctive characteristics of an object, he can do so by stating what other object is suggested by this inscape, what other individual he is reminded of. Thus an object's inscape might recall the shape of another thing; this shape is then part of the object's individual distinctiveness and hence Hopkins will make words as 'loop-locks', 'hornlight', 'moonmarks', 'trambeams', &c.[6] Sometimes it is not the quality of shape that recalls to the poet another object, but a whole group of qualities is so predominant that it reminds him of other objects very much like it in this respect. Keen to depict the very essence of the object, he can never be satisfied with the round-about way of a construction with 'like': it is 'flake-doves' he perceives and not 'doves like flakes'. Similarly he writes of: 'rose-moles', 'flake-leaves', 'lilylocks', 'snow-pinions', 'fawn-froth', 'flint-flake'.[7] Finally there is a group of these 'comparative' compounds in which the likeness between the objects symbolized by the two nouns is not primarily sensory, but is a likeness of instress. To this group belong compounds as: 'wolfsnow', 'earl-stars', 'braggart bugles', 'lovelocks' and 'carrion comfort'.[8] One should be careful not to be too rigid in these divisions; it goes without saying that expressions as 'flake-doves', 'lilylocks', &c., bear out similarity of inscape as well as of instress.

For completeness' sake I add here two more classes of compounds: first there is the adverb-noun combination in 'backwheels', 'after-draught', 'betweenpie', 'uproll', 'downcarol', &c.;[9] secondly there is the verb-noun combination in 'dare-gale', 'spendsavour', 'treadmire', 'fall-gold', 'wring-world', &c.[10] It is impossible to make out how far analogy here influenced the poet; we shall have to make many remarks about analogy in Hopkins's poetry afterwards. It is enough to point out that 'daregale' immediately calls up 'daredevil'; is 'spendsavour' formed on the analogy of 'spendthrift'?

Hopkins once complained that very often he had not the energy nor the inspiration to correct and touch up old sonnets. This is not surprising, because for one thing he was in bad health, tired and jaded, during the greater part of the last four or five years of his life, and for another the stimulus of publication, which implies a careful finishing of a poem, was entirely absent. He let his poems lie for a long time and even when finally he did touch them up so that they were suitable to be seen by Bridges, he did not do this with the care one expects from one who intends to publish. I pass by the inconsistencies in the spelling of words; but the attitude spoken of towards his poems certainly accounts for the at times most annoying absence of any consistent plan of using the hyphen. This is no easy subject in the English language, but the erratic practice of Hopkins foils any attempt at creating order among his numerous compounds. Reading through his autograph poems (and one should remember that Bridges made up his collection of Hopkins's poems from these autographs) I find that in one draft he uses a hyphen to connect the parts of a compound, in another draft, often on the very same page, he drops it altogether, while in the third instance he makes the two parts into one word. Thus I read in drafts of the *Epithalamion* (*Poems* 72), 'kind-cold' and 'kindcold'; in two different drafts of *Poems* 9 I come across 'peartree' and 'pear-tree'; similarly I find 'purple of thunder', and 'purple-of-thunder', 'earl-stars' and 'earlstars', 'lion-foot' and 'lion-hand' but 'lionlimb', 'heavenforce' and 'heavenhandling' but also 'heaven handling', 'bluff hide' and 'bluffhide'; and on one page I read 'fore pangs', 'fore-pangs' and 'forepangs'.[11] Turning to the published poems I find a similar absence of any system in the use of the hyphen: he writes 'windlaced' but 'love-laced', 'self-instressed' but 'selfwrung', 'glass-blue' but 'bugle blue' and 'gluegold'; 'rash-fresh', but 'baldbright' and 'froliclavish'; compare also 'gaygear' and 'gay-gang', 'deft-handed' and 'lighthanded'; and this collection is by no means complete.[12] It is a great pity that Hopkins did not finish his poems with more care, because the absence of any system of using the hyphen often leads to obscurity that has nothing to do with the poetry, an obscurity that only rises from a careless spelling. How much trouble might have been saved many readers of Hopkins, if the poet had used a hyphen in groups as 'lily showers', 'treadmire toil', 'hell-rook ranks', 'gospel

proffer', 'rut peel' and 'shock night'.[13]   This erratic and most unsystematic use of the hyphen involves the danger that we look for a
difference between various kinds of compound formations according
as they are joined by means of a hyphen or not, where in fact there
most likely is none.

So far I have examined a small portion of Hopkins's very numerous
compounds.   But with the remainder I can deal more briefly, because
the principles underlying these formations have been set forth above.
For what I have said about the limiting of a genus to a species by the
addition of a restrictive adjective to the generic noun, is, *mutatis
mutandis*, applicable to the adjective itself.   The adjective can be considered as a genus in the category of quality and thus we are allowed
to speak of a 'restrictive adverb' that limits the generic adjective.
Examples speak for themselves: 'rare-dear', 'lovely-asunder', 'baldbright', 'rash-fresh', 'wilful-wavier', 'lovely-felicitous', 'wild-worst',
'kindcold', 'wet-fresh', 'Tarpeian-fast'.[14]   These adjectival formations
are new specific marks for qualities, just as the noun-compounds of
Hopkins were new specific marks for things.   Let the reader place side
by side, e.g. 'kindly cold', 'kind and cold', and 'kindcold', and he will
agree that there is a falling off in the first two expressions: in the third
he is face to face with that 'terrible crystal' of Hopkins's poetry.
   Another group of adjectival compounds that I must touch upon are
those formations in which the noun preceding the adjective indicates the
degree or measure in which the quality expressed by the adjective
occurs.   Instances abound: 'leaf-light', 'brass-bold', 'tool-smooth',
'herds-long', 'glass-blue', bugle blue', 'moth-soft', 'champ-white', 'jay-
blue', 'beam-blind', 'bellbright', 'gluegold-brown', 'gold-vermilion',
'lashtender', &c.[15]   This mode of composition is common enough even
in normal logical language; I would be the last to maintain that in all
these instances it was only the anxiety to express the inscape that made
Hopkins turn to this formation.   But this admission, that here analogy
undoubtedly influenced Hopkins, does not invalidate my argument.
For leaving analogy alone, I hold that we cannot explain satisfactorily
why Hopkins *consistently* eschewed formations such as 'light as a leaf'.
I say *consistently*; for indeed it is surprising that the drawn-out way of
making such expressions with 'as' is used once only: 'though *as a beechbole firm*' (*Poems* 43), and even here Hopkins deviated from the rule,
for he inverted the order of words.   This consistency can only be
explained by Hopkins's peculiar way of seeing the world around him.
Just as in noun-formations of the type 'flake-doves', 'earl-stars', &c.,

the image through likeness of instress and inscape became fused with the object of perception. And consequently 'leaf-light' became a new *specific* mark for a new specific quality.

Hopkins always desired to achieve the closest parallelism between his perception and its expression; and this drove him to string words together into those many long combinations ending in -ed: 'day-dissolved', 'whirlwind-swivelled', 'wimpled-water-dimpled', 'rook-racked', 'self-instressed', 'not-by-morning-matched', &c. &c. We can easily distinguish two groups: 'star-eyed', 'strawberry-breasted', 'dovewinged', 'carrier-witted', &c., form one group; they should be handled gingerly, for if they fall to pieces they lose their freshness and beauty. The second group is more firmly built: 'no-man-fathomed', 'tear-tricked', 'chancequarried', 'hoar-hallowed', 'ground-hugged', &c.[16] These compounds need never cause obscurity or difficulty provided readers of Hopkins's poetry take their time and do not become nervous as soon as they are seen to approach. They should be taken quietly; Hopkins's own advice may be of use here: 'take breath!' and begin to unravel them quietly. The most monstrous group to my mind occurs in *Poems* 43 at the very end of a very difficult sonnet, when one feels inclined to give up the struggle altogether; the furls or furrows of the new-ploughed land are described as *with-a-fountain's shining-shot*. What Hopkins means to say is that the fur-rows are shot through with the shining as of water falling down in a fountain; incidentally another instance in which the image has become entirely absorbed in the object which it is meant to illustrate.

I now return to Hopkins's perception of inscape and will pursue this subject a little further. I have shown that to Hopkins the indi-vidually distinctive characteristic of any object was often bound up with one dominating quality; I remind the reader of examples of the type of 'whitebeam'. This quality stood out and struck the poet as most expressive of the object's individuality, but—and this is an im-portant point to notice—however striking this one quality was, it never made the poet forget the genus to which the object belonged; the second component part of these compound words proves this beyond any doubt. But at times it did happen that some property of the object or some definite aspect so strongly impressed the poet as being of the very essence of this object, that he completely identifies this property or aspect with the essence of the object itself. The object becomes in Hopkins's perception the very embodiment of this property or aspect. Hence in these cases any reference to its specific or generic nature is entirely left out; the individual essence of the object is expressed by 'substantiation' of a quality. I distinguish two ways in which this complete identification of quality and essence is expressed: Hopkins either uses an abstract noun as 'infinity', 'robbery' or 'variety' (I shall return to these examples), or he converts the adjective into a noun: 'the fair', 'the green', 'the steep', 'the deep', &c. This latter group may well cause misreadings unless one's attention has been directed to this grammatical 'licence'. For to many this use of the converted adjective will be a grammatical licence. Indeed, in systematic language the adjective converted into a noun also occurs, but it then normally indicates a class of persons and not a single concrete object. And it is not likely that analogy with some fixed expressions of logical language as 'the blue' for the sky, has influenced the poet. Here follow some instances, first of the converted adjective:

> Have *fair* fallen, O fair, fair have fallen . . .   *Poems* 21

This example is given for completeness' sake rather than for reasons of clarity; 'fair' here means fair fortune, and for its use Hopkins appealed to the authority of Shakespeare (I. 173). In his sonnets on Binsey Poplars there is a much better example:

> O if we but knew what we do
> When we delve or hew—
> Hack and rack the growing *green*!   *Poems* 19

In that one word *green* Hopkins has expressed the inscape of the landscape around Oxford. He also might have used the abstract noun 'greenness'. One point is clear, that the quality of greenness of the growing trees and flowers dominated the scene to such an extent that its essence as apprehended by Hopkins at this moment could not better be expressed than by a complete identification of this quality with it.

> O the mind, mind has mountains; cliffs of fall
> Frightful, sheer, no-man-fathomed. Hold them cheap
> May who ne'er hung there. Nor does long our small
> Durance deal with that *steep* or *deep*.   *Poems* 41

There is something very effective in this blunt way of describing the frightful precipitous cliffs as 'that steep', 'that deep'. In this example the choice of words is entirely original. In a similar way he calls the seas 'the deeps' in the *Deutschland,* but there is some suggestion in

this case that he may have been influenced by 'depths' and the rather
poetical 'deep'.   Another instance:

> I cast for comfort I can no more get
> By groping round my *comfortless*, than blind
> Eyes in their *dark* can day. . . .   *Poems* 47

Bridges appears to have favoured the opinion that here there was no
room for the noun 'world' after 'comfortless' and 'dark' (*Poems* p.117).
If Hopkins meant to say 'comfortless world', he would have managed
to find room for it, for obscurity without a sufficient reason he hated;
and the omission of 'world' would only obscure the meaning of the
otherwise lucid lines.   But he did not intend to say that he groped
in vain round his comfortless world: that would take away a good deal
of the terror now expressed in this converted adjective 'comfortless'.
Hopkins inscaped the circumstances in which he now lived, and what
struck him as of the essence, indeed, as the essence itself, was not that
they were without comfort, but that they were *comfortlessness* itself.
A parallel instance is found in the *Deutschland* st. 27, where Hopkins
writes: 'in wind's *burly*'.   In the same way and for the same reasons
Hopkins speaks of 'that sweet' referring to the bugler boy he loved and
admired (*Poems* 23); and a soldier he once describes as a 'scarlet'
because he wore a red coat (*Poems* 39).[17]

And here are some examples where Hopkins uses the abstract noun
to express the inscape of a concrete object.

> Brute beauty and valour and act, oh, air, pride, plume . . .
>   *Poems* 12

This is the description of the inscape of the Windhover.   All abstract
nouns with the exception of plume!   The bird's inscape lay in his own
beauty, his valour and his pride and his air.   ('Air' should also be taken
in its concrete sense: the air is as it were background to this bird's
inscape and part of it; about this twofold meaning of 'air' see my
remarks on this subject in the final chapter.)

> Let life, waned, ah let life wind
> Off her once skeined stained veined *variety* upon . . . two spools.
>   *Poems* 32

Here again the abstract noun to express the varied colours.   Gifts of
Providence are called 'providence' by the poet.

> She [Mary], wild web, wondrous robe,
> Mantles the guilty globe,
> Since God has let dispense
> Her prayers his *providence* . . .   *Poems* 37, l. 38

The infinite God is referred to as 'God's infinity' in:

> Of her who not only
> Gave *God's infinity* . . .
> Welcome in womb and breast . . .   *Poems* l. 17

We can now understand why Hopkins also called God 'rescue', and not 'rescuer', 'the *recurb* and the *recovery* of the gulf's sides', and not 'recurber' or 'recoverer' (*Poems* 10 and *Deutschland* st. 32), why he wrote '*robbery's* hand' and not '*robber's* hand' (*Eurydice* st. 23).   Again God is 'sway' of the sea, and not the swayer (*Deutschland* st. 1), just as the thirsty are 'thirst' in *Poems* 47.   In his poem on the portrait of the twins (*Poems* 54) he calls them 'creatures all *heft, hope, hazard, interest*', not '*objects* of heft, hope, of hazard, of interest'; no, here too there is complete identification of a certain quality, if we like to call it so, with the persons themselves: they are inscaped in the given circumstances as *hope*, &c.   And we feel how again 'the rifts are loaded with ore'.

It will need no long discussion to show that another result of Hopkins's inscaping an object must be his employment of what is called the hypallage.

> Thou knowest , . .
> The *swoon of a heart* that the *sweep and the hurl of thee* trod
> Hard down with a *horror of height* . . .   *Deutschland* st. 2

This juxtaposition of abstract noun and what might be called concrete verb (i.e. a verb that can only be properly predicated of a concrete thing) is the best argument in favour of my opinion that here Hopkins expressed the inscape of Christ in His dealings with the poet.   It was Christ, sweeping and hurling down upon the poet, who trod him down, as in another sonnet Christ *rocks* His foot upon him.   But in his vision he inscaped Christ and his mind fastened upon the quality of Christ's eagerness and impetuosity to crush the poet: it is the *sweep* and the *hurl* that now *treads* him down, not 'with a horrible height', but here again, 'with a *horror of height*'.   As a rule this figure of speech does not cause any great obscurity: on the contrary, the danger is that we carelessly overlook it altogether, or if not that, that we take it as a mere roundabout description of a simple fact.   We should, however, take pains in grasping 'the power of forcibly and delicately giving the essence of things', which accounts for the employment of the hypallage as well as of other devices occurring in Hopkins's poetry.

Here follow some more examples of his use of the hypallage:

The *frown of his face*
Before me, the *hurtle of hell*
Behind, where, where was a, where was a place?

Deutschland st. 3

She struck—not a reef or a rock
But the combs of a *smother of sand* . . .
And she beat the bank down with her bows and the *ride of her keel.*

id. st. 14

Similarly, in the *Deutschland* Hopkins speaks of 'the *flood of the wave*', 'the jading and *jar of the cart*', &c.   But notice especially the combination of abstract noun and concrete verb in: 'Christ's *interest eyes* them' (*Poems* 10) and again in:

Though no high-hung bells or *din*
Of *braggart bugles cry it in—*   *Poems* 6

An over-subtle and very prosaic critic might accuse Hopkins of 'false perspective' in imagery, and bring forward that it is nonsense to speak of interest 'eyeing' a man or the 'sweep' 'treading' on someone.   He is right but he has misread the poet.

Hopkins's identification of an object's essence with its prominent quality explains a good many expressions that are by no means clear at a first reading.   In the fourth stanza of the *Deutschland* the poet writes:

I am soft sift
In an hourglass—

Here he does not explicitly compare himself with the softly sifting sands in the hourglass: he caught the inscape of the flowing sand and he identified himself with that continuous motion, that drift, of sand: he is not the sifting sand, he is the sift of the sand.   It is for the very same reason that he could say that he *was* gall, that he *was* heartburn, (*Poems* 45); he did not *have* a disease; no, it was so in him and it caused him such sufferings that he knew that he *was* the disease.   Consider this instance:

God's most deep decree
Bitter would have me taste: *my taste was me.*   *Poems* 45

How strident this identification of himself with his taste tortured by the bitterness that came from God!   He gives this picture of the outcasts of this world:

But no way sped,
Nor mind nor mainstrength. . . .   *Poems* 42

Do not say that here the poet omitted the word *to have*: they have no mind . . . No, they *are* no mind; that is their individually distinctive characteristic, their inscape. What a terrible way of describing the 'undenizened' of society!

In the same fashion Hopkins refers to those men who by their 'wild and wanton work' ruin the beauty and innocence of youth, as 'banes':

> . . . that most in you earnest eye
> May but call on your *banes* to more carouse.   *Poems* 54

In the *Deutschland* he calls the sea 'flint-flake' and this epithet should also in my opinion be explained in this way. We might for clarity's sake have preferred a phrase like 'the sea threw up sprays of flint-flakes', but we should have lost the most effective succinctness of the sea as 'flint-flake' (st. 13).

These remarks are the necessary introduction to my dealing with that vexed question: why in Hopkins do we find all those omissions of the relative pronoun? They are not due to lack of space: if the poet had felt that the pronouns were needed, he would have made room for them in his packed lines. It is his peculiar apprehension of the relation between the antecedent and its relative clause that in most cases accounts for the omission of the relative pronoun. Bridges in his notes to his edition of Hopkins's poems makes some slating remarks about this practice and condemns it wholeheartedly:

> . . . it is easy to see that he banished these purely constructional syllables from his verse because they took up room which he thought he could not afford them: he needed in his scheme all his space for his poetical words, and he wished those to crowd out every merely grammatical colourless or tone-less element; and so when he had got into the habit of doing without these relative pronouns . . . he abuses the licence beyond precedent. . . . (*Poems* p. 97).

But unknowingly Bridges destroys his own case in the very same paragraph where he says: 'This grammatical liberty, *though it is a common convenience in conversation* and has therefore its proper place in good writing . . .' (italics mine). But the language of this poet is the language of 'common conversation', only heightened; Hopkins had other reasons for his omissions than those suspected by Bridges.[18]

The number of omissions has been grossly exaggerated; in fact what we might call 'irregular' omissions are rare. I intend to deal with this subject at some length, first because I hope that it will help many to understand obscure passages in Hopkins, and secondly because it affords an excellent opportunity of summarizing what has so far been shown to be the effect on language of Hopkins's inscaping an object.   Here is a fairly comprehensive list of *regular* omissions of the relative pronoun in its function as object of the relative clause:

> . . . why must
> Disappointment all I endeavour end?   *Poems* 50

> . . . ah! this air I gather and I release
> He lived on . . .   id. 20

> Lovely (is) . . .
> All the air things wear that build this world of Wales.   id. 16

> Father . . . of heart thou hast wrung.
>   *Deutschland* st.9

> . . . the prayer thou hearst me making
> Have . . . heard . . .   *Eurydice* st. 28

> When the thing we freely forfeit is kept . . .   *Poems* 36

> I cast for comfort I can no more get . . .   id. 47

> But be . . . the brand we wield
> Unseen . . .   id. 49

> . . . lovely-felicitous Providence
> . . . , the breast of the
> Maiden could obey . . .   *Deutschland* st. 31

Except in the last instance there is no comma preceding the relative clause, there is no break of any kind.   The relative clause is restrictive and this is a point that should not be overlooked; it confirms what I have said above that no quality was in Hopkins's apprehension ever accidental to the inscape.   Let us just consider one example in detail:

> I cast for comfort I can no more get. . . .

What a bitter qualification of 'comfort' here; he gropes for 'un-get-at-able' comfort, he gropes for a comfort that of its very essence is beyond his grasp.   To realize the poignancy of this line substitute a continuative clause for the restrictive one: 'I cast for comfort, which I can no more get.'   Gone that harsh, terrible tone of hopelessness! for the comfort is not described any longer in its essence; we are only given to understand that, perhaps for accidental reasons, it is at present beyond his reach.

In the following quotations I have placed the omitted relative pronoun within brackets, because it is not always easy to see how Hopkins built these sentences.

> [the wind] . . . stanches, starches
> Squadroned masks and manmarks [that] treadmire toil there
> Footfretted in it.   *Poems* 48

> Not mood in him nor meaning, proud fire or sacred fear,
> Or love or pity or all that sweet notes [that are] not his might nursle:
>   id. 21

> What by your measure is the heaven of desire,
> The treasure [that] never eyesight got . . .?
>   *Deutschland* st. 26

The curious thing is that once the omission is pointed out, 'the meaning of the line explodes at once', to use a favourite expression of Hopkins; what the poet said is so true: 'read it with the ears, . . . and my verse becomes all right' (I. 79).

By saying that these omissions are regular, I do not affirm that consequently the only reason why Hopkins omitted the pronoun is that it was a common convenience of conversation. The explanation which I shall put forward for the irregular omissions may well fit the regular omissions as well, paradoxical though it may sound. But this is a point that cannot always be strictly proved. It can be proved of our last example, however, in which in my opinion the omission of the relative requires a further explanation beyond that of 'convenience'; what this explanation is I shall presently show.

The second group of omissions, regular according to our grammars, consists of those in which the relative is dependent on a preposition:

> It is the blight man was born for,
> It is Margaret you mourn for.   *Poems* 31

> . . . sours
> That neighbour-nature thy grey beauty is grounded
> Best in.   id. 20

In the following instances what obscurity there is arises not so much from the omission as from a certain form of contraction, by which the preposition or the adverbial expression in the main clause functions in the subsidiary clause as well:

> . . . on that path you pace
> Run all your race, . . .   *Poems* 27

> . . . have heard [the prayer] and granted
> Grace that day grace was wanted.   *Eurydice* st. 29

> I greet him the days I meet him . . .   *Deutschland* st. 5

> God rest him all road ever he offended!   *Poems* 29

K

Another group comprises the omissions of the relative as subject of the relative clause: again the omissions are in a sense regular:

There's none but truth can stead you.   *Poems* 54

It is the forgèd feature finds me . . .   id. 21

. . . it is the rehearsal
Of own, of abrupt self there so thrusts on . . . the ear.   ibid.

Is it only its being brighter
Than the most are must delight her?   id. 18

What was the feast followed the night
Thou hadst glory of this nun?
Deutschland st. 30

The last example, though perhaps not strictly regular, is similar to the preceding ones in that the omission follows the verb to be. Note incidentally that also after 'night' the relative is left out.

But here follow the *irregular* omissions of the relative pronoun, which caused Bridges so much trouble. I bracket the omitted relatives.

Save my hero, O Hero [who] savest.   *Eurydice* st. 28

O well wept, mother [you who] have lost son;
Wept, wife; wept, sweetheart [who] would be one: id. st. 27

. . . Here! creep,
Wretch, under a comfort [that] serves in a whirlwind. *Poems* 41

. . . the outward sentence [which] low lays him . . . here.   id. 21

Squander the hell-rook ranks [that] sally to molest him.   id. 23

They were elseminded then . . . the men [who]
Woke thee . . .   *Deutschland* st. 25

. . . I have put my lips on pleas [that]
Would brandle adamantine heaven . . .   *Poems* 23

. . . with a love [that] glides
Lower than death . . .   *Deutschland* st. 33

Why the omissions here? Not for lack of room, nor from freakishness or unbridled desire to be invincibly queer and startlingly original. Hopkins had reasons for them that sprang from his anxiety to describe things in painstakingly precise terms. I must take a slightly roundabout way in order to make this point clear, and first show the reason why Hopkins preferred 'that' to 'who' in the following lines:

> Yet God (*that* hews mountain and continent
> Earth, all, out; . . .   *Poems* 49

> I *that* spend,
> Sir, life upon thy cause.   id. 50

> [Tom] *that* treads through, prickproof, thick
> Thousands of thorns . . .   id. 42

> . . . or me *that* fought him?   id. 40

> . . . youth, *that* to all I teach yields . . .   id. 23

> . . . cries like dead letters sent
> To dearest him *that* lives alas! away.   id. 45

> Wording it how but by him *that* . . .
> Heaven and earth are word of . . . *Deutschland* st. 29

> To man, *that* needs would worship . . .   *Poems* 38

Except in the fifth and last examples, the antecedent and the relative *that* are not separated by a comma.   Now Hopkins was careful about his punctuation, as he once said to Bridges (I. 215), so that I conclude that he had good reason for placing the relative immediately, and without a break, after the antecedent.   Both the omission of the comma and the choice of 'that' argue that the relative clause is restrictive and not continuative.   The relative clause has the function of a restrictive adjective, restrictive, that is, of the *comprehension* of the antecedent noun, which is clearly individualized; the relative clause expresses the person's inscape, which Hopkins identified with one dominating quality.   The use of 'that', the normal restrictive pronoun, has the effect of connecting antecedent and relative clause in such a fashion that together they express one idea.

Above I have spoken at length of how an adjective preceding a proper name was often restrictive of the comprehension of the noun. Here the same desire to single out one quality of the person as most precisely indicating the individual essence of this person drove Hopkins to use the flat 'that' in preference to 'who', which, most frequently and certainly when it follows a proper name, has a continuative or descriptive function.   Hopkins might have used an adjectival group instead of this relative clause and have achieved the same effect.   But no form of sprung rhythm, however 'licentious', could smooth out groups something like 'to dearest living-alas!-away him'.   And even if he could have managed to cast such intricate groups into a presentable form, Hopkins would not have done it, because they left unexpressed one element essential to the inscape of the person in question. What this is I shall show immediately. But to realize the effect of the restrictive clause, we can often do no better than substitute for it a continuative relative clause. Notice, for instance, the difference between: 'I, who spend, Sir, life upon thy cause', (incidentally, this is the reading in an earlier draft), and 'I that spend, &c.'; in the first case the qualification is added to the subject, in the second it is of the essence of it, so that the subject is considered precisely under the aspect of spending life upon the cause of Christ.

Let us now apply this explanation to the example, quoted above on page 128, which in Bridges's opinion was the worst of all and in which the omission of the relative was licentiousness without precedent: 'Save my hero, O Hero savest'. I need not stress that the omission of the comma as well as that of the relative deserve attention. I conclude from the fact that there is no break between 'Hero' and 'savest' that the connexion between these can likewise stand no break whatever; 'savest' restricts the comprehension of Christ as Hero: the Hero is invoked in this line precisely in so far as He saves men. This 'saving' Christ is here implored to save the hero that is drowned in the waves. A few lines above in the same poem we read 'mother have lost son', and here the omission has again the effect of bringing before us the mother under this exclusive aspect of having lost her child: the mother who mourns over the death of her child is inscaped and is called 'mother have lost son'. If then I were asked the question why Hopkins omitted the relative, I should reply that antecedent and relative clause were so intimately bound together that even the use of a purely connective word was an impossibility because it posited, however slightly, some break between the essence and the quality singled out.

But, here again, why did Hopkins not make another monstrous adjectival group instead of this clumsy and rather obscure relative clause without a subject proper? Why not 'men-saving Hero', why not 'child-bereft mother', or something similar? Why a truncated relative clause if a neat regular phrase like 'Save my hero, O Hero Saviour' would do as well? And the reply is that these corrections of the text do not mean the same as the original text. 'Men-saving Hero', or 'Hero Saviour' expresses a permanent quality; the comprehension is restricted, I grant, but a quality is singled out that is in Christ always. A quality is made predominant that has no exclusive reference to the Christ who is here and now bidden to help. 'Men-saving Hero' or 'Hero Saviour' may be a satisfactory expression of the inscape of the

Christ of all times, but only 'O hero savest' expresses the inscape of Christ who here and now must show Himself the saviour of these men, drowned in this shipwreck.   It is the complete identification of the essence with the one activity now necessary that is expressed in this construction.   And be it noted that for this same reason Hopkins used the restrictive clauses introduced by 'that' in the examples on page 129, in preference to an adjectival group.   'To dearest living-alas!-away him', suppose this were rendered into smoothly flowing English, would not express the same as 'that lives alas! away'.   God does not always live away, and that would be expressed or at least implied by the adjectival attributive group.[19]

The other examples I cannot work out for lack of space; nor do I believe it to be necessary.   But I wish to draw the reader's attention to one other instance, not yet quoted, which was a stumbling block to Bridges, because he hardly understood the line:

> This to hoard unheard,
> Heard unheeded, leaves *me a lonely began.*   *Poems* 44

The reason why I have not included this example among those quoted above is that I feel no inclination whatever to shuffle in a relative pronoun here, making something like 'leaves me one who only began'. We consider the line as it stands, and the meaning is evident enough and the phrasing most typical of Hopkins.   'Began' is a noun, and as such properly preceded by an attributive adjective.   But it is the past tense of the verb 'to begin' that is used as a noun; a verbal form expressing activity is thus used to indicate a quality of the poet.   The poet calls himself a 'began', not a beginner; for 'beginner' would express a permanent static quality and would not be the perfect expression of the inscape of the poet whose essential quality here and now is 'I once began', and that is what he is left now: from that aspect his essence is left unaltered.   'Lonely began' as descriptive of the essence is indeed a terrible expression and well fits the terrible sonnet of which it is the closing phrase.[20]

So far I have studied the various ways in which Hopkins expressed the close relation, here and there approaching complete identification, between a quality or activity of a thing or person and the inscaped object itself.   The perfect expression of the inscape could not be channelled into the system of logical language; hence the many irregularities in his poetry.   But an object, once it had been inscaped, began to be active, as I have remarked in the first chapter; it is this aspect that

I shall examine now. There is little difficulty here and for the most part examples will be clear by themselves. Notice the position of the adverb in:

> Do in spare hours *more thrive* than I that spend . . .
>
> Poems 50

> . . . who . . . *most sways* my heart to peace;   id. 20

> Or *less would win* man's mind.   id. 37, l. 109

> Who . . . each one
> *More makes*, when all is done,
> Both God's and Mary's son.   id. 37, l. 71

> May but call on your banes *to more carouse*   id. 54

> My own heart let me *more have* pity on.   id. 47

> . . . the reversal
> Of the outward sentence *low lays* him . . .   id. 21

The reason of the front-position of the adverb of degree is found in Hopkins's perceiving the degree or measure as inseparably connected with the activity expressed by the verb: we should therefore take *more thrive* as a compound verb and do likewise in the other instances. Again, consider the word-order in these lines:

> And *fain will find* as sterling all as all is smart   Poems 39

> . . . God *has let dispense*
> Her prayers his providence: id. 37, l. 40

> . . . and thus *bids reel* thy river   id. 35

> this *bids wear*
> Earth brows of such care, care and dear concern.   id. 35

> . . . *does set dancing* blood   id. 38

> *Have* fair *fallen*, O fair, fair have fallen . . .   id. 21

> *have heard* and *granted*
> Grace that day grace was wanted.   Eurydice st. 29

The last two examples are perfect imperatives, as Hopkins has explained himself. The use of this unusual imperative well shows how he considered auxiliary and main verb as really one word, even though the words were written separately. This explanation accounts for the other changes in word-order as well: the future tense is 'will find' and the adverb 'fain' does not determine the nature of the verb 'find'; it belongs to the one verbal form 'will find' and therefore precedes the group.   Hence Hopkins looked upon the causal aspect of a verb in the same way as on its temporal aspect, and thus he cannot divide the groups 'let live', 'bids wear', &c.   It is again the application of the principle which we have studied before: what he perceived as one and undivided, he tried to express in one word or expression.   If Hopkins refrained from making the combined auxiliary-verbal stem into a proper compound verb, it is presumably only because the change in word-order was proof enough how the verbal expression had to be taken.

I must make some remarks about the activity itself.   In the first chapter I have shown how the objects, once inscaped, began to be active, began even to live, in Hopkins's peculiar perception of them. I have there given numerous examples of this activity, so that it would be superfluous to return to them.   But there is one aspect of this subject that deserves our attention here.   As soon as an object was perceived as 'charged with love, charged with God' (*N.* 342) and thereby began to deal out its own being (*Poems* 34), it consequently affected other beings that became the object of this activity.   To make this clear, we notice how, for instance, a relation of place between this object and another has life instilled into it: from being merely static, it becomes dynamic and expressive of motion.

> . . . her earliest stars, earl-stars, stars principal, *overbend us*,
>
> *Poems* 32

> Now Carisbrook keep goes under in gloom;
> Now it [*sc.* the cloud] *overvaults* Appledurcombe;
>
> *Eurydice* st. 8

Notice: 'overbend' and 'overvaults', and not 'bend over' and 'vaults over'.   I take the change of word-order in the following line not primarily as an inversion for the sake of the rhythm or the music of the line.

> When will you ever, Peace . . . *under be* my boughs ?
>
> *Poems* 22

'Under be' has become a transitive verb expressing activity.

> Tom . . . that *treads through*, prickproof, thick
> Thousands of thorns . . .   id. 42

'Treads through' by its very position demands to be considered as a transitive verb; here as elsewhere a relation of place is altered by the poet's keen awareness of the object's inscape into one of motion and activity.   A similar instance occurs in:

> . . . it is the rehearsal
> Of own, of abrupt self there so *thrusts on*, so throngs the ear.
>
> Poems 21

Another curious example occurs in:

> Fairyland; silk-beech, scrolled ash, packed sycamore, wild wychelm, horn-
>   beam fretty *overstood*
> *By*.   id. 72

Such examples as these are clear enough, but there is another set of instances that requires closer attention.   They are easily overlooked unless one's attention has been drawn to them.   The opening line of the *Deutschland* affords an excellent starting point:

> Thou mastering me
> God!

Here the reader is faced by this question: why did Hopkins use the verb 'to master' (in the sense of 'to be one's master') and why was he dissatisfied with the expression: 'Thou God that art my master'?   The reply is that this latter phrase would express a relation of static dependence between God and the poet and no more.   But Hopkins had inscaped even this relation and now: God 'masters' the poet.   (Cf. also Chapter 5, p. 158.)   Examples of this type abound.   Hopkins could not write: 'Christ, be the East to us' or much less: 'be like the East to us': he must write: 'Let him easter in us' (*Deutschland* st. 35).[21] The poet liked this freshness and suddenness in his diction; it was incomplete, however, and hence he continues to express this thought in a more complete and more picturesque form:

> . . . be a dayspring to the dimness of us, be a crimson-cresseted east,
> More brightening her, rare-dear Britain . . .   *Deutschland* st. 35

Similarly, expressions like: 'to be a trumpet to', 'to be a tongue to', 'to be like a plume', &c., Hopkins discarded altogether.   He writes to 'trumpet', to 'tongue', to 'plume'.[22]   For the same reason he coins the verbs to 'size', to 'justice', to 'leave' (for to 'get leaves'), to 'flesh', to 'day-labour'.   He uses to 'foot' and to 'frock' and to 'selve' instead of long round-about descriptive verbs.[23]   To 'stanch' is preferred to to 'make stanch' and in the same fashion he employs to 'starch', to 'round', to 'weary', to 'brazen' and to 'purple'.[24]

Finally it is for this reason that Hopkins always favours the concrete verb: 'feature' is so much more active than the common verb 'show':

And *features*, in flesh, what deed he each must do.   *Poems* 43

'Breathes' is far better than 'spreads' or 'brings' in these lines:

Comforting smell *breathed* at very entering . . .   id. 16

My winter world, that scarcely *breathes* that bliss . . .   id. 51

'Masks' is more concrete and more active than 'hides', just as 'mantles' is preferred to 'covers':

Patience *masks*
Our ruins of wrecked past purpose.   id. 46

She, wild web, wondrous robe,
Mantles the guilty globe . . . .   id. 37, l. 39

These verbs have besides a picture attached to them. I will give one more example illustrating Hopkins's fondness for this active, concrete verb. In an early draft of the *Deutschland* he had written:

lovely-felicitous Providence
Finger of a tender of, O of a feathery delicacy, the breast of the
Maiden could obey so, be *musical of it* and . . .

He changed the italicized phraze into 'be a bell to'. But to me it is as if in the very act of writing this correction he completed the expression of his version by adding a verb expressing activity as well, and now the line runs:

the breast of the
Maiden could obey so, *be a bell to, ring of it*, and
Startle the poor sheep back!   *Deutschland* st. 31

But I have not yet set forward what to my mind is the strongest evidence of Hopkins's perception of objects as ever active and ever dealing out their own being. The abstract word is not often used where a gerund might be employed, and this seems to me most peculiar to Hopkins. Let us consider this line:

As a dare-gale skylark in a dull cage
Man's mounting spirit in his bone-house, mean house, dwells—
That bird beyond the *recollection* of his free fells . . .   *Poems* 15

which Hopkins altered into:

That bird beyond the *remembering* his free fells . . .

It is hardly necessary to add an explanation here; the alteration speaks for itself.   Yet how typical of Hopkins this change is, considering his very personal way of apprehending external reality!

This predilection for the gerund is one of those devices of Hopkins's that are liable to escape the reader's attention; just because they come so unobtrusively, they are easily slurred over.   Here is a list of instances, which, though not complete, will undoubtedly give a right impression of the frequency of this practice with Hopkins:

> And after it almost unmade, what with dread,
> Thy *doing*:   *Deutschland* st. 1

> and the call of the tall nun
> To the men . . . rode over the storm's brawling.   id. st. 19

The keener to come at the comfort for feeling the *combating* keen.   id. st. 25

> The jading and jar of the cart,
> Time's tasking, it is fathers that *asking* for ease
> Of the sodden-with-its-*sorrowing* heart   id. st. 27

> For how to the heart's *cheering*
> The . . . grey
> Hovers off . . .   id. st. 26

Night roared, with the heart-break *hearing* a heart-broke rabble,
The woman's *wailing*, the *crying* of child without check—   id. st. 17

> Wring thy rebel, dogged in den,
> Man's malice, with *wrecking* and storm.   id. st. 9

> Our make and *making* break . . . down
> To man's last dust . . .   *Poems* 11

> Godhead here in *hiding*, whom I do adore . . .   id. 89

> *Seeing*, *touching*, *tasting* are in thee deceived;
> How says trusty *hearing*? that shall be believed;   ibid.

> It will flame out, like *shining* from shook foil;   id. 7

> Comforting smell breathed at very *entering* . . .   id. 16

> When will you ever, Peace, . . .
> Your round me *roaming* end . . .   id. 22

Those sweet hopes . . . whose least me *quickenings* lift . . .   id. 23

> This *seeing* the sick endears them to us . . .   id. 29

> Comforter, where, where is your *comforting*?   id. 41

Not that hell knows *redeeming*
But for souls sunk in seeming . . .   *Eurydice* final st.

Have, get, before it cloy,
Before it cloud, Christ, lord, and sour with *sinning*,
Innocent mind . . .   *Poems* 9

. . . overflowing boon in my *bestowing* . . .   id. 23

. . . and your sweetest *sendings* . . . befall him!   ibid.

He . . . served this *soldiering* through . . .   id. 39

To keep at bay
Age and age's evils . . . *drooping*, *dying* . . . and *tumbling* to decay;
                                                         id. 36

Not within *seeing* of the sun,
Not within the *singeing* of the strong sun,
. . . or treacherous the *tainting* of the earth's air . . .   ibid.

With-a-fountain's *shining*-shot furls.   id. 43
(another draft reads: with-a-wet-*sheen*-shot)

Foam-falling is not fresh to it . . .   id. 58

. . . it cramps all *doing*   ibid.

There may be readers who are inclined to think that the difference between, for instance, 'asking' and 'demand', 'comfort' and 'comforting', 'combat' and 'combating' is too subtle or too small to require so much attention. I cannot agree: it is these idiosyncrasies of style that tell in Hopkins's poetry and not one of them can we afford to neglect.

There is another point that calls for treatment here; it is the scant use of the adverb throughout Hopkins's poetry. I have taken the trouble of counting the adverbs ending in -ly occurring in the poems; the sum-total is twelve.[25] But I have counted four times as many instances where normally one would have expected an adverb, but where, in fact, Hopkins omitted the adverbial ending -*ly*. It is this apparent dislike of the adverbial ending that often causes great obscurity.

. . . the bright wind *boisterous* . . . beats earth bare.   *Poems* 48

Some candle *clear* burns . . .   id. 26

. . . why wouldst thou *rude* on me thy . . . foot rock?   id. 40

In these lines, and in many like them, the difficulty is whether the word in italics belongs to what precedes or to what follows; is it an adjective belonging to the noun preceding, or is it an adverb without a proper adverbial ending belonging to the verb immediately following? And the answer is that it is both. The adjective used predicatively truly flourishes in Hopkins's poetry. Let me give some more instances and then see why it is that Hopkins so frequently employs it.

The heart rears wings *bold* and *bolder*	*Poems* 14
. . . all the landscape . . . rides *repeated* topsyturvy . . .	id. 5
I muse at how its being puts *blissful* back	
. . . mild night's blear-all black	id. 26
Only the beak-leaved boughs *dragonish* damask the . . . light.	id. 32
. . . nor yet plod *safe* shod *sound*;	id. 42
. . . youth, that . . . Yields *tender* as a pushed peach . . .	id. 23
Christ's . . . foot follows *kind* . . .	id. 10
As a skate's heel sweeps *smooth* on a bow-bend:	id. 12
Comforting smell breathed at very entering,	
Fetched *fresh* . . . off some sweet wood.	id. 16
O then, *weary* then why should we tread?	id. 36
Thou heardst me *truer* than tongue confess . . .	*Deutschland* st. 2
O brace *sterner* that strain!	*Poems* 27
A juice rides *rich* through bluebells, in vine leaves.	id. 54
And scarlet wear the spirit of war there *express*.	id. 39
. . . *rich* it [the air] laps	
Round the four fingergaps.	id. 37, l. 78
. . . this blue heaven The . . . Hued sunbeam will transmit *Perfect*, . . .	
	ibid. l. 86
God, lover of souls, swaying *considerate* scales, . . .	id. 16

The best approach to this question why Hopkins was so keen on the use of the predicative adjective is first to show why it was that he had no use for the adverb proper, that is, the adverb belonging to the verb. The modal adverb proper determines the nature of the verb. This is easy enough. The verb, as qualified by this adverb, is predicated of the subject of the sentence, so that the adverb is in no way directly referred to the subject. In a complete sentence of the type 'the candle burns clearly', the group 'burns clearly' is predicated of the subject, and the adverb 'clearly' has no direct connexion with the subject. But in Hopkins's perception of inscape the quality did not only affect the activity as expressed by the verb, but it directly inhered in the subject as well. When Hopkins inscaped a burning candle, the quality of clearness did not exclusively belong to the burning; as the burning was of the individual essence of this candle as here and now perceived, as, consequently, in his perception there was no separation of activity and essence, the quality that determined the activity necessarily determined the individual essence. 'Some candle *clear* burns': because it defines the nature of the burning, it defines the nature and the essence of the inscaped candle as well: the burning is clear, but the candle is clear too. The quality cannot be sundered from the activity; and because activity and essence are one here, the quality cannot be separated from the subject of the clause. The predicate consequently points to both the activity and the thing; it looks both ways. Unless we take it in this twofold function—of course the functions converge and fall together —we cannot understand the exact expression of the inscapes of this world.

If Hopkins did away with rules of grammar and syntax, it was because they limited the possibilities of language as a medium of poetry; and if the poet transgressed the system of the language, it was never for reasons that cannot stand close scrutiny. The conclusion to be drawn is as obvious as it is important: the serious reader of Hopkins's poetry should slur over no grammatical or syntactical liberty but by careful reading of the poem he must try to find out why it was that Hopkins deviated from common grammar and syntax. Every grammatical and syntactical construction occurring in his poetry should be allowed to assert itself very emphatically in the reader's mind; only then can he hope to grasp the deeper significance of his language. When we now look back on the numerous 'contortions', we are surely impressed by a handling of language which betrays the major artist. Hopkins lays bare 'the naked thew and sinew' of the language. His is no irresponsible playing, no wilful destruction. No, 'current language heightened', and we never realized that current language was so rich a mine, however dark at times. And what holds good of Hopkins's grammar and syntax, also holds good of his words themselves. They never yield up their complete meaning at a first slovenly reading. The sense of words does not lie on the surface. Words should be taken and examined one by one. The reader should take each word by itself until he feels he has sounded its deepest significance, till he is sure that he has *inscaped* it. But I have reserved this subject for the final chapter.

5

INSCAPING THE WORD

'NO one wrote words with more critical deliberation than G. Hopkins', Bridges wrote long after his friend's death.[1] Bridges did not always approve of this critical deliberation of Hopkins, as for example when he spoke of the irrelevant suggestions of homophones (*Poems* p. 98), but he was undoubtedly right in holding that Hopkins never wrote down his words until he had most diligently weighed them. This critical deliberation, with which Hopkins fixed his choice on a word, is the necessary result of his very sensitive and most personal word-consciousness. And this word-consciousness can only be satisfactorily explained by the fact that Hopkins applied his theory of inscape to every element of the language; he could not rest before he had caught the inscape of every word, before, that is, he had tasted the individually distinctive characteristics of every word and expression.

As early as 1868 he wrote down some thoughts on the essence of words that deserve our attention. The date is of importance; the essay was written some six months before he became a Jesuit; he had left the Oratory School at Birmingham where he had been teaching for eighteen months, and had taken no new post. He therefore had plenty of leisure; that he now turned to the problem of language and the nature of words well shows where his interests lay. This interest in language and languages dates from his Oxford days; his notebooks bear out his love of etymology and his predilection for the study of foreign languages and home dialects.[2] The essay is not a complete treatise on the nature and essence of words. It strikes one as fragmentary; it is a collection of ideas on this subject, not worked out, but just put down, presumably in the hope that one day these schematic notes might be properly put together into a complete treatise. The definitions are not precise; he employs various words to indicate what exactly he meant, but nowhere does he attempt a clear-cut definition of his terms. I shall quote some paragraphs of the essay to give the reader an idea how Hopkins considered the word.[3] The essay opens as follows:

All words mean either things or relations of things: you may also say then substances or attributes or again wholes or parts. e.g. *man* and *quarter.*

To every word meaning a thing and not a relation belongs a passion or prepossession or enthusiasm which it has the power of suggesting or producing but not always or in every one. This *not always* refers to its evolution in the man and secondly in man historically.

The latter element may be called for convenience the prepossession of a word. It is in fact the form, but there are reasons for being cautious in using form here, and it bears a valuable analogy to the soul, one however which is not complete, because all names but proper names are general while the soul is individual (*N.* 95).

Prepossession reminds me very strongly of instress; the reason why Hopkins did not use this word is presumably the same reason as warned him against the use of 'form': instress is individually distinctive, while a noun by itself is general or universal. He then continues:

Since every definition is the definition of a word and every word may be considered as the contraction or coinciding-point of its definitions we may for convenience use word and definition with a certain freedom of interchange.

A word then has three terms belonging to it, ὅροι, or moments—its prepossession of feeling; its definition, abstraction, vocal expression or other utterance; and its application, 'extension', the concrete things coming under it.

It is plain that of these only one in propriety is a word; the third is not a word but a thing meant by it, the first is not a word but something connotatively meant by it, the nature of which is further to be explored.

But not even the whole field of the middle term is covered by the word. For the word is the expression, *uttering* of the idea in the mind. That idea itself has two terms, the image (of sight or sound or *scapes* of the other senses), which is in fact physical and a refined energy accenting the nerves, a word to oneself, an inchoate word, and secondly the conception (*N.* 95–6).

Scrappy as the essay is, no one can doubt that Hopkins had very sound, as well as rather original, ideas about the nature of words. To my mind he has to a certain extent forestalled many opinions that were only put forward some forty or fifty years after the date when Hopkins wrote the above remarks, and that are now eagerly discussed in books dealing with the philosophy and psychology of language. This is not the place to discuss these opinions of Hopkins; I am here not concerned with his theory of the word, but with the results of his word-consciousness.

From what I have quoted it is evident that to Hopkins a word was very much more than a sign for a thing.   To this poet a word was as much an individual as any other thing; it had a self as every other object, and consequently just as he ever strove to catch the inscape of a flower or a tree or a cloud, he similarly did not rest until he knew the word as a self.   He attended to the various meanings this word might have, he let its sounds grow upon him and take hold of his ear, he realized its likeness in sound with other words, he felt its instress, in brief, he caught its inscape.   And once a word had been inscaped, it was no longer merely a name for a thing whose only function was to point to this or that object.   When by concentrating on its individual essence Hopkins had succeeded in knowing its individually distinctive characteristics, the word, if used, did not function only as a sign or symbol for a thing, but it functioned with its most complete being; it 'dealt out its own being' (as he himself would say), that is, it was functional in the phrase with its various meanings, its suggestive power, its connotative value, &c.   His words have now a body and bodily they are placed in the text.   If it is true that great poetry will never yield all its beauty at a first reading, we do well to realize that this applies to the poems of Hopkins in a very special manner.   Precisely because he inscaped the words, they could never become mere parts of a whole, of the line or of the stanza; they retained their own individuality as well.   And in order fully to understand what every word, as inscaped by the poet, contributes to the meaning of the line, many readings, and most attentive readings, are necessary.   One should try to catch the inscape of every word that occurs in the poems of Hopkins.   Each word should be allowed to assert itself in our minds with its complex of sounds.   By concentrating on the music of the word in this way, we shall be reminded of other sounds and these will cast round the word a melody that greatly adds to the expression of the experience.   To give one very simple example: let the reader take the words of the following lines one by one, and then repeat the line attending only to the music in the words, and see whether the sounds do not call up the colours that are expressed by the strictly logical contents of the line:

> When drop-of-blood-and-foam-dapple
> Bloom lights the orchard-apple . . .   *Poems* 18

Similarly, the reader should concentrate his attention on the meaning of every word and visualize the object or objects which it symbolizes.   I shall give examples in the course of this chapter, proving that Hopkins must be read in this way, if we wish to understand him properly. No word was to this poet a conventional sign for a thing, handy and useful and no more. Hopkins loved the words, each of them; they were all of them alive; as of other objects which he had inscaped, so it is true of words, that they throw off sparks, if we know how to touch them. Words too are charged with activity, and it is to the reader to allow the words in Hopkins's poetry to exert that activity. Take them one by one, take them as parts of the line, let them quietly grow upon your mind, and you will know how great an artist of words Hopkins is. He did not choose a word because of its meaning only. If he fixed his choice on this particular word or expression, it was because it well fitted the rendering in language of his experience in virtue of its whole being. One cannot escape from the conclusion to be drawn from these facts: we should take pains to take each word by itself and try and 'inscape' it as Hopkins had inscaped it before he used it in his poem. Hopkins should be read with the same critical deliberation with which he wrote.

Devices such as alliteration, assonance, internal rhyme, occurring so plentifully,[4] are not explained by a meaningless, even childish, love of them for their own sake. It has been called 'his worst trick . . . passing from one word to another . . . merely because they are like in sound'.[5] But to my mind no painful search after such combinations could ever have effected the felicity with which they are employed in his poetry as the most natural and the most apt expression of his poetic vision. If any reader of Hopkins's poetry fails to see this, he is not reading in the correct way. Let him try and compare Hopkins's early poetry with his later poems and find out for himself the striking difference in the employment of these devices. In the former alliteration and internal rhyme and assonance are grafted on to the language and are an added ornament; in his later poetry all these devices are essential to the expression of the poetic experience. Let the reader repeat to himself slowly and attentively the following lines and he will see what is meant when we maintain that every aspect of the words is functional in the expression of the poet's vision:

Earnest, earthless, equal, attuneable, vaulty, voluminous . . . stupendous
Evening strains to be time's vast, womb-of-all, home-of-all, hearse-of-all
     night. *Poems* 32

The picture of the coming night is very delicate: one 'senses' the solemn approach of the evening in the music of these lines.

It will be clear from what I have said so far that this chapter must be incomplete. I do not pretend that I have caught the inscape of every word as Hopkins did; for this I should need his very sensitive ear for the music of the language, his delicately attuned sense of rhythm, his love of words as 'selves', his deep insight into the structure of words and expressions, his knowledge too of English, Welsh, the Lancashire and other dialects, and—why not?—of Greek and Hebrew and Coptic: for there is no reason why the inscape of a word did not suggest to Hopkins words from these languages, which he had studied. I am convinced that I have probably never inscaped the words of his poems as Hopkins did; and yet I believe that I have partly discovered the extreme beauty of his language. I can do no more than give the reader some idea of the results of Hopkins's inscaping words. Some very clear instances will be given, which, I hope, will show the reader the way. He can then pursue this fascinating subject further and no doubt make startling and very exciting discoveries for himself.

I shall first deal with the more prosaic results of word-inscape, *sc.* analogy. I have already referred to analogy in dealing with Hopkins's many compound-formations in the foregoing chapter. But though I there pointed out the possibility of analogous formations, no attempt was made to examine why Hopkins should have formed words after the analogy of existing ones; that is the question that concerns us now.

It is clear that not every living word or expression directly fitted the precise rendering of Hopkins's experience. This is not to be wondered at when we recall the demands he made on every element of his language. Often words had to be given the shape required here and now; or at another time new words had to be created, because no amount of shaping would ever give the results desired.[6] 'The poet', thus remarks Mr. Read in his essay on Hopkins,[7] 'seeks absolute precision of language and thought and the exigencies of this precision demand that he should exceed the limits of customary expression, and therefore *invent*—invent sometimes words, more frequently new uses of words, most frequently new phrases and figures of speech which reanimate words . . .' Hopkins wanted language to perform more functions than it was capable of once it had become subject, and tied down, to systematic use. He exhausted all the possibilities of language to make it as pliable a material as he possibly could. And analogy is one of those means that increase the capacity of expression of a language. Without doing violence to the essence of the language, analogy fully exploits the hidden resources of it. If, to take a simple example, the suffix -*y* converts nouns into adjectives, why confine this inherent possibility of the language to some generally accepted cases, as noisy, snowy, fiery, earthy, &c., and why not extend it, if the language profits by it in its essential function of expressing thought and emotion?

Analogy is evident in the many conversions used by Hopkins. Having inscaped a word he could make abstraction of its normal function: no word is of its essence bound to a certain grammatical or syntactical function. I have already shown how freely Hopkins converted nouns into verbs: to 'power', to 'foot', to 'easter', to 'size', to 'front', to 'tongue', to 'trumpet', to 'bugle', to 'frock', to 'justice', &c.[8] The reverse process is likewise by no means rare; 'hurl', 'sweep', 'swoon', may be common enough, but 'achieve', 'plod', 'ride', 'sift', 'breaks' and 'awakes', 'dare', 'furl' and 'heed' as nouns are Hopkins's own formations.[9] He goes even further and converts the verb 'to gaze out of countenance' into a noun:

> . . . where a glance
> Master more may than *gaʒe, gaʒe out of countenance.*
>
> *Poems* 38

To Hopkins there existed no *dead* suffixes, and the range of any living suffix was very much wider in his use of it than in that of common speech or writing. Most of these analogous formations are clear enough. Here are some ending in *-y*: 'towery', 'branchy', 'pillowy', 'barrowy', 'fretty', 'goldy'; these are 'regular' in so far as the suffix is appended to a noun. But Hopkins also conjoins it with adjectives: 'yellowy', 'vasty', 'roundy'.[10] The prefix *a-* forms adverbs: 'astray', 'astrew' and 'abreast', but also 'aswarm', 'astrain' and 'afresh'.[11] Further, Hopkins uses 'to disremember' in the same breath with 'to dismember'; 'disseveral' is used elsewhere. The prefix *un-* is used in: to 'unchild', to 'unleave', to 'unfather', to 'unselve'; also in: 'Unchrist' and 'unchancelling'. The prefix *re-* regains its original meaning in 'recurb' and 'recovery'.[12]

Hopkins appears to have liked to juggle with the suffix *-le* after verbs: it occurs where we do not expect it and it is not found where we naturally expect it. He uses 'nursle', 'girdle' and 'brandle', instead of an expected 'to nurse', 'to gird' or 'to brand'; but the normal 'brindled' and 'curdled' are changed into 'brinded' and 'curded'. Here follow the lines in which these words occur:

> Not mood in him nor meaning, proud fire or sacred fear,
> Or love or pity or all that sweet notes not his might *nursle*:
>
> *Poems* 21

Wild air, world-mothering air,
Nestling me everywhere,
That each eyelash or hair
Girdles; . . .   *Poems* 37, l. 4

Recorded only, I have put my lips on pleas
Would *brandle* adamantine heaven . . .   id. 23

Glory be to God for dappled things—
For skies of couple-colour as a *brinded* cow;   id. 13

Each limb's barrowy brawn, his thew
That onewhere *curded*, onewhere sucked or sank— . . .   id. 43

Slight as these alterations are, they effected precisely what Hopkins aimed at in his poetry.

However well established any one compound-word was in the language, however much the individuality of its component parts had been worn away by use, Hopkins was aware that it was compounded. At times he splits such a compound up again: 'endurance' becomes 'durance', 'enlisted' is shortened to 'listed'; to 'endear' becomes to 'dear', as to 'enfold' becomes to 'fold'; 'lace' is used for 'interlace', 'whelms' for 'overwhelms', 'mines' for 'undermines' and 'ware' for 'aware'.[13] This is not so bad: but Hopkins performs other tricks with compounds that have become part and parcel of the living language. He splits them up, takes them to pieces and patches them together again, but often he does not care where the pieces originally belonged. Some of these new 'creations' are simple and straightforward, others are by no means so easy to understand; but they all of them make this point clear that in every compound word the component parts never lost their individuality for Hopkins. If any word was capable of entering into compound-formation with a word with which it formed a generally accepted new expression, there was no reason why this capacity should be limited to entering into compound-formation with this one word. 'Landscape' and 'seascape' are good compounds, Hopkins will form 'lovescape'; 'rainproof' exists, why then not 'prickproof'? 'Piecemeal' is common, but Hopkins thought that when trees lose their leaves, they lose them 'leafmeal'. 'Mankind' exists and Hopkins makes 'mansex'. 'Worldly-wise' probably suggested 'self-wise'; 'quickgold' undoubtedly was formed on analogy of 'quicksilver' as 'mainstrength' after 'mainstay' or another compound with 'main-'. 'Schoolfellow' is easy to understand, 'fallowbootfellow' needs some more concentration, especially because Hopkins did not use any hyphens; 'to cry havoc' is the standard expression, but when the context asks 'disaster' instead of 'havoc', Hopkins coins the expression 'to cry disaster', which, besides, has the advantage that the verb now suggests 'descry' as well. So 'world without end' very likely begot his 'world without event'. 'Yesterday' is very well, but if on that day the weather happened to be tempestuous, Hopkins will speak of 'yestertempest'.[14]

More complicated, or at least not so evident, are the following expressions: 'God rest him *all road* ever he offended' (*Poems* 29). It is curious how Hopkins inscaped the expression 'in what way'; 'way' never lost its original meaning and 'way' is originally synonymous with road. 'Lay knee by *earth low under*': in that way Hopkins expressed the opposite of 'heaven high above' (*Eurydice* st. 28). Hopkins used to 'ring of it' and I take it to be a formation analogous with 'to sing of something' (*Deutschland* st. 31). 'Sort' and 'way' are often synonymous: and so Hopkins replaces 'in a way' by 'in a sort':

> . . . so I *in a sort* deserve to
> And do serve God. . . .   *Poems* 23

If we normally speak of 'that year' or 'that day' as adverbial expressions of time, Hopkins extends this practice to 'that spell' and 'that weather' —hence I do not think it is accurate to say that these instances can be quoted as mere omissions of the preposition.[15] Formations as 'onewhere', 'by meanwhiles' and 'hard at hand' are probably extensions of 'somewhere', 'by turns' and 'hard by', respectively.[16]

I have spoken of Hopkins's predilection for the concrete word in the foregoing chapter: but let me add a few examples: 'expression of care' is normal English, but to Hopkins it was not concrete enough and so he wrote 'brows of care'; similarly 'cheeks of fire' is not so concrete as 'cheeks of flame'; 'set on fire' is similarly re-created to 'set on a flare'. We can say 'days after', Hopkins will also use 'world after'. If expressions as 'well done!' and 'well caught!' are part of living speech, why then not 'well wept'?; 'your money or your life!' is good, so to Hopkins is 'your offering!' And how very effective is the reminder of 'they took to the boats' in the pathetic line:

To the shrouds they took,—they shook in the hurling and horrible airs.[17]

At times the reader may have been puzzled by Hopkins's use of the preposition:

> I did say yes
> O *at* lightning and lashed rod   *Deutschland* st. 2

Flake-doves sent floating forth *at* a farm-yard scare!   *Poems* 8

Here the preposition 'at' indicates the occasion on which something happens; compare with it expressions as 'she fainted *at* the news', '*at* seeing it happen he ran away', &c.   The preposition 'to' is sometimes used to express a degree as in 'to a nicety', 'to a fault'; this use is extended by Hopkins:

> I steady as a water in a well, *to* a poise, *to* a pane . . .
>
> *Deutschland* st. 4

The meaning here is that the water is so smooth, is so poised, that it is like a pane.

Enough examples have been given to form some idea of how Hopkins examined the workings of the language, how suffix and prefix, preposition or its absence, &c., greatly increased the utility of the language as a system of signs.   It is as if Hopkins had discovered a secret in all these analogous formations.   To him the growth of the language had been artificially impeded by conventional use; a great deal of its wealth as a means of expression and communication was still unexploited.   It was to him as if—with a change of metaphor— language had grown rusty in its joints by bare systematic use.   Now he has discovered how, once loosened from this grip of the system, language is a material with unexpected possibilities.

I have called analogy a more prosaic result of word-inscape; let us see what are its more fascinating results.   A word functions with its whole being.   Thus a word may possess two grammatical or two syntactical functions and Hopkins will employ them both; it may have various meanings and Hopkins will make them converge in his poem; it may call up words like it in sound or instress, and these too function. Before turning to his own poetry to study the effects of word-inscape I shall first make a few remarks about how Hopkins read and studied Homer.   For we are entitled to adopt that attitude towards the poetry of Hopkins which he took up towards the *Iliad*.   We thus safeguard ourselves against the possible, indeed likely, charge of reading into Hopkins's poetry what is not there.

Hopkins refuses to believe in the *epitheton ornans*, for pure luxury is incompatible with real poetry.   Hera may be called again and again λευκώλενος, the leader of the ranks μεγάθυμος, the javelin δολιχόσκιος, and the Gods of Olympus or the heroes of the Greeks and Trojans ποιμὴν λαῶν: never is the epithet mere ornament to Hopkins, or worse, a line-filler.   If it is used, it is used because this word and only this word expresses an essential element of the poet's experience.   No matter how common the epithet, to Hopkins it functions always with its complete being and cannot be replaced by any other.   That he is often more ingenious than convincing in his explanation of such epithets in no way affects my argument; in fact it only confirms it the more.

On λευκώλενος (*Iliad*, Bk. V, 767) Hopkins remarks: 'her arms gleamed as she lashed the horses'.   But in parenthesis he adds that 'just possibly it suggests notion of with clean hands, a good conscience in what she was going to do now'.   This is going pretty far.   The same word occurs some twelve lines before and here the epithet means, or at least suggests, 'seemingly winning by her beauty, or that her white arms gleamed as she holds the reins'.   When in the fourth book (489 ff.) Antiphos aims his javelin at Ajax he is called αἰολοθώρηξ and Hopkins comments: 'for just a flash he matched himself with Ajax'; so this epithet meant to Hopkins more than just 'with glancing breast-plate'.   In V, 268, Anchises is called ἄναξ ἀνδρῶν soon after he had stolen some horses; Hopkins endorses the use of this epithet 'because the theft was so masterly'.   In the same book (V, 445 ff.) it is told how Apollo is going to help Aeneas and is called ἀργυρότοξος 'the silver-bowed Apollo' (449); but to Hopkins it suggested that he is 'as true to Aeneas as his arrows to the mark'.   When Diomedes boasts that either his own blood or that of his enemy must now quench the thirst of the God of War, Ares, he calls the latter ταλαύρινος, usually rendered by 'bearing a shield of bull's hide' (V, 289);[18] for Hopkins it signified that Ares would 'drink the blood by the bucket like out of the hollow of his shield'. In the same book, 504 ff., there is a picture of galloping horses, throwing up clouds of dust to the sky, described as πολύχαλκος, which Hopkins annotates: 'echoing to the horses' hoofs'.

It is hard to agree with all these interpretations of Hopkins; fortunately this is not asked of us.   But one thing stands out clearly from his remarks: he could never look upon a word as a mere expletive; a word was essential to the line as soon as it was placed in it.   He would turn and turn it over till he had found the facet reflecting the experience, or part of it, expressed by this word.   For this purpose he takes the word with its full suggestive power: silver calls up faithfulness, the flash of shining mail courage and valour; the gleam of white arms even suggested a clean conscience.   Compared with these instances of Hopkins, what I adduce will be only child's play; I leave it to the reader himself to apply Hopkins's own standards more rigidly.

I shall begin with some simple instances that can be easily checked, thus to pave the way for some more startling, and at first sight, hardly believable, examples.

> The glassy peartree leaves and blooms, they brush
> The descending blue;   *Poems* 9

These lines are an excellent starting point; they are clear enough and yet they contain a violent 'distortion'.   For what does 'they' refer to? Not to the peartree, which is singular; obviously to 'leaves and blooms'; but these are verbal forms and not nouns.   They are verbal forms in the first sentence, but by themselves they might be plural nouns as well. Now Hopkins transcended the actual function of these words in the line, so that the first time they function as forms of a verb, and immediately afterwards as nouns.   Other instances are not so interesting as this one, because, though Hopkins uses a word in two different functions, he uses the word twice over.   At all events even the instances now following well show how he was always aware of the fact that a word had these different functions:

> . . . out of sight is out of *mind*.
> Christ *minds*;   *Poems* 10

Notice the sudden leap from the noun to the verb.

> God's most deep decree
> Bitter would have me *taste*: my *taste* was me.   id. 45

> . . . rare gold, bold steel, bare
> In both; *care*, but share *care*—   id. 42

> *Mark*, the *mark* is of man's make . . .
>   *Deutschland* st. 22

> *touch* had quenched thy tears,
> Thy tears that *touched* my heart . . .   *Poems* 29

> But in pale water, frail water. . . .
> Thy venerable *record*, Virgin, is *recorded*.   id. 58

> *Wording* it how but by him that present and past,
> Heaven and earth are *word* of, *worded* by?—
>   *Deutschland* st. 29

> The majesty! what did she mean?
> *Breathe*, arch and original *Breath*.   id. st. 25

There is a pleasant and subtle shift in function and meaning in the use of 'while' in:

> Nay, what we had lighthanded left in surly the mere mould
> Will have waked . . .
> What *while* we, *while* we slumbered.   *Poems* 36

'While', used for the second time, is not a mere repetition; it is now a conjunction, whereas in the first place it was a noun.

Slightly more complicated is the use of 'grace' in these lines:

> God with honour hang your head,
> Groom, and *grace* you, bride, your bed
> With lissome scions. . . .   *Poems* 28

'Grace' is in my opinion used as a noun, being on a par with 'honour', so that the sense is: 'God hang you, bride, with grace.'   But I will not believe that Hopkins lapsed into such bad taste as to have us insert another 'hang' before 'your bed'.   Undoubtedly Hopkins transcended, as it were, the use of 'grace' as a noun, and fastens now upon its function as verb, so that the second and third lines mean: 'God grace your bed with lissome scions'.

In all these instances there was question of two grammatical functions of one word; in the same manner Hopkins used a word twice over in two syntactical functions:

> I caught this *morning morning*'s minion. . . .   *Poems* 12

Notice the difference between the functions; the first 'morning' indicates time and is rather flat compared with the 'morning's minion' where the meaning of 'morning' is enriched by being impersonated.

> I cast for comfort I can no more get
> By groping round my comfortless, than blind
> Eyes in their dark can day or *thirst* can find
> *Thirst*'s all-*in-all in all* a world of wet.   *Poems* 47

In the third line 'thirst' stands for 'the thirsty', in the closing line it is a proper abstract noun.   The play upon 'in-all' is clear enough; it calls up the line:

> Whether *at once, as once at* a crash Paul . . .
>   *Deutschland* st. 10

a play upon 'once' also pointed out by G.W.Stonier in his essay on Hopkins, contained in his collection entitled *Gog Magog* (pp. 49–50). I should not like to speak of word-play in the following line where 'my God' is used in two different syntactical functions with extreme felicity and great dramatic effect:

> That night, that year
> Of now done darkness I wretch lay wrestling with (*my God!*) *my God.*
>
> *Poems* 40

In all the above examples the repetition of the word in different functions is such that it betrays the real artist; there is nothing affected or artificial about it, no straining after effect by clever ingenious play upon words.   It is impossible exactly to indicate why the repetition comes off so well; it is only a true poet who can succeed in these daring experiments.

Having pointed out Hopkins's awareness of the various functions that a word could fulfil in the sentence, I now turn to that most interesting subject—Hopkins's consciousness of various meanings words could have, irrespective of their spelling.   Hopkins felt the total weight of each of the words he placed in his sentence; if it had different meanings he was aware of them, and he appears to have taken a pleasure in using them.   Thus he writes:

> On ear and ear *two* noises *too* old *to* end . . .   *Poems* 11

This may strike the reader as rather insipid, but he introduced this repeated echo purposely and unobtrusively.   The repetition of 'end-' is not accidental in:

> . . . why must
> Disappointment all I *end*eavour *end*?   id. 50

More obvious examples are:

> Deep, deeper than *divined*,
> *Divine* charity, . . .   id. 28

> It fancies, *feigns*, deems, dears the artist after his art;
> And *fain* will find as sterling all as all is smart.   id. 39

But this use of homophones is to my taste degraded into freakishness where he writes:

> That *piecemeal peace* is *poor peace*; what *pure peace* . . .   id. 22

Much better is the play upon 'time' in the following quatrain, belonging to *Poems* 54, though not published with this fragment:

> Ah, life, what's like it?   Booth at Fairlop Fair
> Men boys brought in to have each one shy there, one
> Shot, mark or miss, no more.   I miss: and 'there!'—
> 'Another *time* I . . .'   '*Time*, says Death, is done.'

Here the use of time in its twofold meaning is certainly very effective.

But it is probably not correct to speak in this case of a twofold meaning of 'time'; it is better to speak of Hopkins delicately making the most of two nuances of one meaning. And this he often does. Words are uesd in quick succession, and though the fundamental meaning is the same, he manages to use the words with a slight variation, which is often very poetic; thus for instance:

> Thou art indeed *just*, Lord, if I contend
> With thee; but, sir, so what I plead is *just*.   *Poems* 50

In the following lines the verb 'to cheer' is used transitively and intransitively in rapid succession, which well suggests the speed of thought:

Nay in all that toil, that coil, since (seems) I kissed the rod,
Hand rather, my hand lo! lapped strength, stole joy, would laugh, *cheer*.
Cheer whom though? the hero . . .   id. 40

'To build' is used in its literal and metaphorical sense in:

> . . . birds *build*—but not I *build*.   id. 50

and *touch* in the lines also quoted above:

> . . . *touch* had quenched thy tears,
> Thy tears that *touched* my heart, child. . . .   id. 29

an example which I have included among the instances of words used in two grammatical functions (p. 150).

Similarly the verb 'to shine' is used thus, but here the verb is used only once, so that its literal and its metaphorical sense converge:

> And frightful a nightfall folded rueful a day
> Nor rescue, only rocket and lightship, *shone*.
> *Deutschland* st. 15

Again:

> I *lift up* heart, eyes . . .   *Poems* 14

The very fine play upon 'blind' and 'see' may be included here:

> The rash smart sloggering brine
> *Blinds* here; but she that weather *sees* one thing, one;
> Has one fetch in her: she rears herself to divine
> Ears . . .   *Deutschland* st. 19

Hopkins does not always succeed so well; in my opinion the effect of word-play is very jarring in:

> . . . so I in a sort *deserve* to
> And do *serve* God to *serve* to
> Just such slips of soldiery Christ's royal ration.   *Poems* 23

And a phrase as 'it *calls* the *calling* manly' does not sound quite genuine (*Poems* 39).   I single out two instances that are not so easy to understand:

> The majesty! what did she mean?
> *Breathe,* arch and original Breath.
> Is it love in her of the being as her lover had been?
> *Breathe,* body of lovely Death.   *Deutschland* st. 25

The lines are obscure if we take 'breathe' to mean to inhale, draw breath, in both cases; this meaning only fits the fourth line in which the poet implores the lifeless body to come to life again, to breathe again, that it may tell the poet why it was that the sister called Christ to come, and to come quickly.   In the second line he asks the Holy Ghost to *breathe,* that is, to inspire him to understand the secret of the nun.   Even more obscure is the play upon the word 'part' in the following lines:

> If I have understood,
> She holds high motherhood
> Towards all our ghostly good
> And plays in grace her *part*
> About man's beating heart . . .
> Yet no *part* but what will
> Be Christ our Saviour still.   *Poems* 37, ll. 46–54

The expression 'to play a part' is rather violently pulled to pieces in these lines and here Hopkins is certainly not at his best.   Rather clumsy and ugly is the pun in:

> With the sweetest air that said, still *plied* and pressed,
> He swung to his first poised purport of *reply.*   *Poems* 27

But ugly or not, what is of importance to note is the fact that Hopkins detected these nuances in meaning and brought them into his poetry. In the following lines the words 'flame', 'grace' and 'keen' are twice used in the same sense, though each time they refer to different things. Thus desolation is called a flame, but so is the soul's presence with God. Suffering is referred to as grace, but so is the joy of intimate friendship with Christ:

> My heart, but you were dovewinged, I can tell,
>   Carrier-witted, I am bold to boast,
> To flash from the *flame* to the *flame* then, tower from the *grace* to the *grace.*
>   *Deutschland* st. 3

The meaning of 'keen' is clear enough:

> Or is it that she cried for the crown then,
> The *keener* to come at the comfort for feeling the combating *keen?*
> *Deutschland* st. 25

The use of the *syllepsis* entirely fits in with Hopkins's word-consciousness, for the *syllepsis* clearly argues that Hopkins has so inscaped the expression that the parts never lost their individuality. I have not found one instance where I would say that Hopkins is successful; it always falls rather flat:

> he *came to* us *after* a boon . . .   *Poems* 23

where 'to come' is used joined with the preposition 'to' to indicate direction, and with 'after' to express the object of the coming, and the strong suggestion of 'to be after' is all too evident. A very startling example is given in *Poems* 37:

> Of her who not only
> *Gave* God's infinity
> Dwindled to infancy
> *Welcome* in womb and breast,
> Birth, milk and *all the rest.* . . .   ll. 17–22

To give welcome, birth, milk and all the rest is putting a terrible strain on the meaning of 'to give'; but there it is, and it is a typical result of Hopkins's word-consciousness.

These examples of *syllepsis* are the first traces of Hopkins's making various meanings converge in the single use of the word. In the *syllepsis* the meanings are at least connected, but Hopkins manages to make various meanings, wide apart, converge. I shall give many examples and work them out because it is so easy to overlook them in reading his poetry. This practice of Hopkins is very common, and ingenious as it may appear, it is never a trick, and here Hopkins is hardly ever guilty of bad taste.

Having described the beauty of harvest-time, he turns his thoughts to man who is not impressed by the 'barbarous beauty' of nature:

> These things, these things were here and but the beholder
>   Wanting; which two when they once meet,
> The heart *rears* wings bold and bolder
> And hurls for him, O half hurls earth for him off under his feet.
> *Poems* 14

I have printed the verb 'rears' in italics; it signifies not only that the heart 'grows' wings, it at the same time means that it 'raises' them.

Unless we take this twofold meaning into account, the line will not bear minute analysis.   For if we take 'rears' in the first sense exclusively, the transition to the thought expressed in the closing line is very abrupt, too abrupt to be quite logical.   If we take the verb in its second meaning of 'to raise' only, we may well ask how the poet came to speak of the heart rearing its wings, whereas we should expect the wings to rear, that is, to raise, the heart, just as we speak of wings raising the bird.   It is only by making the two senses of 'to rear' converge that the line becomes clear.

> Oh, the sots and thralls of lust
> Do in spare hours more thrive than I that *spend*,
> Sir, life upon thy cause.   *Poems* 50

> Not today we need lament
> Your wealth of life is some way *spent*:   id. 6

In both quotations 'spend' has the sense of to pass time, so much is evident from the use of the word 'life' which is joined to the verb in either case.   But we miss much if we overlook the sense of 'to spend' as synonymous with 'to lay out money': life, as if it were money, has been laid out without stint in gaining the greater glory of God.   It is of no concern here that one fundamental meaning historically underlies this twofold use of the verb; in time these meanings have drifted far enough apart to allow us to speak of a twofold sense of one word.   But the reader must be careful not to misunderstand the term 'twofold meaning'; I prefer to speak of convergence of meanings, which implies that the word is re-created, re-animated and now has a meaning which is not merely the sum of two converging senses; they intermingle and become fused so that we had better speak of an altogether new significance which the word has now gained.   Here is another fine instance:

> This to hoard unheard,
> Heard unheeded, *leaves* me a lonely began.   *Poems* 44

'Leaves' does not only indicate the result of ill-success, as when we use it in such a phrase as 'the war left him a broken man'.   'Leaves' here expresses moreover that the poet was left in the same state in which he was before he began to do all he possibly could for the conversion of relatives and friends: it *left* him what he was at the beginning, and thus expresses that he had made no progress whatever.   A similar employment of the two meanings occurs in:

> The fine delight that fathers thought; the strong
> Spur, live and lancing like the blowpipe flame,
> Breathes once and, quenchèd faster than it came,
> *Leaves* yet the mind a mother of immortal song.   *Poems* 51

'Quenched faster' clearly suggests that 'leaves' here means: 'goes away'.   But the addition of 'yet', expressing some contrast, has the effect of bringing out that other meaning of 'leaves', *sc.* of leaving behind in a specified state.   Mark the exact significance of 'mind' in:

> Let life, waned, ah let life wind
> Off her once skeined stained veined variety upon, all on two spools; part,
>   pen, pack
> Now her all in two flocks, two folds—black, white; right, wrong; reckon
>   but, reck but, *mind*
> But these two; . . .   *Poems* 32

The verb 'to mind' is used in combination with various nouns and accordingly it is given a certain nuance markedly affecting its core of meaning, which is something like to think of, bear in mind (cf. expressions as: 'mind your own business', 'mind your steps', 'mind the expenses', &c.).   In the above quotation Hopkins appears to have hardened this central meaning; 'to mind' here has nothing of the vagueness of 'to think about', because the original meaning has been most successfully re-created.   This re-created word contains in itself all the freshness which it originally possessed but which it lost by being tied down to systematic use.   This instance seems to me a very good illustration of what has been called the 're-creation of word' and of which Cecil Day Lewis has remarked that it is the last secret of poetic technique.[19]   Some more instances:

> The frown of his face
> Before me, the hurtle of hell
> Behind, where, where was a, where was a place?
> I whirled out wings *that spell* . . .   *Deutschland* st. 3

We have already seen how 'that spell' with its supposed omission of the preposition was an extension of the way we say 'that time'.   The reason why 'spell' was preferred to 'time' is clear from the foregoing lines: there was no way out for the poet, held as he was as if by a charm, by hell hurtling behind and God's frowning face before him.   To express that awful moment by 'time' was impossible; 'spell' suggests both that moment of time as well as its awfulness.

After these examples I venture a little more:

> And though the last lights off the black West went
>   Oh, morning, at the brown brink eastward, *springs*— *Poems* 7

and I take 'springs' not only to be synonymous with, though much more expressive than, 'rises'; it calls up the likeness of the morning to spring-time.   Intentional or not, this suggestion certainly enhances the beauty and the freshness that these lines breathe.

> Brute beauty and valour and act, oh, *air*, pride, plume, here
>   Buckle! . . .   *Poems* 12

'Air' refers not only to the sky as the background of the hawk's flight; the proximity of the other qualities of the bird clamours for the meaning of 'behaviour, impressive attitude' as well.

In the opening line of *The Wreck of the Deutschland, mastering* should be taken in its twofold sense of 'overcoming, reducing to subjection', but also, as pointed out in the previous chapter (p. 134) of 'being a master'.

There can be no doubt that Hopkins intended the twofold meaning of 'told—tolled' to function in this line:

> A prophetess towered in the tumult, a virginal tongue *told*.
>   *Deutschland* st. 17

How strange that Bridges could speak of 'the irrelevant suggestions' of homophones (*Poems* p. 98).   The tolling is heard in the repeated t's of the line.   And notice how the comparison of the nun's voice to a ringing bell is logically complete: 'a prophetess *towered* in the tumult', that is, in Hopkins's keen apprehension, the nun rose *like a tower*, was like a belfry.   And if the nun is like a belfry, her voice is like the tolling bells.   A parallel instance is given in *Poems* 24:

> Both thought and thew now bolder
> And *tolled* by Nature: Tower . . .

Here we have again the association of 'tolled' and 'tower', but here too Hopkins wrote 'told'.   We should not overlook the homophone in what, to my mind, are some of the finest lines Hopkins ever wrote:

> Brute beauty and valour and act, oh, air, pride, plume, here
>   Buckle! AND the fire that breaks from thee then, a billion
> Times *told* lovelier, more dangerous, O my chevalier!   *Poems* 12

In the first chapter I remarked how 'tolled 'appeared to be demanded by Hopkins's peculiar association of the instress of fire, bells, and activity;

in the third I showed how it fitted in with the underthought of the poem.   In the *Eurydice* there occurs this stanza:

> She had come from a cruise, training seamen—
> Men, boldboys soon to be men:
>   Must it, worst weather,
>   *Blast* bole and bloom together?   st. 4

How appropriate the use of 'blast'!   The fact that bad weather causes the shipwreck makes one take the verb in its primary sense of 'to be like a strong gust of wind', but by its being used transitively it has moreover the sense of 'to ruin, to wreck'.   It is again a clear instance of how Hopkins renewed the word altogether by withdrawing it from the meaning in systematic use.

In his sonnet on Oxford there occur these lines:

> Thou hast a base and brickish skirt there, sours
> That neighbour-nature thy grey beauty is *grounded*
> Best in; . . .   *Poems* 20

The verb in italics suggests more than merely 'established': Oxford's surroundings are nothing less than 'grounds', one beautiful park, in the midst of which the 'towery city' is laid out.

> As kingfishers catch fire, dragonflies draw flame;
> As tumbled over rim in roundy wells
> Stones *ring*: . . .   *Poems* 34

—'ring' here should be taken not only to mean 'make a noise', but also 'make rings'.

In Hopkins's poem on the unemployed he expresses his pity with the outcasts of society, describing them as follows:

> But no way sped,
> Nor mind nor mainstrength; gold go garlanded
> With, perilous, O no; nor yet plod safe shod sound;
>   Undenizened, *beyond bound*
> Of earth's glory, earth's ease, all; . . .   *Poems* 42

Why did Hopkins write 'beyond bound', and why did he not use the normal 'beyond bounds' with a plural -*s*?   The outcasts have not only been placed outside the pale, the *bounds*, of the comfort of this earth; there is a strong and most dramatic suggestion that, however clever and scheming these poor people may be, no matter how talented, no matter what they do, no matter how they 'jump', earth's glory and earth's ease are beyond their reach, are beyond their 'bound'.

M

Another instance, this time again from the *Eurydice*:

> No Atlantic squall overwrought her
> Or rearing billow of the Biscay water
> Home was at hand
> And *the blow* bore from land.   st. 5

And 'the blow' is not only the wind; how strident the line becomes if
we take blow in its meaning of calamity or disaster as well. Again,
how the following line gains in beauty and significance if 'folded'
is properly inscaped:

> And frightful a nightfall *folded* rueful a day
>
> > *Deutschland* st. 15

I have hinted above (p. 146) that 'folded' was a simplified form of
'enfolded'.   And this is true enough; but Hopkins had his reasons for
preferring folded to enfolded.   The frightful nightfall was the *fold*,
the shelter, for a rueful day; what an image!   We might have expected
that a calm night would have received such a dreadful day into its
shelter: but no, the shelter of the night was worse than the day.

Notice the fugitive meaning, so hard to fix, of 'find' in the following
quotations:

> Over again I feel thy finger and *find* thee.
>
> > *Deutschland* st. 1

> It is the forged feature *finds* me . . .   *Poems* 21

There is here a curious mingling of the meanings 'to experience' and
'to come across'.

The original meaning of 'dear' is restored in:

> Deep, deeper than divined,
> Divine charity, *dear* charity,
> Fast you ever, fast bind.   id 28

> We hear our hearts grate on themselves: it kills
> To bruise them *dearer*.   id. 46

How effective the choice of the verb 'strikes' in:

> and thrush
> Through the echoing timber does so rinse and wring
> The ear, it *strikes* like lightnings to hear him sing;   id. 9

The meaning 'to impress' and its literal sense as evident from its combination with lightnings here fall happily together.

I take the verb 'to beat' in its twofold sense of 'to strike' and 'to win a fight' in:

Delightfully the bright wind boisterous ropes, wrestles, *beats* earth bare
Of yestertempest's creases; . . .   *Poems* 48

The second meaning of 'to win a fight' appears to me to be very clearly suggested by the preceding verb 'wrestles'.   Hopkins coined a new verb 'to stead' with the meaning of both 'to steady' and 'to be of (good) stead':

> Where lies your landmark, seamark, or soul's star?
> There's none but truth can *stead* you.   Christ is truth.
>
> *Poems* 54

Readers have wondered at the intransitive use of the verb 'to mould' in:

> what lovely behaviour
> Of silk-sack clouds! has wilder, wilful-wavier
> Meal-drift *moulded* ever and melted across skies ?   *Poems* 14

But apart from its intransitive use, 'mould' suggests something well defined in shape, and this hardly fits the thought: 'wilder', 'wilful-wavier', 'meal-drift', 'melted' are all of them words that call up the reverse of definite shape.   The solution of this apparent contradiction is that in 'mould' various meanings meet; it means that the clouds take on various shapes; it further reinforces the idea of whiteness and shapelessness, suggested by meal-drift, because to Hopkins the sense of mould as synonymous with fungi and mildew, white and of no fixed shape, was never absent.   If we look at the original draft of this poem, which reads:

> has wilful, *swanwing-whiter*
> Meal-drift moulded ever &c. . . .

I believe that this convergence of various meanings of 'mould' was intentional, and that the whiteness of the clouds and their unsubstantiality was compared to the frothiness of mildew.

> One stirred from the rigging to save
> The wild *woman-kind* below, . . .   *Deutschland* st. 16

Is the hyphen placed in 'woman-kind' lest we should miss the suggestive force of 'kind' as affable? Did the poet intend us to interpret these lines in this way, that the sailor was impelled to risk his life also

because these women had been kind to him? Three stanzas farther on
there occurs this line:

> The rash *smart* sloggering brine
> Blinds her . . .

Why 'smart', while the sense appears to demand 'smarting'? It is as if
the sea took pride in being so smart, so clever, in ruining the ship with
all the people it carried; nevertheless the sense of 'smarting' should not
be left out of consideration.

> Star-eyed strawberry-breasted
> Throstle above her nested
> Cluster of *bugle blue* eggs thin
> Forms and warms the life within.   *Poems* 18

In the first chapter I adduced these lines as containing a fine instance
of synaesthesia in Hopkins and put it on a par with 'thunder-purple'.
One should not conclude that 'bugle' should only be taken in this
sense of 'horn'; of course, in the very first place 'bugle' stands here for
the plant, and the choice of the word 'cluster' undoubtedly confirms it.
But the suggestion of the other sense should not be missed; if this
should strike some readers as far-fetched, let them remember that
Hopkins's first version read 'bugled blue'.

   Dr. Gardner points out another example.   In the unfinished poem
on Margaret Clitheroe occurs the line:

> Being to her virtue clinching-blind . . .   *Poems* 86

' "clinching-blind" ', so remarks Dr. Gardner, '. . . suggests the eyes
of a bigot fast shut; but when we unmask a pun on the name Clinch
(the judge who condemned Margaret) the same gains a clarity which is
of dubious value' (op. cit., p. 192).

   Here is another instance, concealed, but, once detected, very
effective

> Summer ends now; now, *barbarous* in beauty, the stooks arise
> Around; . . .   *Poems* 14

It is not unlikely that most readers of Hopkins have never been greatly
troubled by the word 'barbarous'.   By its association with 'barbaric'
they have very naturally come to take this word as more or less
synonymous with 'wild', well knowing how Hopkins loved 'things
wild':

> What would the world be, once bereft
> Of wet and of wildness?   Let them be left,
> O let them be left, wildness and wet . . .   *Poems* 33

There appears to be little doubt that this was the meaning intended by the poet; but in this sense 'barbarous' does not normally occur.   Let us ask ourselves this question: why did Hopkins prefer 'barbarous' to 'barbaric'? Apart from reasons of euphony and rhythm, I hold that 'barbaric' with its accent on the second syllable could not call up the 'barbs', that is, the ears of the bearded corn that was gathered in sheaves; but 'barbarous' with its main stress on the first syllable 'barb' so easily suggested the ears of corn bundled together.

Another instance:

> For how to the heart's cheering
> The down-dugged ground-hugged grey
> Hovers off, the jay-blue heavens appearing
> Of pied and *peeled* May!
>
> *Deutschland* st. 26

The sense of 'peeled' seems to be that in May the buds of trees and flowers open out and thereby loose their peels, their outward coverings. Dr. Gardner has changed the spelling (is it a printer's mistake or has he made the change himself—perhaps unknowingly?) and his text reads 'pealed'.[20]   Here again we have an excellent instance of the very relevant suggestion of homophones: the freshness of May is closely associated with the ringing of happy bells.

> Be adored among men,
> God, three-numberèd form;
> Wring thy rebel, *dogged* in den,
> Man's malice . . .   *Deutschland* st. 9

This instance will hardly need any comment; 'dogged' well expresses the tenacity with which man clings to his malice.   But in a very fine picture we see vividly portrayed how this malice shuns daylight and like a dog crouches in its kennel.   Be it noticed, incidentally, how Hopkins inscaped fallen man and expressed this inscape by means of hypallage.   Hopkins did not write 'Wring thy rebel malicious man', but 'Wring thy rebel, man's malice' (cf. Chapter 4, p. 123).

Another example taken from the *Deutschland*:

> . . . is the *shipwrack* then a harvest, does tempest carry the grain for thee?
>
> st. 31

Why 'shipwrack', and why not 'shipwreck'?   To me it is as if Hopkins meant a kind of highest common factor of 'shipwreck' and 'rack'. The word as it stands now unmistakably calls up the shipwreck, but as unmistakable is the suggestion that those wrecked were 'racked' with pain and sufferings, having to face an untimely death in the waves.

Another instance from the *Deutschland*, st. 23:

> and these thy daughters
> And five-livèd and leavèd favour and pride,
> Are sisterly *sealed* in wild waters, . . .

Hopkins has called the number five 'the finding and sake of suffering Christ' (st. 22) and in the line previous to the ones just quoted it is the seal of St. Francis's 'seraph arrival'.   Hence these *five* Franciscan sisters have received the impress of suffering Christ, have been sisterly 'sealed'.   But at the same time, who can miss the picture of the wild waters closing over these sisters and thus 'sealing' their common grave? And again from the *Deutschland*, st. 3:

> The frown of his face
> Before me, the hurtle of hell
> Behind, where, where was a, where was a place?
> I *whirled out* wings that spell. . . .

And while we read these lines and feel the poet's terror, we see him wildly rise out of this *world* 'to flash from the flame to the flame then'.

As my last instance I quote the opening lines of *Spelt from Sibyl's Leaves (Poems* 32):

> Earnest, earthless, equal, attuneable, vaulty, voluminous, . . . stupendous
> Evening strains to be time's vast, womb-of-all, home-of-all, hearse-of-all
>   night.
> Her fond yellow hornlight wound to the west, her wild hollow hoarlight
>   hung to the height
> Waste; . . .

By its exquisite choice of vowelling this couplet gives a very fine impression of how the coming darkness gradually spreads smoothly and soothingly over the evening scene; by and by the blackness of the night will obliterate everything: all things will be made *even*, level, and smooth, by the *evening*.   In proof that Hopkins was aware of this suggestiveness of the   word 'evening', I would adduce the   choice of 'equal' in the first line.   But there is music in these lines.   Is it because we do not only see the moon setting, but hear her go down on the tones of the 'horn' that is 'wound'?   How well the choice of 'strains' fits here! And this wonderful strain of music explains the use of 'attuneable' as well.

One of the defects that Bridges detected in the poetry of his friend was, as I have said before, the irrelevant suggestion of homophones. At one time he grows so impatient with them that he throws them out; Hopkins had written:

> Nine months she then, nay years, nine years she long
> Within her wears, bears, cares and *combs* the same: *Poems* 51

Bridges substitutes 'moulds' for 'combs','having no doubt that G. M. H. would have made some such alteration' (*Poems* p. 119). It is very much to be doubted whether Hopkins would have made this flat alteration; in fact he appears to have put 'combs' in very intentionally, for an earlier draft of the poem reads:

> Nine months it may be then or nine years long
> She wears within, she bears and cares the same,

which is good enough, though we prefer the alteration. Now the word 'combs' is queer in the context, certainly when we first stumble upon it. F. R. Leavis writes on this point; he would not have the word changed for 'moulds' or for any other word; he is not worried about its meaning so much, but suggests that the term *prolepsis* 'suitably invoked, would suffice to settle any qualms'.[21] This solution does not entirely satisfy me. I have already had occasion to point out that it is disastrous if in Hopkins's poetry we sunder the image from that which it is meant to illustrate; image and object were not represented by two parallel strings of thought, each with an existence untouched by the other. The image and the object illustrated by the image became fused; consequently in the above lines, where the poet is compared to a mother, we should not make the mistake of keeping the fundamental idea rigidly separated from the illustration. In working out the image, how the mother surrounds the child in her womb with loving care, the poet never lost sight of the 'mind, a mother of immortal song'. With these preliminary remarks, I interpret 'combs' as follows; it first calls up, not the mother combing her child, but the poet 'combing' his immortal song; he goes through it with the comb, to put it very bluntly and very prosaically—but that is what is meant. During those long years of waiting, the poet is ever rearranging the lines, is ever rejecting what is imperfect, is ever endeavouring to find the perfect expression. This makes excellent sense. But there is more: 'combs' calls up the honeycomb: the poetic mind 'wears, bears, cares' the immortal song, and most lovingly shelters and fosters it: but this is a weak circumscription: the mind 'combs' her immortal song, till it can fly forth, and—here I take over an image of Bridges'—display its 'plumage of far wonder and heavenward flight' (*Poems*, Introductory Sonnet by Bridges).[22]

I have given many examples, though not all of them. Often I feel that I am treading slippery ground, because the things which I have so far pointed out cannot be strictly proved.   At times they sound incredible and a sense of diffidence creeps over me: am I not interpreting the text of Hopkins's poetry in a way that would have startled the poet himself?   Yet the mass of instances given, the example set by Hopkins himself in explaining Homer, and the theory of inscape applied to words, are reassuring; besides, if reading Hopkins in the way I have done increases the beauty of his poetry, who is to forbid doing so?   I am quite willing to run the risk of reading too much in him, if thereby he gains so much in beauty and significance.

The reader may be dismayed, or, if he has surrendered to this wonderful practice of Hopkins, he may be glad, to hear that I have not yet exhausted this subject, that I am going even further.   But I want to feel solid ground before making some remarks about a most precarious aspect of it: how far can any word call up other words like it in sound, and how far do these words, thus suggested, affect the meaning of the line?   I return then once again to Hopkins's notes on Homer.

Μώνυχας (*with single, i.e. uncloven, hoof*) is a common enough epithet for horses; it occurs in *Iliad*, Bk. V, lines 236 and 581; Hopkins comments as follows: l. 236: 'there is a thought like "the poor dumb beasts" after their master's death and no doubt a suggestion in *μών-υχας* of *μόνος*'; l. 581: 'here too I think there is a play on *μόνος*: they were left masterless.'   It also occurs in line 321 and here Hopkins remarks that in it 'there may be a suggestion of a lonely spot'. How far can *μώνυχας* suggest *μόνος*?   But of far greater interest it is that, once this possibility of suggestive power has been pointed out, *μόνος* undoubtedly does add some nuance to the meaning of *μώνυχας*. Another instance comes from the *Iliad*, Bk. V, 256:

$$\ldots \ \tau\varrho\varepsilon\tilde{\iota}\nu \ \mu' \ o\dot{\upsilon}\varkappa \ \dot{\varepsilon}\tilde{\alpha} \ \Pi\alpha\lambda\lambda\grave{\alpha}\varsigma \ \ 'A\theta\acute{\eta}\nu\eta.$$

Here Hopkins asks himself: 'is there a suggestion of *πάλλειν*?', which can have the same meaning as *τρεῖν*.   Indeed, can and does 'Pallas' suggest the verb *πάλλειν* and was this word 'Pallas' instinctively chosen as very apposite to the whole line, even though the poet did not perhaps fully realize why it was that it so well fitted the contents? But Hopkins goes even further: in the simile of the mountain stream destroying bridges and dykes, to which I referred in the second chapter, there occur these lines (V, 87–8):

$$\Theta\tilde{\upsilon}\nu\varepsilon \ \gamma\grave{\alpha}\varrho \ \mathring{\alpha}\mu \ \pi\varepsilon\delta\acute{\iota}o\nu \ \pi o\tau\alpha\mu\tilde{\omega} \ \pi\lambda\acute{\eta}\theta o\nu\tau\iota \ \dot{\varepsilon}o\iota\varkappa\grave{\omega}\varsigma$$
$$\chi\varepsilon\iota\mu\acute{\alpha}\varrho\varrho\omega, \ \mathring{o}\varsigma \ \tau' \ \mathring{\omega}\varkappa\alpha \ \varrho\acute{\varepsilon}\omega\nu \ \dot{\varepsilon}\varkappa\acute{\varepsilon}\delta\alpha\sigma\sigma\varepsilon \ \gamma\varepsilon\varphi\acute{\upsilon}\varrho\alpha\varsigma.$$

'For he stormed across the plain like a winter torrent at the full, that in swift course scattereth the causeys.'

Hopkins commentary runs: '*ἐκέδασσε* makes one suspect things like *σκάμανδρος*'. Hopkins is very cautious here, but he has the courage to make this striking remark.

Turning now to Hopkins's own poetry I first take two instances which are safe enough. In the closing stanza of the *Deutschland* Hopkins writes:

> Dame, at our door
> Drowned, and among our shoals,
> Remember us in the roads, the heaven-haven of the Reward:
> *Our King back, oh, upon English souls!*

Why, we ask, 'upon' English souls, and why not 'in'?; and I answer: because the expression running through Hopkins's mind is: 'Our king back *upon* English *soil*'. It is as if at the very last moment Hopkins changed 'soil' to 'souls'.

> In a flash, at a trumpet crash,
> I am all at once what Christ is, since he was what I am, and
> This *Jack, joke, poor potsherd*, patch, matchwood, immortal diamond,
> Is immortal diamond. *Poems* 48

Here again we can see the poet at work: 'Jack' suggested through assonance 'joke', but his mind searching for words expressive of man's abject state combined 'joke' and 'Job', the type of man in deepest misery. But Job irresistibly called up the potsherd with which he scraped his wounds and thus the poet comes to identify himself with this worthless piece of pottery.

These two examples are 'solid ground' enough in so far as the word suggested is expressed: namely 'souls' in the first quotation and 'potsherd' in the second. But more doubtful are from their nature those examples where the word suggested is not expressed at all. Let us go warily and pick out the safer instances first:

> Again, look overhead
> How air is azurèd;
> O how! nay do but stand
> Where you can lift your hand
> Skywards: rich, rich it *laps*
> Round the four fingergaps. *Poems* 37, l. 77

Indeed, 'laps' in the sense of 'surrounds' well fits the context; but the swift and lively rhythm of the lines makes me expect 'leaps', a word also suggested by the line 'lift your hand skywards'. The suggested

form 'leaps' markedly influenced the structure of the phrase. If 'laps'
is used intransitively, it hardly gives sense; if we take 'laps round'
together and thus have a transitive verb in the sentence, we get an
ugly break in the rhythm of these otherwise smoothly running lines
and the rhyme 'laps—gaps' becomes a false rhyme in so far as 'laps' is
now no longer strongly stressed: in 'laps round' the heavy stress falls
on 'round'. If we make 'leaps' coincide with 'laps', sense, rhyme,
and rhythm gain by it.

The following instance is taken from the *Eurydice*. The poet has
described how the captain refused to leave the ship; he then comments
as follows:

> It is even seen, time's something server,
> In mankind's medley a duty-swerver,
>   At downright 'No or yes?'
> Doffs all, *drives* full for righteousness.   st. 14

There is a very evident and obvious suggestion of 'dives' here; 'doffs'
by assonance is closely associated with 'dives'. Moreover, the captain
going down of his free will with the ship is compared to a swimmer
about to take the plunge: he doffs everything as the immediate preparation for the dive. The suggestive force is here so strong that it was
only after many readings that I found that I had been myself distorting
the text: I had always read 'dives'. Why then, we may ask, did
Hopkins write 'drives' instead of 'dives'? It is not unlikely that
Hopkins was himself aware that 'dives' was so obviously demanded by
the sense and by the music of the line that he thought it entirely superfluous to write it down; 'drives' was sufficiently like 'dives' to call up
the latter word, and besides 'drives' better expressed that the captain
had quite made up his mind to do the right thing. His resolution
might have been coloured with a certain inevitable fatality from which
there was no escape, if the poet had written 'dives'.

Another instance from the same poem:

> No Atlantic squall overwrought her
> Or *rearing* billow of the Biscay water: st. 5

This is a case which I feel inclined to gloss in a way so often used by
Hopkins in his annotations of Homer: 'Excellent; rearing suggests
roaring'. Similarly this line from the *Deutschland*, st. 13:

> Into the snows she sweeps,
> *Hurling* the *haven* behind,
> The Deutschland, on Sunday . . .

Does 'haven' call up 'heaven'? The choice of the brusque 'hurling' does, to my mind, suggest that the proud ship undaunted by the snow-storm was not only leaving the haven, but also the one place where she could be safe under such trying circumstances. It is certainly interesting to note that the combination 'heaven—haven' occurs in the final stanza of the *Deutschland.*

There can be no doubt that Hopkins was aware of the combination 'furls—furrows' in the description of Harry Ploughman steering his plough through a ploughed field (*Poems* 43). And similarly in the lines which will be quoted immediately, taken from the Eurydice, 'rivelling' is so like 'revelling' and the latter completes the picture of the storms so cruelly that this likeness cannot have escaped the poet.

Let me now add an example which at first sight may appear to be too far-fetched to be quite credible, but of which Hopkins may yet have been aware. It occurs in the *Eurydice*, st. 17. The sailor-boy 'takes to the seas and snows as sheer down the ship goes'; he has managed to get hold of a life-belt and now 'he gasps and gazes everywhere', if rescue is near at hand:

> But his eye no cliff, no coast or
> *Mark* makes in the rivelling snowstorm.

Is there a suggestion of 'ark'? or perhaps better, was there such a suggestion contained in the lines for the sensitive ear of Hopkins? Here many a reader will shrug his shoulders and wonder what will be the end of this method of interpretation. And yet, let us look at it more closely. I grant that normally 'mark' does not call up 'ark'; but if we observe that Hopkins could separate the 'm' from 'mark' and use it as the final element of his ryhme-group 'st-or-m', this example may grow less incredible and admittedly possible. Those who remain stubborn and refuse to give it any credit, I advise to remember that Pallas called up πάλλειν for Hopkins. And so there is a mournful intimation of *soft*-ringing bells and *soft*-beating drums in:

> And flockbell*s* *off* *t*he aerial
> Downs' forefalls beat to the burial.   *Eurydice* st. 2

In *The Lantern out of Doors* occur the lines:

> They rain against our much-thick and marsh air
> Rich beams, till death or distance *buys* them quite.   *Poems* 10

The meaning is clear; any obscurity is dispelled by the line following: 'Death or distance soon consumes them . . .', but whereas 'consumes' is plain enough, I find it hard to understand how Hopkins could ever choose the word 'buys'. If this word is taken in its normal sense, it must be granted that the image of death or distance buying up men is very curious and queer.   If the line is intended to convey the idea that men are no longer visible because they have either died or otherwise gone from our sight, it is indeed very strange to express this form of disappearance by the image of buying; what is bought does not disappear.   In spite of Bridges's irrelevant suggestions of homophones, I prefer to spell the verb *by's* or *byes* and take it as the adverb made into a verb; this makes sense, and even more than that, I think that this certainly enhances the beauty of the line.   Even if this slight change accounts for the sound-complex, it does not account for the queer spelling; and I can see no entirely satisfactory way of explaining it, unless he thought the image of buying rather effective.   I believe it is possible that 'buys' is a kind of contracted form: death suggests 'bury' and distance may well call up 'hide'; is 'buys' a kind of highest common factor of these two?

It is slippery ground we are standing on now; but Hopkins did not much mind it, so why should we not venture to tread it carefully? Here is another instance:

> Hard as hurdle arms, with a broth of goldish flue
> Breathed round; . . .   *Poems* 43

thus runs the description of the ploughman 'at stress', with tucked-up sleeves, his sinewy strong arms ready to steer the plough through the clods of heavy earth.   To me these lines always depict the hairy arms with the blue veins standing out; but apparently not a word is spoken of blue veins.   One day I discovered that I had been unconsciously mixing the following versions:
'with a broth of goldish flue'—and this is Hopkins's version
'with a froth of goldish blue'—which was my own, but which may have been in Hopkins's mind as well.   It is impossible to prove such point, but the ἐκέδασσε—σκάμανδρος case makes me feel that possibly I am not far out.

In the *Deutschland*, stanza 9, God is called 'fondler of heart thou hast wrung'.   I cannot help seeing God wringing the stubborn heart and *founding* it in the furnace.   Again, in stanza 31 God's care is said to be 'of a feathery delicacy'; can we miss here the *fatherly* delicacy of the Heavenly Father?

One more instance: why does 'behaviour' so strikingly depict the cloudscape in *Poems* 14?   We see the silk-sack clouds *heave* along the *bays* in the heavens.   Did we unconsciously interchange the vowels of 'behaviour'?

The following lines are, in my opinion, among the most dramatic and most pathetic in Hopkins's poetry:

> I wake and feel the fell of dark, not day.
> What hours, O what black hours we have spent
> This night! what sights you, heart, saw; ways you went!
> And more must, in yet longer light's delay.   *Poems* 45

These lines are truly terrible, and the terror I cannot explain by reference to the contents only; there is something very strident and painful in them, which I have never met with in any other of the terrible sonnets. I found out the secret when I caught myself reading:

> And more must, in yet longer *day's delight.*

It was as if day rejoiced at darkness covering the poet.[23]

Hopkins once wrote to Patmore that 'on these mutual bearings of words in a passage the beauty of diction depends' (III. 165); he did not work out how far words could influence each other. It is a subject about which it will always be very hard to make remarks that will carry conviction with all. I have apparently strayed very far from 'current language' in adducing these instances of word-consciousness; but Hopkins has added 'heightened, to any degree heightened and most unlike itself', and I have tried to show to what this logically led. In spite of some very striking, and sometimes very startling, examples, I believe that I have done little more than give a glimpse of how Hopkins created beauty through a most apt use of words. There is much left to be detected, and only repeated and most attentive readings, demanding intense concentration on every aspect of the poet's highly-wrought language, will gradually yield the full crop of poetic beauty. But I hope that I have successfully shown the way. Purposely I have refrained from applying the standards of Hopkins to his own work as rigidly as he himself applied them to Homer; but the instances given will convince most readers that Hopkins's poetry can successfully stand the closest scrutiny. The deeper we enter into the meaning of the lines, the more eagerly we allow the music of his verse to grow upon us, the more we succeed in catching the flow of his verse, in a word, the more truly we 'inscape' his poetry, the greater our reward and the more intense our joy in reading his poems. There is no need to fear that we shall exhaust the treasures in his poetry: if the best test of the greatness and excellence of a poet lies in increased pleasure in repeated readings, Hopkins triumphantly passes this test.

NOTES

INTRODUCTION

1. (p. xi) *New Bearings in English Poetry*, p. 159.   In a similar strain the critic of *The Times Literary Supplement* writes: 'Not until . . . 1918 did the world know that the second half of the nineteenth century had possessed another major poet whose achievement in bulk and quality can perhaps best be compared with Matthew Arnold's' (*T.L.S.*, 25 Dec. 1930, p. 1099).
2. (p. xi) Plowman, M., *Adelphi*, vol. ix, p. 360.
3. (p. xi) *London Mercury*, vol. xxxviii, p. 217.
4. (p. xi) O'Neill, G., *Essays on Poetry*, p. 117.
5. (p. xi) *Aspects of Literature*, p. 60.
6. (p. xii) Pryce-Jones, *London Mercury*, vol. xxiv, pp. 45–6, 48.
7. (p. xii) *Form in Modern Poetry*, p. 45.
8. (p. xii) *English Critical Essays: Twentieth Century*, p. 374.
9. (p. xii) op. cit., p. 193.
10. (p. xiii) *Aspects of Modern Poetry*, p. 53.
11. (p. xiii) loc. cit., p. 361.
12. (p. xiii) *Modern Poetry. A personal Essay*, p. 125.
13. (p. xiii) Roberts, M., Introduction to *The Faber Book of Modern Verse*, p. 3.
14. (p. xiv) ibid., p. 4.   MacNeice, op. cit., p. 125.
15. (p. xvi) op. cit., p. 52.
16. (p. xvi) Introduction to the second edition of *Poems*, p. xiv.
17. (p. xvii) Phare, E., *The Poetry of G. M. Hopkins*, pp. 47, 19; Deutsch, B., *This Modern Poetry*, p. 197.   W. J. Turner writes: 'It is evident that Hopkins resembled Keats more than any other English poet both in his strength and weakness' (*The Spectator*, 14 July 1944, p. 33), and Dr. Gardner sides with Miss Phare as far as likeness with Worsdworth is concerned: 'But altogether, he stands in a much closer relationship to Wordsworth, both in his choice of subjects and in his consistently metaphysical apprehension of natural phenomena' (op. cit., vol. I, p. 156).
18. (p. xvii) *After Strange Gods*, p. 48
19. (p. xvii) W. de la Mare in his Introduction to the *Poems* by Eileen Duggan, p. 8. O. Burdett, *Nineteenth Century and After*, vol. 117, p. 234.
20. (p. xvii) Phare, op. cit. pp. 13 ff.; B. Ifor Evans, *English Poetry in the Later Nineteenth Century*, p. 218.
21. (p. xvii) Bridges first launched this comparison, but Hopkins repudiated it (I. 154–5).   Cf. also: Fletcher, *American Review*, Vol. VI, No. 3, p. 339; *New Verse*, No. 14, p. 18; P. Henderson, *The Poet and Society*, pp. 103 ff.   This essay by Mr. Henderson deals at great length with the likeness between Whitman and Hopkins.   It has been called 'excellent' by the reviewer of *The Times Literary Supplement* (8 July 1939), though to my mind it is one of the worst that have so far appeared.   The reader should compare the article with the second chapter of this book and decide for himself whether the analysis of Mr. Henderson is borne out by facts.

22. (p. xvii) Fletcher, loc. cit.

23. (p. xvii) Terence Heywood, *English*, vol. III, No. 13, pp. 16–24; cf. Barker Fairley, *London Mercury*, vol. XXXII, pp. 128 ff.

24. (p. xvii) Gweneth Lilly, *The Modern Language Review*, vol. 38, pp. 192–205.

25. (p. xvii) Stanford, W. B., *Studies*, vol. XXX, pp. 359–68.

CHAPTER 1

1. (p. 1) G. W. Stonier in his essay on G. M. Hopkins in *Gog Magog* writes: 'The landscape expressed for him God's presence: *inscape* or *instress* (words he is fond of using) is not merely the artist's apprehension of vital form, but of divine shape. Wherever he can find *inscape*—in the eternal yet ever-changing forms of tree, river, and cloud—he finds God' (page 55). The inaccuracy of these descriptions of inscape and instress and especially of their identification will become evident in the course of my explanation of these terms. Miss E. E. Phare in her *G. M. Hopkins: A Survey and Commentary* has this passage: 'The oddness of Hopkins, then, is connected with his theory of "inscape", a word which he coined himself to describe the pattern which makes every fragment of creation, every "bead of being", to use his own phrase, individual and unique' (p. 81). I have no serious fault to find with this description of inscape; it should be pointed out, however, that to explain the oddness of Hopkins by his theory of inscape is, indeed, possible, but then the theory should be worked out to its logical conclusions and be applied to his writing poetry. This point has been overlooked by Miss Phare: a theory of inscape which only concerns the peculiar attitude of Hopkins towards created reality does account for some oddities, as for instance his many compound words, but by no means for all of them.

In an article on the poetry of Hopkins in the *New Review*, Vol. VII, p. 4, there occurs this passage: 'He used words with new connotations, he even invented words when the ordinary vocabulary failed him: "sake" referred to the unique attribute of a thing that struck an observer, "instress" to the design cohering the particulars of a scene, and "inscape" to the core of creative purposeness underlying the design.' I do not see how these definitions can possibly fit the instances I have given later in this chapter.

Dr. Pick and Dr. Gardner have paid more attention to the exact meaning of 'inscape' and 'instress'. The former writes: ' . . . usually he employs the word (viz. inscape) to indicate the essential individuality and particularity or "selfhood" of a thing working itself out and expressing itself in design and pattern' (op. cit., p. 33). And Dr. Gardner rightly maintains that inscape is more than a delightful sensory impression; he then continues: ' . . . it was an insight, by Divine grace, into the ultimate reality—seeing the "pattern, air, melody" in things from, as it were, God's side' (op. cit., p. 27). In the main I agree with Dr. Pick as is clear from my own exposition. Dr. Gardner's explanation of an *insight*, something subjective therefore, I cannot accept.

2. (p. 1) Euphony is a subject which will be passingly dealt with in the third and in the final chapter.

3. (p. 2) *Scape* in the sense of the scholastic *species* occurs in the following instances:

After death the soul is left to its own resources, with only the scapes and *species* of its past life. (Unpublished retreat notes, Sept. 1883.)

Our action leaves in our mind scapes or species, the extreme intention or instressing of which would be painful and the pain would be that of fire. (Unpublished annotations to the *Spiritual Exercises* of St. Ignatius.)

Cf. Several strong thrills of light followed the flash but a grey smother of darkness blotted the eyes if they had seen the fork, also dull furry thickened scapes of it were left in them (*N.* 178).

It (the meteor) was a firework . . . But its seeming to pass the crest of Pendle is curious. It may be because the eye taking up the wellmarked motion and forestalling it carries the bright scape of the present and past motion . . . on to a part of a field where the motion itself has not or will not come (*N.* 176).

Scape also occurs in the sense of 'pattern', in which the other aspect of this suffix in 'landscape' comes more to the fore: 'at sunset in the same quarter of the sky I saw, as far as I could remember it, almost the very same scape, the same colour and so on . . .' (*N.* 136).

4. (p. 3) "Scaping" in this sense is also found in these quotations:

. . . my eye was caught by the scaping of the leaves that grow in allies and avenues. . . . They fall from the two sides of the branch or spray in two marked planes which meet at a right angle or more (*N.* 124).

. . . by watching hard the banks began to sail upstream, the scaping unfolded (*N.* 135).

The pond, I suppose from over pressure when it was less firm, was mapped with a puzzle of very slight clefts branched with little sprigs : the pieces were odd-shaped and sized—though a square angular scaping could be just made out in the outline . . . (*N.* 137).

I looked long up at it (cloud) till the tall height and the beauty of the scaping—regularly curled knots springing if I remember from fine stems, like foliation in wood or stone— had strongly grown on me (*N.* 140).

5. (p. 4) Describing Michelangelo's 'Entombment' Hopkins makes mention of his masterly 'inscape of drapery' (*N.* 188). In his essay on 'Poetry and Verse' he speaks of the inscape of speech and the inscape of verse (*N.* 249). Here 'inscape' does not refer to what is distinctive of an individual but of what is distinctive of the species. This use of 'inscape' need not cause any difficulty: it is a logical extension of its use. Hopkins has himself pointed out how very often a species struck him more as a self than the individuals composing the species: ' . . . I am inclined to believe . . . that the specific form, the form of the whole species, is nearer being a true Self than the individual' (*N.* 316). Hence the apparent contradiction occurring (*N.* 322), where Hopkins contrasts 'natures or essences or inscapes' with the 'selves, supposits, hypostases', is to be explained in the light of what goes immediately before where he says that the self not overlaid with a nature is a zero; 'inscape' is consequently here, as in the passages above, employed with reference to what is distinctive of the specific essence.

6. (p. 6) 'God's utterance of Himself in Himself is God the Word, outside Himself is this world. This world then is word, expression, news of God. Therefore its end, its purpose, its purport, its meaning and its life and work is to name and praise him.' (From his unpublished retreat notes: dated 17 August 1882.)

7. (p. 7) The close relationship between inscape, beauty and the Creator has been commented on by many critics, often in a learned terminology and with seemingly profound investigations into its source. Cf., for example, Mr. Kliger's article: ' "God's Plenitude" in the Poetry of G. M. Hopkins', *Modern*

Language Notes, Vol. LIX, No. 6.   Dr. Gardner writes: 'It would have been possible for Hopkins to arrive at this metaphysical fusion of God the Word and nature without the aid of specific external suggestion; though that suggestion might have come from a number of very early sources, such as the more spiritual forms of pantheism.   It is most probable, however, that a direct stimulus came from the Schoolman, Scotus, . . .' (op. cit., p. 21).

To anyone who is at home in the *Spiritual Exercises* of St. Ignatius and has *undergone* the 'Contemplatio ad amorem spiritualem obtinendum' it must be clear that here, more than anywhere else, is to be found the source of the spiritual appreciation of beauty in nature.   The reference to St. Matthew vi. 27–30 will not be out of place here.

8. (p. 10) I do not hold that the absence of the article in the poems of Hopkins should always be explained by impersonation, or that the rhythm of the line had no influence upon its insertion or omission.   But one should never be too hasty in explaining them as convenient means to improve the rhythm.   Thus where Hopkins calls Christ 'hero of Calvary' (*Deutschland* st. 8), the omission has the effect of making this epithet a kind of title.   Similarly I should like to draw the reader's attention to the omission in the following three lines: 'Pitched past pitch of grief', 'pining till time when . . . some Fatal four disorders . . . contended', 'It dates from day Of his going in Galilee' (taken from *Poems* 41, 29 and *Deutschland* st. 7, respectively).   I am inclined to believe that Hopkins uses the words *pitch*, *time* and *day* as if they were proper names indicating place and date.

9. (p. 12) In his diary we likewise come across passages in which this perception of things as active is evident.   A few typical instances follow:

. . . endless ranges of part-vertical dancing cloud . . .
a slender race of fine flue cloud . . . (*N.* 110).
. . . the moon was roughing the lake with silver and dinting and tooling it with sparkling holes (*N.* 114).
. . . fine afternoon with snow-white flying scarf-ends in the clouds (*N.* 115).
I saw the phenomenon of the sheepflock . . .   It ran like the water-packets on a leaf— that collectively, but a number of globules so filmed over that they would not flush together is the exacter comparison: at a gap in the hedge they were huddled and shaking open as they passed outwards they behaved as the drops would do (or a handful of shot) in reaching the brow of a rising and running over (*N.* 118).
The brow was crowned with that burning *clear* or silver light which surrounds the sun, then the sun itself leapt out with long bright spits of beams (*N.* 162).

'Hopkins's faith in the ultimate identification of Christ with perfect beauty and ideal activity seems to have occasioned in the poet, and also in nature, an inspired restlessness or impetuosity—a gust to hurl and be hurled, as if God were participating with his creatures in some jubilant cosmic sports or circus', thus writes Dr. Gardner (op. cit. p. 195).   For the refutation of this explanation of Hopkins's peculiar view of reality I refer the reader to the concluding remarks of Note 7.

10. (p. 13):

It is plain it (*sc.* the mind) might have more perfection, more being.   Nevertheless the being it has got has a great perfection, a great stress . . .' (*N.* 312).
Chance applies only to things possible; what must be does not come by chance and what cannot be by no chance comes.   Chance then is the ἐνέργεια, the stress, of the intrinsic possibility which things have (*N.* 310).

11. (p. 14) This meaning of *to instress* is further illustrated by the passages printed above (page 175) where I was dealing with the meaning of *scape*.

12. (p. 18) And this solemn and sonorous line has been called bombastic (*Studies,* vol. xxx, p. 362).

13. (p. 19) That 'bugle' does not refer to the plant, or at least does not refer solely to it (see final chapter) is proved by the reading of this line in the first draft of the poem, where Hopkins wrote 'bugled-blue'.

14. (p. 19) Dr. Gardner draws his reader's attention to something similar: 'wind-beat whitebeam, airy abeles set on a flare' (*Poems* 8). 'An association of *wind* and *fire* is recurrent in this poet's work ("white-fiery . . . snow", "a blown beacon", "lanced fire . . . black Boreas") and is probably due to Biblical influence —the whirlwind and fire of Ezekiel (I. iv), the rushing wind and tongues of flame in the Pentecostal visitation (Acts II. ii.–iii.)' (op. cit. p. 195). The examples are to my mind not convincing; their explanation even less.

15. (p. 22) To my knowledge two articles have so far appeared on the influence of Scotus on Hopkins: C. Devlin, S.J.: *New Verse,* April 1935, and W. H. Gardner: *Scrutiny,* 1936, pp. 61–70. Dr. Pick and Dr. Gardner both deal with Scotist influence at some length and rightly see in it an important factor in Hopkins's development.

Works consulted on the philosophy of Scotus:

C. R. S. Harris : *Duns Scotus.* 2 vols. Oxford, 1927.
R. Seeberg : *Die Theologie des Johannes Duns Scotus.* Leipzig, 1900.
F. Ueberweg : *Grundriss der Geschichte der Philosophie der patristischen und scholastischen Zeit.* Zweite Teil. Berlin, 1915. (pp. 571–85).

16. (p. 27) The passage referred to occurs among the unpublished notes on the *Spiritual Exercises* and reads as follows:

'The fall from heaven of the rebel angels was for them what death is for man. As in man all that energy or instress with which the soul animates and otherwise acts in the body is by death thrown back upon the soul itself: so in them was that greater stock of activity with which they act, intellectually and otherwise, throughout their own world . . . (there follow some illegible lines). This throwing back or confinement of their energy is a dreadful constraint or imprisonment, and as intellectual activity is spoken of under the figure of sight, it will in this case be an imprisonment in darkness, a being in the dark. But this constraint or blindness will be most painful when it is the main stress and energy of the whole being which is thus baulked. This is its strain towards God . . .'

And on the following page, having explained how after the fall the devils are ever confronted by the scape of the 'act which blotted out God and put darkness in the place of light', he thus describes a fallen angel left to himself entirely: 'against these acts of its own lost spirit dashes itself like a caged beast and is in prison, violently instresses them and burns, stares into them and is the deepest darkened'.

CHAPTER 2

1. (p. 29) To Bridges he once wrote: 'Perhaps you are so barbarous as not to admire Thomas Hardy—as you do not Stevenson; both, I must maintain, men of pure and direct genius' (I. 251).

2. (p. 30) Hopkins clearly distinguished obscurity from want of clarity at first

sight (I. 54). 'Plainly if it is possible to express a subtle and recondite thought on a subtle and recondite subject in a subtle and recondite way and with great felicity and perfection, in the end, something must be sacrificed, with so trying a task, in the process, and this may be the being at once, nay perhaps even the being without explanation at all, intelligible' (I. 266).

3. (p. 30) Patmore wrote to Hopkins as follows: 'Much meditating on the effect which my MS. "Sponsa Dei" had upon you, when you read it while staying here, I concluded that I would not take the responsibility of being the first to expound the truths therein contained: so, on Xmas Day, I committed the work to the flames without reserve of a single paragraph' (III. 236–7). Hopkins replied: 'Your news was that you had burnt the book called *Sponsa Dei*, and that on reflection upon remarks of mine. I wish I had been more guarded in making them. . . . My objections were not final, they were but considerations . . . even if they were valid, still if you had kept to yr. custom of consulting your director, as you said you should, the book might have appeared with no change or with slight ones' (III. 237). Patmore then put Hopkins at ease by telling him that he did not burn *Sponsa Dei* altogether without the further consultation mentioned (III. 242).

4. (p. 32) Hopkins here identifies *inscape* with beauty of style. The extension of the meaning of inscape is not surprising. A poet's inscape reveals itself in his style and if the true poet succeeds in expressing his inscape, there will necessarily be an exquisite beauty of style.

The quotation here in question proves that one should not hold rigidly to inscape as being synonymous with design or pattern. I have spoken about this point in the first chapter. In his essay on *The Wreck of the Deutschland* (*Essays and Studies*, 1935, pp. 124–52) W. H. Gardner had been led astray to such an extent that he omits the notion of inscape altogether and fastens on that of design and pattern, so that to him Hopkins's aim consisted in the realization of a 'seemingly precious yet entirely organic system of tone-values' (loc. cit. 129). This involves a serious misunderstanding of Hopkins's attitude towards the function of poetry.

5. (p. 32) Patmore's precise objection to the genius of Barnes cannot be given; the letter containing it has been lost (cf. III. 220).

6. (p. 33) It is astonishing how W. J. Turner could write: 'His work has no philosophical or intellectual content; it is purely physical and verbal' (*The Spectator*, loc. cit., p. 32).

7. (p. 33) Cf. II. 8, I. 39, I. 96. Among the Greek tragedians Hopkins's favourite was Aeschylus: 'Besides the swell and pomp of words for which he is famous there is in him a touching consideration and manly tenderness; also an earnestness of spirit . . .' (I. 256).

8. (p. 34) Cf. also I. 89, II. 117, II. 37.

9. (p. 34) With reference to Bridges cf. I. 216, II. 147, I. 93, 97; with reference to Dixon: I. 280, II. 73, II. 55.

10. (p. 35) In many places Hopkins criticizes Patmore for his frigidity: see I. 21, III. 155, 200, 173 and 174.

11. (p. 40) In a letter to Bridges dated 30 September 1884 he adds: 'I believe I shd. not disavow but retouch "Elected silence" and St. Dorothy' (I. 198).

12. (p. 41) Thus he wrote once to Bridges: ' . . . for I find myself that when I am tired things of mine sound strange, forced, and without idiom which had

pleased me well enough in the fresh heat of composition. But then the weaker state is the less competent and really critical' (I. 137). Cf. his remarks about *Eurydice*, I. 50, and about *Harry Ploughman*, I. 263.

13. (p. 42) Expressions like 'towering pillow clouds . . . in fine snowy tufts' (*N.* 136), 'lovely damasking [of clouds] in the sky' (*N.* 143, also 181, 145, &c.), 'pied skies' (*N.* 140, 179), 'tossed clouds' (*N.* 181), 'flinty waves' (*N.* 181), 'cobbled foam' (*N.* 180), 'mealy white' (*N.* 144), his predilection for words as dapple, pied, to rinse, shire, strain, lash and so on; all this recalls many a passage in his poems. Cf. Gardner: op. cit. pp. 164–5.

14. (p. 44) Bridges has placed among the poems of this group *Spelt from Sibyl's Leaves* (*Poems* 32), in which Hopkins refers to the night that comes over him. In a note Bridges confesses that the date of this poem is unrecorded (*Poems* p. 111). Undoubtedly the poem is of later date: it was sent to Bridges on 26 November 1886 with the remark that he (Hopkins) had 'at last' completed it. But he cannot have begun it much earlier, because the first drafts of the poem occur in his notebooks of the Dublin lectures, in company with a rough copy of his notice of Dixon written for Arnold's *Manual*; this notice Hopkins wrote in the latter half of 1884 (I. 198).

15. (p. 45) Cf., for example, W. G. Hanson, *The London Quarterly and Holborn Review*, 1944, pp. 64 ff.; the anonymous reviewer of Dr. Pick's book in *The Durham University Journal*, Vol. XXXV, pp. 34–5. Dr. Pick's book deals explicitly with the subject *Poet-Priest*.

16. (p. 45) Op. cit., pp. 1–2.

17. (p. 47) Cf., for example, II. 28 and II. 93.

18. (p. 47) Max Plowman in an article on Hopkins in *Adelphi*, Vol. IX, pp. 356 ff.

19. (p. 48) With reference to this study he wrote to Baillie: 'I try, and am even meant to try, in my spare time (and if I were fresher or if it were anyone but myself there would be a good deal of spare time taking short and long together) to write some books; but I find myself so tired and harassed I fear they will never be written. The one that would interest you most is on the Greek Lyric Art or on, more narrowly, the art of the choric and lyric parts of the Gk. plays. I want it to be in two parts, one the metre, the other style. It is, I am afraid, too ambitious for me, so little of a scholar as I am . . .' (III. 105).

20. (p. 49) It should be borne in mind that Hopkins made a clear distinction between his truly inspired poetry and 'popular pieces', in which, as he says, he felt himself to fall short (I. 78). Such popular pieces are *Penmaen Pool*, *The Silver Jubilee*, *The May Magnificat*, *Morning Midday and Evening Sacrifice*, *St. Alphonsus Rodriguez*, *Inversnaid*, and *The Blessed Virgin compared to the air we breathe* (I. 179).

21. (p. 50) Cf., for example, 'You are my public and I hope to convert you' (I. 46). 'You understand of course that I desire to see you a Catholic or, if not that, a Christian or, if not that, at least a believer in the true God . . .' (I. 60). Cf. also I. 114. In one of his letters he wishes Dixon a 'speedy conversion' (II. 49).

22. (p. 51) Dr. Gardner writes on this point as follows: '. . . . we have an amazing "metaphysical" digression—a musical fantasy, like a piece of elaborate ornamentation by Mozart, on the fortuitously mystical theme of Five. We say "fortuitously" because if there had been only *four* nuns to lament, or if they had

chanced to be Benedictines instead of Franciscans, the charm could not have been wound up' (op. cit., p. 63). I disagree *toto cœlo*: if there had been four Benedictines, Hopkins would have inscaped them just the same though no one can say what depths of thought this inscape would have stirred in the poet.   To call this 'intellectual alchemy which transmutes the factitious into the fundamental' (ibid.) is not to grasp the poet's mind.

23. (p. 52) More instances of Hopkins's careful analysis of imagery are found on pages I. 243, I. 35, III. 67, III. 155, and II. 77.

24. (p. 53) The Greek text is taken from the edition of Homer by D. B. Monro (Oxford, Clarendon Press, 1906).   The translation is from *The Iliad of Homer* done into English Prose by Andrew Lang, Walter Leaf and Ernest Myers (Revised Edition, London 1929).

CHAPTER 3

1. (p. 63) Hopkins failed in the use of *do* and *did* sometimes, though rarely; it is not for the sake of emphasis that he had recourse to this auxiliary in, for example, the following lines:

. . . thrush *does* so rinse and wring the ear	*Poems* 9
. . . each grace that *does* now reach our race	*Poems* 37

Their magnifying of each its kind
With delight calls to mind
How she *did* in her stored
Magnify the Lord.   *Poems* 18

2. (p. 64) Illustrative examples are:

Heart, go and bleed at a bitterer vein for the
Comfortless unconfessed of them—
No not uncomforted: lovely-*felicitous Providence*
Finger of a tender of, O of a feathery delicacy . . .

Deutschland st. 31

Notice the solemnity expressed by the apposite use of Latin words in this gorgeous passage taken from *Poems* 48:

. . . all is in an enormous dark
Drowned.   O pity and *indignation*!   Manshape, that shone
Sheer off, disseveral, a star, death blots black out; nor mark
Is any of him at all so stark
But vastness blurs and time beats level.   Enough! the *Resurrection*,
A heart's *clarion*!   Away grief's gasping, joyless days, *dejection*.
Across my foundering deck shone
A beacon, an eternal beam.   Flesh fade, and mortal trash
Fall to the *residuary* worm;

But there is no poem of Hopkins's that is 'crammed with Latin words', always a fault in his view (I. 284).

3. (p. 64) The words occur in the following poems:
        angel-warder 23, hie 23, ghost 31, thew and brawn 43, thew 24, and *Deutschland* st. 16, lade *Eurydice* st. 3, brine id. st. 20.

As the following words so rarely occur in English, I have thought that it might serve a useful purpose to give their meaning:

to fettle: *C.O.D., dial.*: to put right.   *Poems* 29

to pash: *O.E.D., obs. exc. dial.*: to hurl or throw violently.   id. 32

to mammock: *O.E.D., now chiefly dial.*: to break, cut, or tear into fragments or shreds.   id. 42

to rivel: *C.O.D., archaic*: to wrinkle, crumple, shrivel.   *Eurydice* st. 17.

to rive: *C.O.D.*, rend, cleave, wrench away, strike asunder. (*archaic, poet.*)   *Eurydice* st. 25

to reeve: see Bridges's remarks: *Poems*, p. 100.   *Deutschland* st. 12

to wend: *C.O.D.*, direct one's way (*archaic*), go.   *Poems* 37

heft: *O.E.D., dial.* weight; *obs., fig.*: stress, pressure of circumstances.   id. 54

sillion : *O.E.D., obs.* form of selion : a portion of land . . . lying between furrows . . .   id. 12

shive: *C.O.D., obs.* slice.   id. 72

bole: *C.O.D.*, stem, trunk.   *Eurydice* st. 4.

to tuck: *O.E.D., now dial.*: to touch, to sound.   *Poems* 34

to burl: *O.E.D., obs.*: to bubble as a spring or fountain out of which water flows gently.   *Deutschland* st. 16

to buck: *O.E.D., obs. exc. dial.*: to drench, soak.   ibid.

(I have failed to find the reference to 'Dixonary'; I give it on the authority of R. L. Mégroz: *Modern English Poetry*, p. 18.)

4. (p. 67) The terms 'logical' and 'affective' language are taken from J. Vendryes: *Le Langage—introduction linguistique à l'histoire* (1921). Cf. Ch. IV, 'Le Langage affectif', pp. 162–83.

I have not adhered to the distinction as drawn and discussed by Vendryes, but have considerably simplified matters.

5. (p. 72) These terms are used with predilection by many critics: e.g. 'he *distorts* language constantly to pack his thought more densely . . .; but a careful reading . . . yields at once the poet's thought and the justification of his *tortured* syntax'. J. O'Brien in *The Bookman* 1931, p. 207.—'Against him the equally obvious *torture* of words, *torture* of meaning and rhythm . . . make no less strong an objection.' Pryce-Jones in *The London Mercury*, May 1931, p. 45.—' . . . we may forgive him his use of dialect words and invented words, but not his *maltreatment* of order and syntax . . . not such *contortions* as

Commonweal

Little I reck ho! lacklevel in, if all had bread.'

Herbert J. C. Grierson and J. C. Smith, *A Critical History of English Poetry*, p. 508.

6. (p. 72) Daiches, *New Literary Values*, p. 30.—In a similar strain F. R. Leavis

writes: 'He aimed to get out of his words as much as possible unhampered by rules of grammar, syntax and common usage' (*New Bearings in English Poetry*, p. 162). I have no serious objection to make here, provided 'unhampered' is understood correctly.

7. (p. 85) W. Empson, *Seven Types of Ambiguity*, p. 286. D. Sargent, *Four Independents*, p. 148. W. Gardner, op. cit., pp. 180 ff.

8. (p. 85) G. Murphy, *The Modern Poet*, pp. 147-9. J. Pick, op. cit., p. 71.

9. (p. 86) W. Empson, op. cit., p. 285.

10. (p. 86) Cf. *Deutschland* st. 5 and 11, *Eurydice* st. 16 and 27, *Poems* 6, 7, 9, 10, 11, 14, 15, 21, 23, 29, 34, 39 and 51.

11. (p. 87) Cf. Overdiep, *Stylistische Grammatica*.

12. (p. 88) wisest my heart: *Poems* 44; far with fonder a care: id. 36; idle a being: id. 44; wide the world's weal: id. 42.

13. (p. 90) We give some lines in which the conjunction *that* is left out:

. . . we dream we are rooted in earth	*Deutschland* st. 11
. . . it finds The appealing of the Passion is tenderer in prayer apart:	id. st. 27
From life's dawn it is drawn down, Abel is Cain's brother . . .	id. st. 20
Not today we need lament Your wealth of life is . . . spent:	*Poems* 6
. . . I yield you do come sometimes	id. 22
They say who saw . . . He was all of lovely manly mould,	*Eurydice* st. 19
. . . would say The marvellous Milk was Walsingham way. . . .	id. st. 26
Of the best we boast our sailors are.	id. st. 19
A windpuff bonnet of fawn-froth Turns and twindles over the broth Of a pool so pitchblack, fell-frowning, It rounds and rounds Despair to drowning	*Poems* 33

14. (p. 100) Gardner, op. cit., p. 124.

15. (p. 102) *like* is found in the following few lines, occurring in his non-popular poetry:

But it rides time like riding a river . . .	*Deutschland* st. 6
. . . it strikes like lightnings to hear him sing;	*Poems* 9
What the heart is! which, like carriers let fly—	id. 27
It will flame out, like shining from shook foil;	id. 7
. . . cries like dead letters sent To dearest him . . .	id. 45
. . . a May-mess, like on orchard boughs!	id. 8

16. (p. 103) Wolfgang Clemen, *Shakespeares Bilder. Ihre Entwicklung und Ihre Funktionen im Dramatischen Werk.* Bonn, 1936.

17. (p. 105) 'Dauphin is a variant of dolphin', writes Mr. Downey ('A Poem not

Understood', *Virginia Quarterly Review*, vol. 11, p. 512). Jones's *Pronouncing Dictionary* does not give this pronunciation of dolphin; I do not even believe that it is likely that to Hopkins *dauphin* in this connexion carried the suggestion of dolphin, which would only tend to confuse the imagery. But I should like to point out that *caught*, the second word of the poem, and *court* are pronounced similarly and this strong suggestion of *court* is confirmed by the choice of 'dauphin', 'reign', 'chevalier'.

18. (p. 106) From what I have said it will be clear that I cannot agree with Dr. Gardner's conception of Hopkins's *underthought*; cf. op. cit. p. 175.

CHAPTER 4

1. (p. 109) Dr. Pick annotates in a footnote: 'The small tree, *Pyrus Aria*, having large leaves with white silky hairs on the under sides' (op. cit., p. 56). I do not reject this interpretation of *whitebeam*, though I do not think it likely that Hopkins should use the word 'beam' to express the inscape of a tree which struck him not by its massiveness but by the delicate whiteness of its leaves.

2. (p. 115) The compounds occur in the following poems: gaygear 36, gay-gangs 48, wanwood 31, boldboys *Eurydice* st. 4, barebill 25, sweet-fowl 15, bluffhide 43, silk-ash 24, greenworld 18, Goldengrove 31, silk-sack 14, fineflower 61, gaylink 61, silk-beech 72; grimstones: rejected draft of the *Eurydice*; dimwoods, id. of *Poems* 8.

3. (p. 116) heaven-handling 40, neighbour-nature 20, winter world 51, wonder wedlock 28, hoarlight 32, couple-colour 13, favour-make: rejected draft 54, gold-wisp 24, gold-dew: rejected draft 8, goldnails 61.

4. (p. 116) flockbells *Eurydice* st. 2, manmarks 48, girlgrace 36, manshape 48, beechbole 43, dayspring *Deutschland* st. 35, meadow-down 15; wind-walk 14, sea-swill *Eurydice* st. 16, lipmusic and limbdance 58, bloomfall 23, gospel proffer *Deutschland* st. 4.

5. (p. 117) foam-fleece *Deutschland* st. 16, meal-drift 14, raindrop-roundels 5, lily showers *Deutschland* st. 21, bone-house 15, shadowtackle 48, fire-folk 8, hailropes *Eurydice* st. 7.

6. (p. 117) loop-locks 72, hornlight 32, moonmarks 21, trambeams 26.

7. (p. 117) flake-doves 8, rose-moles 13, flake-leaves 72, lilylocks 43, snow-pinions 21, fawn-froth 33, flint-flake *Deutschland* st. 13.

8. (p. 117) wolfsnow *Eurydice* st. 7, earl-stars 32, braggart bugles 6, lovelocks 36, carrion comfort 40.

9. (p. 117) backwheels 23, afterdraught *Eurydice* st. 16, betweenpie 47, uproll and downcarol 58.

10. (p. 117) dare-gale 15, spendsavour 26, treadmire 48, fall-gold *Deutschland* st. 23, wring-world 40.

11. (p. 118) purple-of-thunder 21, earl-stars 32, lionlimb and heaven-handling 40, bluffhide 43, forepangs 41.

12. (p. 118) windlaced 43, love-laced 30, self-instressed 27, selfwrung 32, glass-blue 37, bugle blue 18, gluegold 72, rash-fresh 11, baldbright, *Eurydice* st. 7, froliclavish 72; gaygear 36, gay-gang 48; deft-handed 26, lighthanded 36.

13. (p. 119) lily showers *Deutschland* st. 21, gospel proffer id. st. 4, hell-rook ranks 23, treadmire toil and rut peel 48, shock night *Deutschland* st. 29.

14. (p. 119) rare-dear *Deutschland* st. 35, lovely-asunder id. st. 5, baldbright,

Eurydice st. 7, rash-fresh 11, wilful-wavier 14, lovely-felicitous *Deutschland* st.
31, wild-worst id. st. 24, kindcold 72, wet-fresh 38, Tarpeian-fast *Deutschland*
st. 29.

15. (p. 119) leaf-light 23, brass-bold 30, tool-smooth 32, herds-long 41, glass-
blue 37, bugle blue 18, moth-soft *Deutschland* st. 26, champ-white *Eurydice* st.
12, jay-blue *Deutschland* st. 26, beam-blind 26, bellbright and gluegold-brown
72, gold-vermilion 12, lashtender 56.

16. (p. 120) day-dissolved 54, whirlwind-swivelled *Deutschland* st. 13, wimpled-
water-dimpled 36, rook-racked 20, self-instressed 27, not-by-morning-
matched 36; star-eyed and strawberry-breasted 18, dovewinged and carrier-
witted *Deutschland* st. 3; no-man-fathomed 41, tear-tricked 30, chancequarried 72,
hoar-hallowed *Eurydice* st. 23, ground-hugged *Deutschland* st. 26.

17. (p. 122) I should like to remark about a line in which a somewhat similar
instance occurs that requires closer examination because it has been misunderstood, according to my views, by Bridges.

> And she beat the bank down with her bows and the ride of her keel:
> The breakers rolled on her beam with ruinous shock;
> And canvas and compass, the whorl and the wheel
> Idle for ever to waft her or wind her with, these she endured.
>
> *Deutschland* st. 14

Bridges remarks here that 'the words between *shock* and *these* are probably
parenthetical' (*Poems*, p. 104). This explanation is most unsatisfactory as it
entirely overlooks the semi-colon after *shock*. Moreover, what is the meaning
of the parenthetical sentence, and why this parenthetical sentence at all? Why
should, as Bridges would have it, *these* refer to the breakers that have been dealt
with two lines before? Bridges tried to solve a problem that had arisen from his
misunderstanding the word *idle*. He could very rightly not make *these* refer
simply to the canvas and compass, whorl and wheel, for this would make no
sense at all. But if one remembers what I have said about the expression of an
object's inscape by bringing forward its predominant quality, it is not difficult to
see that logically the interpretation of the lines should be this: *these* refers to the
canvas and compass, the whorl and the wheel in so far as they are *idle*, incapable
of guiding the ship any longer. It is the *idleness* of these parts that the ship had
to endure. The position of *idle* made Bridges stumble and was the cause of his
misinterpretation; yet this position is to be preferred to that of attribution which
might have been more in accordance with Hopkins's normal practice. But
Hopkins had too sensitive an ear not to be aware of the clumsiness and un-
manageableness of a phrase of this type: the 'idle-for-ever-to-waft-her-or-wind-
her-with canvas and compass'.

18. (p. 125) Most critics are in this matter faithful followers of Bridges. Dealing
with the expulsion of the relative pronoun after *feast* (*Deutschland* st. 30) Dr.
Gardner commentates: 'Hopkins had no use for the colourless, otiose word' (op.
cit., p. 49).

19. (p. 131) Hopkins did once have the courage to make such a compound word;
the result is to my taste certainly not preferable to a relative clause, even if we
have to do without the relative pronoun.

> To what serves mortal beauty —dangerous; does set danc-
> ing blood—*the O-seal-that-so-feature* . . .
>
> *Poems* 38

The feature of the face set the seal on mortal beauty, but I think that Hopkins expressed it very awkwardly in this ugly formation.

20. (p. 131) In this connexion Dr. Gardner refers his reader to *also ran* (op. cit., p. 141). The parallelism is to my mind very superficial, I should say, purely accidental, and explains nothing.

21. (p. 134) I do not deny that this verb may not recall Easter as well as the East. The meaning intended appears to me to be the one propounded in the text.

22. (p. 134) to tongue and to trumpet both occur in *Poems* 49, to plume 22.

23. (p. 134) to size 18 and 47, to justice 34, to leave 50, to flesh 29, to day-labour 15, to foot 58, to frock 5, to selve 34.

24. (p. 134) to stanch and to starch 48, to round 32, to weary, to brazen and to purple 58.

25. (p. 137) They are:

unteachably after evil	*Deutschland* st. 18
thickly falling flakes	id. st. 24
Christ, come quickly	ibid.
when the thing we freely forfeit	*Poems* 36
lustily he his low lot swings	id. 42
delightfully the bright wind beats . . .	id. 48
dearly thou canst be kind.	id. 30
deeply, surely, I need to deplore it	*Eurydice* st. 25
freighted fully . . .	id. st. 3
kind, but royally reclaiming . . .	*Deutschland* st. 34
dangerously sweet	*Poems* 36

CHAPTER 5

1. (p. 140) Robert Bridges, *Three Friends*, O.U.P., 1932.

2. (p.140) Cf. his remarks bearing on Welsh (*N*. 207), the Lancashire dialect (*N*. 145, 149), Irish (*N*. 133), Maltese (*N*. 212), and the many letters to Baillie in which he discusses philological problems of the Coptic and Egyptian languages. An interesting detail is that Hopkins, when a theological student, won a 'spelling competition'. The difficult words were: epaulet, phlegm, catarrh, contemporary, supererogatory, connoisseur, unparalleled, sempstress, and lieutenant.

3. (p. 140) The essay is printed in *The Note-books & Papers of Gerard Manley Hopkins*, pp. 95–7; it is dated 9 Febr. 1868.

4. (p. 143) It is almost unbelievable how constantly Hopkins is fully exploiting rhyme and assonance: a few combinations, many of which are camouflaged by a disguised spelling: pool—peel (48), feel—fell (45), rare—bare and gold—bold (42), waked—waxed—walked (36), waned—wind (32), least—lost (36), buy—boy (27), forms—warms (18), world—wield (14), fall—gall (12), first—fast (10 and 11), wide—wade (10), gnarls—nails (*Deutschland* st. 23), Rhine—ruin—Orion (id. st. 21), yore—year (id. 32), heeds—hides, bodes—abides (id. 32), shower—shire (id. 34), far—fair (54), mark—make (*Deutschland* st. 22 and *Eurydice* st. 17), deal—dale (35), looks—locks (36), lash—lush (*Deutschland*

st. 8), broth—breathe (43), look—like (8), felled—furled (*Eurydice* st. 2), grieve—grove (31), fire—fear (21). These are by no means the complete collection. Lash—lush—plush—gush—flush—flash—flesh occur in quick succession within five consecutive lines (*Deutschland* st. 8). For frequency of alliteration the following line will be hard to surpass:

> a warning waved to
> One once that was found wanting when Good weighed (*Poems* 54).

No fewer than eight words begin with the sound of *w-*.

5. (p. 143) Cf. *T.L.S.* 9 Jan. 1919, p. 19.

6. (p. 144) New words invented by Hopkins are, fortunately, very rare, if we exclude those coinages that are formed on the analogy of existing words, or at least, are improvements only on words generally in use and easily recognizable. Real inventions are to my mind 'unchancelling' (*Deutschland* st. 21) and 'shivelight' (*Poems* 48). *Unchancelling* I take to mean steady, unwavering; in my opinion Hopkins derived it from *chance*: 'leaving nothing to chance', 'not influenced by chance'. A similar sense is given if the French *chanceler* is taken as starting point; but I do not think that Hopkins had this word in mind, for this reason that in his diaries and his letters there was no evidence of his knowing French well. *Shivelight* is not so difficult to explain. I pronounce the word with a short *i* in the first syllable because this better reflects frail rays of light that fall through the branches and twigs of the trees. I have remarked before that Hopkins was none too scrupulous with the endings of some verbs (cf. p. 145); I believe that in this coinage we should see remnants of the verb *to shiver*. Here Hopkins thought it better to leave out the iterative ending just as in another place he thought it better to put it in (see *Deutschland* st. 19: 'The rash smart *sloggering* brine blinds her').

Hopkins thought that *louched* was entirely his: '*Louched* is a coinage of mine, and is to mean much the same as slouched, slouching . . .' Bridges remarks here. 'But *louch* has ample authority, see the *English Dialect Dictionary*' (*Poems*, p. 112).

7. (p. 144) Herbert Read, *Defence of Shelley and other Essays*, p. 159.

8. (p. 145) to power *Poems* 20, to foot 58, to easter *Deutschland* st. 35, to size 47, 18, to front 37, to tongue and to trumpet 49, to bugle *Deutschland* st. 11, to frock 5, to justice 34.

9. (p. 145) Cf. hurl, sweep, swoon *Deutschland* st. 2, achieve, plod *Poems* 12, sift *Deutschland* st. 4, ride id. st. 14, dare 72, breaks, awakes: *rejected draft of* 22, furl 43, heed 43.

10. (p. 145) towery, branchy *Poems* 20, pillowy 25, barrowy 43, fretty 50, goldy 5; yellowy 26, vasty 37, roundy 34.

11. (p. 145) astray, aswarm 32, abreast 23, astrew *Deutschland* st. 21, astrain id. st. 2, afresh id. st. 1.

12. (p. 145) to disremember 32, disseveral 48, to unchild, to unfather *Deutschland* st. 13, to unleave 31, to unselve 19, Unchrist *Eurydice* st. 24, unchancelling *Deutschland* st. 21, recurb and recovery id. st. 32.

13. (p. 146) durance *Poems* 41, listed 21, dear 39, fold *Deutschland* st. 15; lace 48, whelms 32, mines *Deutschland* st. 4, ware 32.

14. (p. 147) love-scape *Deutschland* st. 23, prickproof 42, leafmeal 31, mansex 23, self-wise 23, quickgold 8, mainstrength 42, fallowbootfellow 42, cry disaster 23,

yestertempest 48, world without event 49; cf. also on this subject Gardner, op. cit. 121 ff.

15. (p. 147) ring of it *Deutschland* st. 31, that spell id. st. 3, that weather id. st. 19.

16. (p. 147) onewhere 43, by meanwhiles 30, hard at hand *Eurydice* st. 5.

17. (p. 147) brows of care 35, cheeks of flame 30, set on a flare 8, world after 35, well wept *Eurydice* st. 27, your offering 24, to the shrouds they took *Deutschland* st. 15.

18 (p. 149) Translations are taken from Liddell and Scott, *Greek-English Lexicon*. New Edition, Oxford, 1925–36.

19. (p. 157) Cecil Day Lewis, *A Hope for Poetry* (1924), p. 6.

20. (p. 163) 'The Wreck of the Deutschland'. *Essays and Studies*, 1935, p. 146.

21. (p. 165) *New Bearings in English Poetry*, p. 192.

22. (p. 165) Here follows an instance given by Dr. Gardner:

'low-*latched* . . . at first sight means "dwelling humbly in a thin wafer as behind the latched door of a cottage". . . . but Hopkins had in mind the stronger Shakespearian meaning of *latch*—"to catch, to lay hold of": so that apart from the simile in "leaf-light" the whole line can be taken *literally:* "God, in condescending humility, allows himself to be held, imprisoned in the Host" ' (op. cit. pp. 132–3).

23. (p. 171) Those acquainted with Mr. Empson's book *Seven Types of Ambiguity* may perhaps have drawn a parallel between his theory of ambiguity as of the essence of poetry and the many examples of the ambiguous use of words I have put forward in this chapter. They may even have wondered at my not mentioning his theory in the text and may feel inclined to hold that what I have adduced as peculiar to Hopkins is in fact common to all poets. My reply to these possible objections is that I have made no mention of Mr. Empson's theories because the author has failed to prove them. Indeed, very fine examples have been brought forward by Mr. Empson of the use and effect of ambiguity in poetry and these examples constitute, to my mind, the value of his book. But in order to prove that ambiguity is essential to poetry, he has started from a definition of the word ambiguity that is too vague and of too wide an application to demand serious consideration. Prose is as ambiguous as poetry, if we take ambiguity in Mr. Empson's sense. In the opening paragraph of his study he writes: 'I propose to use the word (*sc.* ambiguity) in an extended sense and shall think relevant to my subject any consequence of language, however slight, which adds some nuance to the direct statement of prose. . . .' But the situation in which words are used always and necessarily adds some nuance to the 'direct statement of prose', and it is precisely this nuance that makes it possible for men to interpret a direct statement of prose. I might end this note with a famous adage: *qui nimis probat, nihil probat;* but that criticism would be too harsh on a book that has helped me in appreciating poetry better.

BIBLIOGRAPHY

Note.

I have tried to present a complete list of books and articles that have so far been published dealing with Hopkins. With only a few exceptions articles that have appeared in weekly papers have, however, not been mentioned. It is possible that some article has escaped my attention, in which case I apologize to its author.

An explanation of the way in which I have drawn up this bibliography seems to be called for. The books mentioned under the first two headings have been arranged (with one exception only) in chronological order, for this reason that thus a survey of the growing interest in Hopkins is given and that at a glance the reader may see how far any author could profit by the research of other writers. The alphabetical order of authors in the third group is accounted for by my wish to place together articles by the same author that were published in different books. In the fourth and most numerous group I followed neither the chronological nor the alphabetical order. To give some guidance in this mass of articles I have thought it best to give an indication of the nature of the article written, whether critical, appreciative, merely introductory, &c. Hence I have based this list of articles on the character of the periodicals in which they appeared, which in most cases will be an indication of the nature of the article. Essays in foreign languages have been placed at the end. As regards the final group, there was no reason to abandon the obvious alphabetical order.

Articles or books marked with an asterisk I have not been able to read.

I. HOPKINS'S OWN WRITINGS

A. *Published sources*

Poems by Gerard Manley Hopkins, edited with notes by Robert Bridges. Second Edition. With an appendix of additional poems, and a critical introduction by Charles Williams. O.U.P., 1930.

The Letters of Gerard Manley Hopkins to Robert Bridges, edited with notes and an introduction by Claude Colleer Abbott. O.U.P., 1935.

The Correspondence of Gerard Manley Hopkins and Richard Watson Dixon, edited with notes and an introduction by Claude Colleer Abbott. O.U.P., 1935.

Further Letters of Gerard Manley Hopkins including his Correspondence with Coventry Patmore, edited with notes and an introduction by Claude Colleer Abbott. O.U.P., 1938.

The Note-Books and Papers of Gerard Manley Hopkins, edited with notes and a preface by Humphry House. O.U.P., 1937.

A Vision of the Mermaids. An edition in full facsimile, limited to 200 copies. O.U.P., 1920.

Selections from the Note-books of Gerard Manley Hopkins, edited by T. Weiss. New Directions Books, James Laughlin, New York, 1945.

B. *Unpublished or partly published sources*

MS. book, called B (see *Poems,* p. 94).

MS. book, called H.

Collection of miscellaneous papers in possession of Mr. G. W. S. Hopkins. I have had access to all the papers mentioned by Mr. Humphry House in the first Appendix to his edition of *The Note-Books and Papers,* pp. 423–8. I have made use of the following unpublished papers: D I, X, D XII, F, G I, G II, L, M 5 and R.

II. BOOKS DEALING WITH THE LIFE AND/OR POETRY OF HOPKINS

(in order of publication)

Lahey, G. F., S.J.	. *Gerard Manley Hopkins.* O.U.P., 1930.
Phare, E. E. .	. *The Poetry of Gerard Manley Hopkins.* A Survey and Commentary. Cambridge U.P., 1933.
MacGuire, D. P.	. *The Poetry of G. M. Hopkins.* English Association, Adelaide Branch, Pamphlet No. 2. Hassell Press, 1934.
Kelly, B. . .	. *The Mind and Poetry of G. M. Hopkins.* Pepler & Lewell, Ditchling (Sussex), 1937.
Karp, Georg. .	. *Germanisches Formgefühl bei Gerard Manley Hopkins.* Wilhelm Postberg, Bottrop i.W., 1939.
Baldi, Sergio .	. *Gerard Manley Hopkins.* 'Morcelliana', Brescia, 1941.
Pick, J. . .	. *Gerard Manley Hopkins: Priest and Poet.* O.U.P., 1942.
Gardner, W. H. .	. *Gerard Manley Hopkins.* A Study of Poetic Idiosyncrasy in Relation to Poetic Tradition. Martin Secker & Warburg, London, 1944.
Ruggles, Eleanor	. *Gerard Manley Hopkins. A Life.* W. W. Norton & Co., New York, 1944.
'Kenyon Critics'.	. *Gerard Manley Hopkins.* New Directions Books, Norfolk, Connecticut (Publ. James Laughlin, New York), 1945. This collection contains the following essays: Austin Warren: Gerard Manley Hopkins (1844–1889).

'Keynon Critics' .   . Herbert Marshall McLuhan: The Analogical
(*contd.*)   Mirrors.
                         Harold Whitehall: Sprung Rhythm.
                         Josephine Miles: The Sweet and Lovely
                            Language.
                         Austin Warren: Instress of Inscape.
                         Robert Lowell: Hopkins' Sanctity.
                         Arthur Mizener: Victorian Hopkins.
                         F. R. Leavis: Metaphysical Isolation.

III. Books containing an essay on Hopkins
                    (in alphabetical order of authors)

Alexander, C., S.J.   . *The Catholic Literary Revival*, pp. 71–84.
                         The Bruce Publishing Company, Mil-
                         waukee, 1935.
Brégy, Katherine.   . *The Poet's Chantry*, pp. 70–88. Herbert &
                         Daniel, London, 1912.
D'Arcy, Martin, S.J. . *Archivum Historicum S.J.*, Vol. I, pp. 118–22.
                         Romae, 1931.
     id.   *Great Catholics*, edited by C. Williamson,
                         O.S.C., pp. 438–47. Nicholson & Watson,
                         London, 1938.
Daiches, David .   . *New Literary Values*, pp. 23–51. Oliver &
                         Boyd, Edinburgh–London, 1936.
Deutsch, Babette   . *This Modern Poetry*, pp. 183–98. Faber &
                         Faber Ltd., London (n.d.).
Fausset, H. I'Anson . *Poets and Pundits.** Jonathan Cape, London,
                         1946.
Gilkes, M. .   .   . *A Key to Modern English Poetry*, pp. 20–39.
                         Blackie & Son, London, 1937.
Henderson, P. .   . *The Poet and Society*, pp. 103–31. Secker &
                         Warburg, London, 1939.
Kenmare, D.   .   . *The Face of Truth*, pp. 92–100. Shakespeare
                         Head Press, Oxford, 1939.
Kilmer, J. .   .   . *The Circus and other Essays*, pp. 180–85.
                         Doubleday, Hamilton, Kent & Co. Ltd.,
                         New York, 1929.
Leavis, F. R.   .   . *New Bearings in English Poetry*, pp. 159–94.
                         Chatto & Windus, London, 1938.
Murry, Middleton   . *Aspects of Literature*, pp. 52–61. Collins &
                         Co. Ltd., London, 1920.
O'Neill, G., S.J.   . *Essays on Poetry*, pp. 117–38. Talbot Press,
                         Dublin, 1919.

Read, Herbert . . *The Defence of Shelley and other Essays.*
Heinemann, London, 1936 (the same essay
first appeared in *Form of Poetry*).

id. *English Critical Essays: Twentieth Century*,
pp. 351–73. World's Classics, O.U.P.,
1933.

Roggen, F. N. . . *Studies in English Literature*, pp. 517–34.
Imperial University Tokyo XV. Tokyo,
1935.

Sargent, D. . . *Four Independents*, pp. 117–83. Sheed &
Ward, London, 1935.

Shuster, G. N. . . *The Catholic Spirit in Modern Literature*,
pp. 115–21. Macmillan, London, 1922.

Sitwell, Edith . . *Aspects of Modern Poetry*, pp. 51–72. Duck-
worth, London, 1934.

Southworth, J. G. . *Sowing the Spring.** Studies in British Poets
from Hopkins to MacNeice. Blackwell,
Oxford, 1940.

Stonier, G. W. . . *Gog Magog and other critical Essays*, pp. 43–63.
Dent, London, 1933.

Treece, H. . . *How I see Apocalypse.** Lindsay Drummond,
London, 1946.

IV. Articles in periodicals

(see remarks, p. 188, for arrangement)

Gardner, W. H. . . The Wreck of the Deutschland. *Essays and
Studies*, Vol. XXI (1936), pp. 124–52.

id. Gerard Manley Hopkins as a Cywyddwr.
*Transactions of the Honourable Society of
Cymmrodorion*, 1940, pp. 184–8.

Heywood, Terence . Gerard Manley Hopkins: His Literary
Ancestry. *English*, Vol. III, No. 13 (Spring
1940), pp. 16–24.

Lilly, Gweneth . . The Welsh Influence in the Poetry of Gerard
Manley Hopkins. *The Modern Language
Review*, Vol. XXXVIII (July 1943),
pp. 192–205.

Kliger, Samuel . . God's 'Plenitude' in the Poetry of Gerard
Manley Hopkins. *Modern Language Notes*,
Vol. LIX, No. 6 (June 1940), pp. 408–10.

Walker, R. S. . . Introduction to the Poetry of Gerard Manley
Hopkins. *Aberdeen University Review*,
Vol. XXV (July 1938), pp. 232–43.

Abbott, C. C. .   .   Gerard Manley Hopkins: A letter and drafts
                        of early poems. *The Durham University
                        Journal*, New Series, Vol. I (Jan. 1940), pp.
                        65–73.

Anonymous   .   .   ibid., Vol. III (Dec. 1942), pp. 34–5.

Downey, H.   .   .   A Poem not Understood. *Virginia Quarterly
                        Review*, Vol. 11 (Oct. 1935), pp. 506–17.

     id.   Gerard Hopkins: A Study of Influences.
                        Southern Review (Louisiana State Univer-
                        sity), Vol I (Oct. 1936), pp. 837–45.

Binyon, L.   .   .   Gerard Hopkins and his Influence. *University
                        of Toronto Quarterly*, Vol. VIII (April 1939),
                        pp. 264–70.

Collins, J. .   .   .   Philosophical Themes in G. M. Hopkins.
                        Thought (Fordham University Quarterly),
                        Vol. XXII (March 1947), pp. 67–106.

Tillemans, Th. .   .   Is Hopkins a Modern Poet? *English Studies*,
                        Vol. XXIV (June 1942), pp. 90–5.

Heywood, Terence   .   On approaching Hopkins. *Poetry Review*,
                        Vol. XXX (June 1939), pp. 185–8.

Sapir, Edward   .   .   *Poetry*, Sept. 1921.*

Zabel, M. S.   .   .   ibid., Dec. 1930.*

     id.   ibid., July 1935.*

Sturge Moore, T.   .   Style or Beauty in Literature. *Criterion*,
                        Vol. IX (July 1930), pp. 591–603.

Auden, W. H. .   .   Review of E. E. Phare's book. ibid., Vol.
                        XIII (April 1934), pp. 497–9.

Read, H. .   .   .   The Letters of G. M. Hopkins. ibid., Vol.
                        XIV (July 1935), pp. 478–82.

Gardner, W. H. .   .   Early Poems and Extracts. ibid., Vol. XV
                        (Oct. 1935), pp. 1–17.

     id.   A Note on Hopkins and Duns Scotus.
                        Scrutiny, Vol. V (June 1936), pp. 61–70.

     id.   The Religious Problem in G. M. Hopkins.
                        ibid., Vol. VI (June 1937), pp. 32–42.

Lienhardt, R. G.   .   Hopkins and Yeats. ibid., Vol. XI (June
                        1943), pp. 220–4.

Read, Herbert   .   .   Poetry and Belief in G. M. Hopkins. *New
                        Verse*, No. 1 (April 1933), pp. 11–15.

Various Authors   .   ibid., No. 14 (April 1935). This Hopkins
                        number contains the following essays :
                        Humphry House: A note on Hopkins'
                        Religious Life.

Various Authors *(contd.)*	André Bremond, S.J.: Art and Inspiration in Hopkins.
	Christopher Devlin, S.J.: Gerard Hopkins and Duns Scotus.
	Charles Madge: What is all this Juice?— Hopkins and Victorian Conceptions of Nature.
	Geoffrey Gregson: Blood and Bran: Hopkins and Hopkinese.
	Louis MacNeice: A Comment.
	Ll. Wyn Griffith: The Welsh Influence in Hopkins's Poetry.
Weiss, T. . . .	G. M. Hopkins: Realist on Parnassus.* *Accent*, Vol. V (1945), pp. 135–44.
Darby, Harold S. .	A Jesuit-Poet—Gerard Manley Hopkins. *The London Quarterly and Holborn Review*, Vol. 162 (April 1943), pp. 110–22.
Hanson, W. G. . .	Gerard Manley Hopkins and Richard Watson Dixon. ibid., Vol. 163 (Jan. 1944), pp. 63–7.
Brown, A. . . .	G. M. Hopkins and Associative Form.* *Dublin Magazine*, April 1928, pp. 6–20.
Pryce-Jones, A. .	Gerard Manley Hopkins. *The London Mercury*, Vol. XXIV (May 1931), pp. 45–52.
Fairley, Barker .	Charles Doughty and Modern Poetry. ibid., Vol. XXXII (June 1935), pp. 128–37.
Young, G. M. .	Forty Years of Verse. ibid., Vol. XXXV (Dec. 1936), pp. 112–22.
MacColl, D. S. .	Patmore and Hopkins: Sense and Nonsense in English Prosody. ibid., Vol. XXXVIII (July 1938), pp. 217–24.
Jones, Glyn . .	Hopkins and Welsh Prosody. *Life and Letters To-day*, Vol. XXI (June 1939), pp. 50–4.
Plowman, Max .	G. M. Hopkins. *Adelphi*, Vol. IX (March 1935), pp. 356–61.
Finlay, Ida . .	Gerard Manley Hopkins: Poet and Priest. *The Cornhill Magazine*, Vol. 59 (April 1939), pp. 467–78.
Turner, W. J. .	Some Modern Poetry. *The Nineteenth Century and After*, Vol. CIX (Feb. 1931), pp. 243–52.
Burdett, O. . .	The Letters of Gerard Manley Hopkins. ibid., Vol. CXVII (Feb. 1935), pp. 234–41.

O'Brien, J.   .   .   G. M. Hopkins. *The Bookman*, Vol. LXXX
                             (April 1931), pp. 207–9.
Kent, Muriel   .   .   Gerard Manley Hopkins: Poet and Prosodist.
                             ibid., Vol. LXXXI (March 1932), pp. 312–13.
Fletcher, J. G.   .   .   G. M. Hopkins—Priest or Poet. *The American
                             Review*, Vol. VI (Jan. 1936), pp. 331–46.
Richards, I. A.   .   .   Gerard Hopkins. *The Dial*, Vol. 81 (Sept.
                             1926), pp. 195–203.
Ogden, C. K.   .   .   *Psyche* (editorial), Vol. XVI (1936), pp. 1–50.
Waterhouse, J. F. .   .   G. M. Hopkins and Music. *Music and Letters*,
                             Vol. XIX (July 1937), pp. 227–35.

Kelly, H., S.J.   .   .   Father Gerard Hopkins in his Letters.
                             Studies, Vol. XXV (June 1936), pp. 239–52.
id.   Gerard Manley Hopkins, Jesuit-Poet. ibid.,
                             Vol. XXXI (Dec. 1942), pp. 438–44.
Stanford, W. B.   .   .   Gerard Manley Hopkins and Aeschylus.   ibid.,
                             Vol. XXX (Sept. 1941), pp. 359–68.
H., J. J.   .   .   ibid., Vol. XXXIII (Dec. 1944), pp. 558–61.
Page, F., Hopkins, G.,   Father Gerard Hopkins (a symposium of four
    and Plures   articles). *The Dublin Review*, Vol. 167
                             (Feb. 1920), pp. 40–66.
Grisewood, H.   .   .   Gerard Manley Hopkins, S.J.   ibid., Vol. 189
                             (Nov. 1931), pp. 213–26.
Clarke, E.   .   .   Gerard Hopkins, Jesuit. ibid., Vol. 198
                             (March 1936), pp. 127–41.
Turner, V., S.J. .   .   Gerard Manley Hopkins, 1844–1944.   ibid.,
                             Vol. 215 (Oct. 1944), pp. 144–59.

Keating, J.   .   .   Impressions of Father Gerard Hopkins, S.J.
                             The Month, Vol. CXIV (July 1909),
                             pp. 59–68; Vol. CXIV (Aug. 1909),
                             pp. 151–60; Vol. CXIV (Sept. 1909),
                             pp. 246–58.
id.   G. M. Hopkins: Priest and Poet. ibid.,
                             Vol. CLXV (Feb. 1935), pp. 125–36.
id.   Fr. Gerard Hopkins and the *Spiritual Exercises*.
                             ibid., Vol. CLXVI (Sept. 1935), pp. 268–70.
Guiney, L. J.   .   .   G. Hopkins: A Recovered Poet. ibid.,
                             Vol. CXXXIII (March 1919), pp. 204–14.
Harting, E. M.   .   .   G. Hopkins and Digby Dolben. ibid.,
                             Vol. CXXXIII (April 1919), pp. 285–9.
Bliss, G.   .   .   In a Poet's Workshop. ibid., Vol. CLXVII
                             (Feb. 1936), pp. 160–7; Vol. CLXVIII (June
                             1936), pp. 528–35.

Crehan, J. . . .	Poetry and Religious Life. The case of Gerard Manley Hopkins, S.J. ibid., Vol. CLXVIII (Dec. 1936), pp. 493–503.
Pick, J. . . .	The Growth of a Poet: Gerard Manley Hopkins, S.J. ibid., Vol. CLXXV (Jan. 1940), pp. 39–46; Vol. CLXXV (Feb. 1940), pp. 106–13.
Phillipson, W. (Dom).	Gerard Manley Hopkins. *The Downside Review*, Vol. LI (April 1933), pp. 326–48.
id.	The Letters of Gerard Hopkins. ibid., Vol. LIII (April 1935), pp. 210–28.
id.	The Journals of G. M. Hopkins. ibid., Vol. LV (Oct. 1937), pp. 526–36.
id.	Gerard Hopkins, Priest. ibid., Vol. LVI (April 1938), pp. 311–23.
id.	Gerard Hopkins and Coventry Patmore. ibid., Vol. LVII (July 1939), pp. 389–98.
Scrinivasa Iyengar, K. R.	Gerard Manley Hopkins. *The New Review* (Calcutta), Vol. VII (Jan. 1938), pp. 1–11; ibid. (Feb. 1938), pp. 115–25; ibid. (March 1938), pp. 264–73.
Shewring, W. H. .	The Letters of Father Hopkins. *Blackfriars*, Vol. XVI (April 1935), pp. 265–71.
Devlin, C., S.J. . .	The Ignatian Inspiration of Gerard Hopkins. ibid., Vol. XVI (Dec. 1935), pp. 887–900.
Kelly, B. . . .	Gerard Manley Tuncks. ibid., Vol. XVIII (June 1937), pp. 424–9.
Hope, F. . . .	Gerard Manley Hopkins. *The Irish Ecclesiastical Record*, Vol. 37 (June 1931), pp. 561–70.
Scott, M., S.J. . .	Gerard Manley Hopkins. *The Irish Monthly*, Vol. LXI (Nov. 1933), pp. 715–20; ibid. (Dec. 1933), pp. 786–92.
Leahy, M. . . .	Father Gerard Manley Hopkins, Jesuit and Poet. ibid., Vol. LXIII (Sept. 1935), pp. 567–76.
MacManus, F. . .	Return of a Victorian. ibid., Vol. LXV (May 1937), pp. 327–35.
id.	The Poet who knew too much. ibid., Vol. LXV (June 1937), pp. 389–99.
Hughes, E. . .	The Innovators. ibid., Vol. LXVI (Dec. 1938), pp. 820–4.

Williamson, C. .   .   Gerard Manley Hopkins.   *Pax*, Vol. XXVIII
                        (March 1938), pp. 87–91; ibid. (April 1938),
                        pp. 107–10.

[Anon.]   .   .   .   *The Times Literary Supplement:* No. 886,
                        9 Jan. 1919; No. 1619, 9 Feb. 1933; No. 1669,
                        25 Jan. 1934; No. 1722, 31 Jan. 1935;
                        No. 1892, 7 May 1938; No. 2099, 25 Dec.
                        1940; No. 2232, 11 Nov. 1944.

Porter, Allan   .   .   Difficult Poetry.   *The Spectator*, 13 Jan. 1923.

Turner, W. J. .   .   Gerard Manley Hopkins 1844 to 1889.   ibid.,
                        14 July 1944.

House, H. .   .   .   G. M. Hopkins.   *New Statesman*, 9 June 1917.

Stonier, G. W. .   .   ibid., 26 Jan. 1935; 4 Nov. 1944.

Ginneken, J. van, S.J. .   'Barbarous in Beauty'.   *Onze Taaltuin*,
                        Vol. V (Juli 1936), pp. 65–73.

Pompen, A., O.F.M. .   Gerard Manley Hopkins, S.J.   ibid., Vol. VI
                        (Mei 1937), pp. 95–102.

Etman, A. .   .   .   Haunting Rhythm.   *Tijdschrift voor Taal en
                        Letteren*, Vol. 27 (April 1939), pp. 30–7.

Panhuysen, J.   .   .   De Poesie van Gerard Manley Hopkins.
                        Boekenschouw, Vol. 32 (Nov. 1938),
                        pp. 313–18.

Peters, W.   .   .   G. M. Hopkins.   De Controverse rond zijn
                        Persoon.   *Studien*, Vol. CXXXII (Nov.
                        1939), pp. 448–59.

Brauns, M.   .   .   De dichter Gerard Manley Hopkins.   *Streven*,
                        Jaargang XII (Aug. 1945), pp. 238–47.

Bremond, A.   .   .   La Poésie Naïve et Savante de G. Hopkins.
                        Études, Tome 221 (Oct. 1934), pp. 23–49.

id.   Quelques Réflexions sur la Poésie et les Styles
                        Poétiques.   A Propos d'une Correspond-
                        ance.   ibid., Tome 242 (Feb. 1940),
                        pp. 310–17.

Behn, I   .   .   .   G. M. Hopkins und seine Dichtung.   *Hoch-
                        land*, Vol. XXXII (May 1935), pp. 148–69.

Croce, B. .   .   .   Un gesuita inglesa poeta, Gerard Manley
                        Hopkins.   *La Critica*, Vol. XXXV (1937),
                        pp. 81–100.

V. BOOKS IN WHICH THE POETRY OF HOPKINS IS DISCUSSED PASSIM

Bailey, R. .   .   .   *A Dialogue on Modern Poetry.*   O.U.P., 1939.

Bateson, F. N. W.   .   *English Poetry and the English Language.*
                        O.U.P., 1934.

Bullough, G. . . *The Trend of Modern Poetry.* Oliver & Boyd, Edinburgh–London, 1934.

Castelli, Alberto . *Scrittori Inglesi Contemporanei.* Messina, 1939.

D'Arcy, M. C., S.J. . *The Mind and Heart of Love.* Faber & Faber, Ltd., London, 1945.

Desmond, F. . . *The Pursuit of Poetry.* Cassell & Company Ltd., London, 1939.

Drew, E. . . . *Discovering Poetry.* O.U.P., 1933.

Eliot, T. S. . . *After Strange Gods.* Faber & Faber Ltd., London, 1939.

Elton, Oliver . . *The English Muse.* Bell & Son, London, 1933.

Empson, W. . . *Seven Types of Ambiguity.* Chatto & Windus, London, 1930.

Evans, Ifor B. . . *English Poetry in the Later Nineteenth Century.* Methuen, London, 1933.

Grierson, H., and Smith, J. *A Critical History of English Poetry.* Chatto & Windus, London, 1940.

Lewis, C. Day . . *A Hope for Poetry.* Blackwell, Oxford, 1934.

MacNeice, L. . . *Modern Poetry. A Personal Essay.* O.U.P., 1938.

Mégroz, R. L. . . *Modern English Poetry,* 1882–1932. Ivor Nicholson & Watson, London, 1933.

Murphy, G. . . *The Modern Poet.* Sidgwick & Jackson, London, 1938.

O'Donnell, M. J. . *Feet on the Ground,* being An Approach to Modern Verse. Blackie & Son, London and Glasgow, 1946.

Olivero, F. . . *Correnti Mistiche della Letteratura Inglese Moderna.* Bocca, Torino, 1932.

Read, H. . . . *Form in Modern Poetry.* Sheed & Ward, London, 1932.

Richards, I. A. . . *Practical Criticism.* Kegan Paul, London, 1935.

Riding, L., and Graves, R. *A Survey of Modernist Poetry.* Heinemann, London, 1927.

Roberts, M. . . *The Faber Book of Modern Verse.* Faber & Faber, London, 1938.

Schlauch, M. . . *The Gift of Tongues.* George Allen & Unwin, London, 1943.

Selincourt, E. de. . *Oxford Lectures on Poetry.* Clarendon Press, Oxford, 1934.

Yeats, W. B. . . *The Oxford Book of Modern Verse.* Clarendon Press, Oxford, 1936.

1844.	11 June. Born at Stratford, Essex.
1854.	At Highgate School.
1857.	Visited the Rhineland.
1859.	Wrote *The Escorial.*
1860.	Visited South Germany.
1862.	Wrote *A Vision of the Mermaids.*
1863.	To Oxford, Balliol College.
1866.	21 October. Converted to the Catholic Faith and received into the Catholic Church by John Henry Newman.
1867.	First Class Honours in Classics. A master at the Oratory School, Birmingham.
1868.	Toured Switzerland. Burned his poetry. 8 September. Joined the Society of Jesus.
1868–70.	Two years' novitiate at Roehampton, London.
1870–3.	Studied philosophy at Stonyhurst, Lancs.
1873–4.	Taught classics at Roehampton.
1874.	Began his course of theology at St. Beuno's, Treimeirchion, North Wales.
1875.	Wrote *The Wreck of the Deutschland.*
1877.	23 September. Ordained Priest.
1877–81.	Preacher at various parish churches of the Society of Jesus in London, Oxford, Liverpool and Glasgow.
1881.	Third year of novitiate at Roehampton.
1882–4.	Taught classics at Stonyhurst College.
1883.	Visited Holland.
1884.	Appointed Professor of Greek at University College, Dublin.
1889.	8 June. Died of typhoid fever.

1918.	*Poems*, edited by Robert Bridges.
1930.	*Poems*, second edition, with additional poems: reprinted in 1931, 1933, 1935, 1937, 1938, 1940.
1935.	*The Letters of Gerard Manley Hopkins to Robert Bridges* and *The Correspondence of Gerard Manley Hopkins and Richard Watson Dixon*, edited by C. C. Abbott.
1937.	*The Note-Books and Papers of Gerard Manley Hopkins*, edited by Humphrey House.
1938.	*Further Letters of Gerard Manley Hopkins*, edited by C. C. Abbott.

CHRONOLOGY OF THE POEMS

(the date mentioned is the date of inception)

1875. TREIMEIRCHION (N. WALES)
    December   *The Wreck of the Deutschland.*

1876. 19 June   *Moonrise* (*Poems* 65).
    5 July   *The Woodlark* (id. 64).
    28 July   *The Silver Jubilee* (id. 6).
    BARMOUTH (N. WALES)
    August   *Penmaen Pool* (id. 5).

1877. TREIMEIRCHION (N. WALES)
    23 February   *God's Grandeur* (id. 7).
    24 February   *The Starlight Night* (id. 8).
    May   *Spring* (id. 9).
         The Lantern out of Doors (id. 10).
         The Sea and the Skylark (id. 11).
         In the Valley of the Elwy (id. 16).
    30 May   *The Windhover* (id. 12).
    Summer   *Pied Beauty* (id. 13).
    1 September   *Hurrahing in Harvest* (id. 14).
         The Caged Skylark (id. 15).

1878. SPRINKHILL (SHEFFIELD)
    April   *The Loss of the Eurydice* (id. 17).
    STONYHURST (LANCS.)
    May   *The May Magnificat* (id. 18).

1879. OXFORD
    13 March   *Binsey Poplars* (id. 19).
    April   *Henry Purcell* (id. 21).
    27 July   *The Bugler's First Communion* (id. 23).
         Duns Scotus's Oxford (id. 20).
    12 August   *Andromeda* (id. 25).
         Morning, Midday and Evening Sacrifice (id. 24).
         The Handsome Heart (id. 27).
    2 October   *Peace* (id. 22).
         The Candle Indoors (id. 26).
         St. Winefred's Well (id. 58).
    BEDFORD LEIGH AND LIVERPOOL
    21 October   *At the Wedding March* (id. 28).

1880. 28 April   *Felix Randal* (id. 29).
    HAMPSTEAD
    August   *Brothers* (id. 30).

	NEAR LIVERPOOL	
	September	*Spring and Fall* (id. 31).
1881.	INVERSNAID	
	28 September	*Inversnaid* (id. 33).
	HAMPSTEAD	*The Leaden Echo and the Golden Echo* (id. 36).
1882.	STONYHURST	
		Ribblesdale (id. 35).
	13 October	*The Leaden Echo &c.* (see above).
1883.	May	*The Blessed Virgin compared to the Air we Breathe* (id. 37).
1884.	DUBLIN	
		Spelt from Sibyl's Leaves (id. 32).
1885.	May	*(Carrion Comfort)* (id. 40).
		'No worst, there is none' (id. 41).
	CLONGOWES	
	13 August	*To what serves Mortal Beauty?* (id. 38).
	DUBLIN	
	August	*(The Soldier)* (id. 39).
	August	*Poems* 44, 45, 46, 47 (see note below).
1886.	December	*On the Portrait of Two Beautiful Young People* (id. 54).
1887.	DROMORE	
	September	*Harry Ploughman* (id. 43).
		Tom's Garland (id. 42).
1888.	DUBLIN	
	May	*Epithalamion* (id. 72).
	July	*That Nature is a Heraclitean Fire &c.* (id. 48).
	August	*Poems* 59.
	September	*In honour of St. Alphonsus Rodriguez* (id. 49).
1889.	17 March	*Poems* 50.
	3 April	*Poems* 69.
	22 April	*Poems* 51.

The list is not complete for this reason that it is impossible to ascertain the date of most of the fragments.

As to dating the 'Terrible Sonnets', I think that the solution given by R. Bridges (*Poems*, pp. 114 and 116) is the most probable. For this reason I have adopted it here.

INDEX OF REFERENCES TO THE POEMS

Numbers preceding the titles refer to the number of the piece in *Poems*, 2nd ed., 1930. (A comparative table showing the corresponding numbers in the 3rd edition is placed at the end of the book.) References in each poem are to the lines unless otherwise stated (st = stanza).

TABLE OF NUMBERING OF THE POEMS

Comparative table showing the numbers given to the poems referred to in this book in the second edition (ed. Robert Bridges and Charles Williams, 1930) and in the fourth edition (ed. W. H. Gardner and N. H. Mackenzie, 1967) of the *Poems of G. M. Hopkins*.

Second Edition	Fourth Edition	Second Edition	Fourth Edition
4	28	31	55
5	30	32	61
6	29	33	56
7	31	34	57
8	32	35	58
9	33	36	59
10	40	37	60
11	35	38	62
12	36	39	63
13	37	40	64
14	38	41	65
15	39	42	70
16	34	43	71
17	41	44	66
18	42	45	67
19	43	46	68
20	44	47	69
21	45	48	72
22	51	49	73
23	48	50	74
24	49	51	76
25	50	54	157
26	46	56	149
27	47	58	152
28	52	61	142
29	53	72	159
30	54		

DATE DUE

GAYLORD			PRINTED IN U.S.A.